Badges and Insignia
of the Third Reich
1933–1945

Badges and Insignia of the Third Reich 1933–1945

Brian Leigh Davis

**colour plates by
Malcolm McGregor**

BLANDFORD PRESS
POOLE · DORSET

First published in the U.K. 1983 by Blandford Press,
Link House, West Street, Poole, Dorset, BH15 1LL.

Copyright © 1983. Blandford Books Ltd.

Distributed in the United States by
Sterling Publishing Co., Inc.,
2 Park Avenue, New York, N.Y. 10016.

British Library Cataloguing in Publication Data

Davis, Brian Leigh
    Badges and insignia of the Third Reich, 1933-45.
    1. Germany. *Heer*—Medals, badges, decorations, etc.
    I. Title
    355.1'5'0943   UC535.G/

ISBN 0 7137 1130 2

Typeset in 11/13pt Monophoto Baskerville by
Asco Trade Typesetting Ltd., Hong Kong
Printed in Great Britain
by Shenval Marketing Ltd.

Contents

Preface

This book is about cloth badges and insignia and as such is divided into eleven main sections dealing with the different types of badges and insignia, as will be seen from the contents listing.

These main sections have been sub-divided into separate compartments devoted to the insignia and badges as worn and used by various German uniformed formations. The master index shows the extent of these formations together with their related insignia.

The text accompanying the sixty-four plates of colour artwork contains the basic information upon the 1297 individually illustrated items, which in most cases consists of:

1 The name of the item, preceded by the reference number used on the colour illustration.
2 The period when it was worn or, wherever possible, the date when the item was known to have been introduced into service.
3 Who wore the item.
4 The reason for its use, and what it represented.
5 How it was worn, together with any other relevant information.

Coloured artwork was decided on in preference to photographic representation to illustrate the badges and insignia. It would have proved almost impossible to have gathered together all the required information needed to illustrate this book by means of colour photographs. Colour artwork permits a far greater range of subject matter and a more consistent finish.

Great care and attention to detail has been expended upon the colour artwork. Malcolm McGregor has painted the items on each plate in scale with each other. On every plate there is a scale marker, one half of which is in centimetres, the other half in inches, 5 cm compared to 1 inch. This gives the relative scale of the items illustrated on that plate. These scale markers only apply to items on the plate on which they appear. Thus, unless the scale marker on one plate happens to be identical to that on another plate, items on one plate should not be compared for size with items on any other illustrated plate.

The limitation of space has forced me to illustrate and explain only a representative selection of items from amongst the vast range of badges and insignia that were known to have existed. As an example of just a small portion of the huge volume of material available it would have been possible to have filled the entire 64 plates of colour illustrations with nothing other than SS cuff-titles, which at the rate of thirteen titles to a plate would have given a total of 832 items, and this would not have covered all the 850 known examples that existed before the outbreak of World War II.

The one hundred contemporary black and white photographs have been specially selected in order to show to the best advantage actual badges and insignia as worn.

It is hoped therefore that this book will prove to be a useful companion to my last Blandford Press book, *German Uniforms of the Third Reich, 1933–45*.

Introduction

Throughout military history, wherever men – and women – have been organised into disciplined bodies of troops, various means have been used in order to identify the leaders, to show who belonged to separate groups, and to indicate those who held special appointments or who undertook specialist work. Divisions within these groups were made by wearing identifying marks. Ranks and appointments, specialist functions and skills were all visibly indicated.

In more recent times this practice has become refined, and by the time World War II enveloped the world badges and insignia were an important and necessary aspect of regulated uniform dress.

German Third Reich badges and insignia were mulitfarious for their use was extended beyond the military armed forces to Germany's para-military formations and political organisations, and they were also used by almost all of their administration and ancillary uniformed groups.

The quality, design and manufacture of German badges and insignia was almost always of a very high standard. The design was usually the responsibility of established military artists and designers, one of the most famous being Egon Jantke. The manufacture and quality control was the responsiblity of the many types of factories within Germany producing high quality metal and cloth insignia, some of which are still operating even today. Two of the most important and famous were Assmann & Sons of Lüdenscheid, manufacturer of many metal items, and Ewald

Vorsteher of Wuppertal. The latter specialised in producing silk woven insignia on a continuous band which gave rise to their trade mark, the now familiar term BeVo, an acronym derived from *B*andfabrik *E*wald *Vo*rsteher.

The quality of German badges and insignia can be divided into certain basic types:

1 Hand-embroidered designs, sometimes in gold or silver metallic threads, on cloth items;
2 Metal emblems mounted on to a cloth backing;
3 Machine-embroidered designs on a cloth backing;
4 Machine-woven silk or cotton designs, usually worked on to a continuous band of cloth;
5 Silk-screen-printed cloth badges;
6 Hand-stencilled or hand-painted items – seldom encountered.

Colours played an important part in the design of these items. Each uniformed organisation tended to have a particular colour which it used as its organisational colour. Other colours or colour combinations were employed to indicate internal divisions, precedence of ranks, or levels of responsibility. Gold normally took precedence over silver, although in the case of the SA gold and silver insignia were used to differentiate between districts that shared the same SA district colour.

Numerals used in the design of badges were either Roman or Arabic. Roman numerals usually indicated a more senior formation than did Arabic numerals.

Lettering used on badges and insignia came in a variety of styles. Block Roman lettering, referred to as 'Latin' script, block Gothic letters, copper plate handwritten script, German handwritten script, known as Sutterlin, and, on a number of Foreign Volunteer items, lettering in Cyrillic (Russian-style) script are all encountered.

Runic emblems were a feature of some of the designs of certain badges worn by personnel of a number of Nazi Party uniformed formations.

The Swastika and the German eagle were both important emblems, the former the official emblem of the National Socialist German Workers Party (NSDAP) and the latter the historic emblem of the German nation. Combined together they were officially established as the State emblem of National Socialist Germany. The actual design, colour and style of both these emblems varied considerably with their use by different uniformed organisations.

Acknowledgements

I am indebted to the following persons who have kindly assisted me directly or indirectly both in the past and the present in the preparation of this book. Eric Campion; Jean Pierre Chantrain; Dieter Deuster; the late Colonel Cliford M. Dodkins, C.B.E., D.S.O.; William 'Bill' Dodkins; Albert Eyns; James Van Fleet; Peter Giddings; Ken Green; James H. Joslyn; David Littlejohn, M.A., A.L.A.; Andrew Mollo; Hans Joachim Nietsch; Tony L. Oliver; Jost Schneider: Prof. René Smeets; Tom Stubbs; Hugh Page Taylor; Lt Commander W. Maitland Thornton, M.B.E., R.D.*, R.N.R.; W. 'Bill' Tobin; Herbert Walther; Jan Winters; and Alan Beadle.

The photographs that appear in this book are from the author's own collection, the Imperial War Museum, the Bundesarchiv, E.C.P.A. and from other private collections.

National and Organisational Emblems

It was common practice for the personnel of all German uniformed organisations to wear a distinguishing emblem of some sort on their main item of uniform apparel. These emblems were usually one of two types. The first was a version of the German National Emblem, which, during the period of the Third Reich, consisted of an eagle – historically the national emblem of Germany – clutching in its talons a Swastika, the emblem of the National Socialist German Workers Party.

The second type of emblem was the Organisational Emblem. Where they were worn, these varied considerably in form, colouring and size. Sometimes it happened that both the National Emblem and the Organisational Emblem were used together.

The emblems illustrated here have been chosen to show the variance in the types of National Emblem, and something of the diversity of design and colour used with the Organisational Emblems. Many more examples existed, but space precludes showing and listing them all.

Plate 1. National and Organisational Emblems

1 The German Naval breast emblem (National Emblem). Worn above the right breast pocket on uniform tunics and in the corresponding position on other forms of clothing without breast pockets. A hand-embroidered version in yellow threads on dark navy-blue badge cloth to match the dark navy-blue uniforms was worn by all Naval personnel up to the rank of commissioned officer. Officers tended to wear the Naval National Emblem in gilt threads.

2 German Army breast emblem. Machine-woven in fine silver-aluminium-coloured metallic threads with a backing of dark blue-green badge cloth, it was worn above the right breast pocket of all tunics with the exception of fatigue jackets and greatcoats. This type was a common feature of pre-war uniforms usually worn by troops up to the rank of commissioned

1 The German Army National Emblem, worn here by Oberleutnant Hoffmann on the right breast of his special field-grey jacket, standard issue for wear by crews of German tank destroyer and self-propelled assault gun units (5 September 1942).

2 Naval, Air Force and Army Panzer officers in conversation. The German Naval and the Luftwaffe National Emblems can be seen, both types of which were worn over the right breast on their respective tunics. From left to right are Kapitänleutnant Kraus, RKT, Major Hradak, RKT, Kapitänleutnant Strelow, RKT, Kapitänleutnant Witte, RKT, and Hauptmann Grüner, RKT (8 February 1943).

officer, although officers were known to make use of this version which was less expensive to purchase than the hand-embroidered version that they normally wore.

3 Air Force officers breast emblem. Hand-embroidered in silver-coloured metallic threads.

4 Waffen-SS (Armed-SS) arm eagle as normally worn by W-SS officers. Hand-embroidered in silver-aluminium-coloured metallic threads on a backing of black badge cloth, this emblem was worn on the left upper arm half way between the shoulder seam and the elbow on all uniform tunics including the greatcoat.

5 The NSFK (Nationalsozialistische Flieger Korps) organisational arm and breast emblem. Officially referred to as a 'Flying Man' emblem, it has been said to represent Icarus, the person in Greek mythology who attempted

3 The Waffen-SS National Emblem. Always worn on the upper left arm of tunics and greatcoats, it is seen here being worn by a Waffen-SS Artillery soldier under training (6 March 1941).

to fly to the sun on wings made from birds' feathers and wax. Two different coloured versions existed. The type shown here, machine-woven on to a backing of blue-grey cloth, was used on the NSFK blue-grey uniform tunics. Those 'Flying Man' breast emblems with a backing of tan material were for use on the tan-coloured work shirt.

6 Breast emblem for Marine-Artillery personnel. These naval personnel were distinguished from their sea-going compatriots by wearing field-grey uniforms and gold-coloured buttons and insignia.

7 NSKK (Nationalsozialistische Kraftfahr Korps) eagle arm badge worn on the right upper arm of the tan shirt and light-weight tan jacket. Other backing colours existed in order to match or blend in with the colour of the uniform. This emblem was also produced as part of the NSKK 'Old Fighters' arm chevron (for details see Plate 58, nos 4 and 5). War-time NSKK units including NSKK Transport Regiments wore a black-edged emblem on the upper left arm of the tunic and greatcoat.

4 An NSKK guard outside the offices of the National Socialist Public Assistance Organisation, Paris. The NSKK emblem was worn on the upper right arm of tunics and greatcoats.

8 NSDAP Political Leaders metal cap eagle, late pattern.

9 German National Railways arm eagle badge. This badge, worn together with a cuff-title (see Plate 29, nos 3 to 6), was in use for a very short time. Introduced in February 1941, it was withdrawn along with the cuff-titles eight months later in September 1941 and replaced by a whole new series of arm eagle badges that also displayed the names of important Railway Divisions together with the initial letters of the wearers' railway Directorate (see Plate 56, nos 1 to 6). When in use it was worn on the left upper arm of the railway tunics and greatcoat.

10 NS-RKB (Nationalsozialistische-Reich Krieger Bund) metal breast eagle badge. The white metal eagle and Swastika badge with a black enamelled Iron Cross motif was worn pinned to the right upper breast at the same level as the medal ribbon bar on the left breast of the dark blue suit worn by members of the National Socialist Empire War Association.

11 The Reichsarbeitsdienst (National Labour Service) cap emblem, cloth version. This machine-woven cap badge featured the blade of a shovel (see also Plate 38) bearing a Swastika set between the angle made by two ears of wheat.

12 Organisational Emblem as used by the Sicherheits-und Hilfdienst (Security and Help Service) and the Luftschutz Warndienst (Air Raid Warning Service) collectively referred to as the 'Luftschutz'. The emblem was worn on the front of the special pattern RLB/SHD/LSW steel helmet as a transfer applied to the metal surface. As a machine-woven cloth badge, it was worn over the right breast of certain uniforms and on the left upper arm of other uniforms of both services. It was also worn as a cap emblem.

13 German Police National Emblem, late pattern. This white metal badge was worn on the peaked cap by all ranks of the Police with the exception of the Waterways Police up to

General of Police. (For the design of the Police eagle within a wreath of oakleaves featured on other police items, especially the arm badges, see Plate 57.)

5 Two members of the Berlin Police adjust the air-raid warning siren mounted on their motor vehicle. Both Policemen are wearing the late pattern Police emblem as their cap badges (24 February 1939).

14 Landwacht (Land Watch or Guard) metal cap badge (see also Plate 34, no. 8).
15 Deutsche Jägerschaft Organisational Emblem arm badge (see Plate 54, nos 7 and 8).
16 Sturm Abteilung (SA) Organisational Emblem here used as a sports vest emblem. Various SA districts were appointed selected colours and from 1934 they had a system of abbreviated letters used officially to distinguish each district. The letters 'KP' that appear on this SA sports vest emblem stand for the SA district of Kurpfalz which was also appointed to use the colour of 'Stahlgrün' – steel-green – a dark shade of green and the same colour shared by the SA district of Nordsee, but whose district initials were No. This SA organisational emblem which was worn on the front of the SA sports vest and on the track suit featured a pseudo-runic emblem combining the letters 'S' and 'A'. The same emblem was used on certain shoulder straps (see Plate 9, no. 12).

Plate 2. National and Organisational Emblems

1 The Deutsche Arbeitsfront (German Labour Front) Organisational Emblem. This Swastika within a cog-wheel design only appeared on DAF uniforms as a small white or gilt metal shoulder strap mount and on DAF waist belt buckles (see Plate 15, nos 14 to 17). The emblem as illustrated here was used on DAF flags and car pennants.
2 NS-Studentenbund (National Socialist Students League) Organisational Emblem. The distinctive feature of this emblem was the lozenge-shaped Swastika, a device appearing on the arm bands and belt buckles used by members of this league (see Plate 32, no. 12).
3 German Air-Sea Rescue cap emblem.
4 Breast eagle National Emblem as worn by German Army female auxiliaries (Nachrichtenhelferinnen des Heeres) from the rank of Nachrichten-Helferin to Nachrichten-Haupthelferin. (See also Plate 46, no. 4.)
5 Cap emblem for members of the Reichsautobahnen. (See also Plate 54, nos 2 and 3.)
6 The Organisation Todt emblem, a combination of the letters 'O' and 'T' as used on the late pattern collar patch for lower ranks of the Organisation Todt. (See also Plate 19, nos 8 to 11.)
7 Bahnschutzpolizei arm eagle emblem worn on the upper left arm of the Bzp jacket and tunics but not on the greatcoat by officer class ranks from Bzp-Oberzugführer to Bzp-Stabsführer.
8 The Deutscher Luftsport-Verband cap emblem in metal.
9 The Hitler-Jugend emblem, shown here as a

6 The Hitler Youth emblem worn on the sports vest of a junior member of the Junge Mädel.

7 The RLB Organisational Emblem, shown here worn on the left cuff of an RLB Officer (8 October 1943).

sports vest emblem. This emblem was also worn as an arm badge by members of the BDM (Bund Deutsche Mädel).

10 Technische Nothilfe (TeNo—Technical Emergency Corps) arm eagle emblem worn on the upper left arm of the dark blue uniform and greatcoat as well as the field-grey tunic.

11 Zollbeamte (Customs) emblem, here as used on Customs officials cuff-title. (See also Plate 27, no. 11.)

12 Postschutz (Postal Protection) arm badge.

13 NSBO emblem as featured on sleeve badge (see Plate 37, no. 2).

14 The Reichsluftschutz Bund (National Air Protection League) arm eagle worn on the left forearm. (See also Plate 53, nos 1 and 2.)

15 The Deutsche Rote Kreuz (German Red Cross) emblem, as used as a hat badge. This same emblem was the main feature on all German Red Cross flags and stick-pin badges.

16 Werkschutz (Factory Guard) arm badge.

17 Cap emblem for personnel employed in State Service, Government officials, etc.

18 Breast badge rank emblem as worn by members of the BDM. (See also Plate 41, nos 14 to 17.)

Shoulder Straps and Collar Patches

Practically every uniformed formation that existed in Germany before and during the Third Reich period made use of shoulder straps and collar patches. It was undoubtedly the main method of displaying a person's rank. These items were also used to indicate such things as the wearer's unit, and, by the use of colour, his branch of service or particular qualification. Levels of responsibility, military or political status such as being an active or reserve member of an organisation, the wearer's district or special appointment, could all be read from shoulder straps and collar patches.

Not every formation wore both shoulder straps and collar patches together. Some like the NSDAP Political Leadership eventually settled for wearing only collar patches. Other formations like the early Reichsbahn (German National Railways) uniformed personnel wore only collar patches of a set design for all ranks. The membership of the Stahlhelm for instance wore only collar patches in ascending order of rank. Quite a few formations chose to use a detailed system of collar patches that showed both the wearer's unit as well as his individual rank where the shoulder straps were shared between groups of ranks. Such formations included the General-SS, the NSKK and the NSFK. The completely opposite system was used by the German Red Cross and the Waterways Air Raid Protection Service where the shoulder straps were used for every separate rank and the few collar patches used were shared between these ranks. Yet again other formations took to wearing only shoulder straps without the aid of collar patches. Such a formation was the Hitler Youth. It is, therefore, almost impossible to arrive at a specific observation about shoulder straps – and shoulder cords and collar patches – and 'passants' as to their method of wear. However, what is apparent is that in one combination or other they played an important part in the sartorial design of German uniforms and had a very practical aspect to their use.

Plate 3. NSDAP Political Leaders' Shoulder Straps and Collar Patches

During the 12-year period from 1933 (or possibly just before) to 1945, four sets of rank insignia were introduced at different times for use by the Political Leadership personnel of the Nazi Party. Each of these sets of insignia varied in design and in colouring. The first two issues were simple and their numbers small in comparison with the complex system finally introduced with its 97 separate sets of collar patches.

1st Pattern, 1933–34

The first pattern of rank insignia used by early Political Leaders made use of shoulder straps, a feature not found with other issues of insignia of later dates (the exception being the shoulder straps used by personnel of NSDAP Political Leadership schools – Ordensburgen). These narrow shoulder straps and their corresponding collar patches were worn in conjunction with a special arm badge (see Plate 37, no. 3) and cap cords worn on the early Political

Leaders Kepi, with their system of cap cord knots indicating ranks (not illustrated).

The first pattern rank insignia was a short lived system, introduced in 1933 or thereabouts and phased out during 1934–35.

1 Ortsgruppenleiter.
2 Kreisleiter.
3 Gauleiter.
4 Landesinspektor.
5 Reichsinspektor und Reichsorganisationsleiter.
6 Blockwart.
7 Zellenwart.
8 Ortsgruppenleiter.
9 Kreisleiter.
10 Gauleiter.
11 Landesinspektor
12 Reichsinspektor
13 Reichsorganisationsleiter. (Prior to the use of collar patches with a double oak-leaf pattern being worn by this rank, the holders of the appointment of Reichs Organisations Leader wore the same pattern of collar patches as those used by Reichsinspektor, no. 12 above. The Organisation Leader was distinguished, however, by wearing a three, gold-braided, chevron sleeve badge worn on the left cuff – not illustrated.)

It will be noticed that the facing colours of light brown, dark brown, bright red and carmine red altered little during the development of the ranking system from 1933 to 1945. It was the increase in, and complexity of the badges of rank that was a reflection of the growth of the Political Leadership movement. The first design collar patch system was simple compared with the complex arrangement introduced as the final pattern. Although the Political Leadership system was nation-wide the complex sub-division had in the first year or so not been fully established and only eight grades of responsibility existed.

(The NSDAP Political Leadership system employed in Germany during the Third Reich period has been explained in some detail in my previous book *German Uniforms of the Third Reich, 1933–1945*, pages 12 to 16, published by Blandford Press.)

By 1934 the German nation had been divided up into four areas of responsibility, three based on territorial areas and one on leadership responsibility. Germany, and later the annexed and occupied territories, was divided into a number of Gauen. These in turn were subdivided into numerous Kreise, and in turn the Kreis was subdivided into a number of Ortsgruppen.

2nd Pattern, 1934–36

The second pattern of collar patches mirrored the newly established division of responsibility

8 Early pattern NSDAP Political Leaders collar patches, 3rd pattern series. Party Member Bohl who as a Gauleiter in June 1939 became the new Landesgruppenleiter der Auslands-Organisation der NSDAP in Spain.

within the Political Leadership system throughout the German Reich, a system that was to
last until Germany's defeat in 1945.

14 Unterabteilungsleiter in Ortsgruppenleitung.

15 Abteilungsleiter in Kreisleitung.

16 Amtsleiter in Reichsleitung.

17 Stellvertr. Gauleiter.

18 Gauleiter.

19 Reichsleiter.

3rd Pattern, 1936–38

The third pattern of collar patches introduced
during 1936 were in use officially until 1938,
although the insignia of the lower ranks of
responsibility tended to be kept in use right up
to 1945.

20 Mitarbeiter Ortsgruppenleitung.

9 2nd pattern NSDAP Political Leaders collar
patches for the rank of Gauleiter, worn here by
Gauleiter Dr Alfred Meyer.

10 3rd pattern Reichsleiter collar patches worn here by Dr Robert Ley (right).

16

21 Hauptstellenleiter in Kreisleitung.

22 Stützpunktleiter (in Ortsgruppenleitung).

23 Hauptamtsleiter in Kreisleitung.

24 Stellvertr. Gauleiter in Gauleitung.

25 Reichsleiter.

Special Insignia, 3rd Pattern, 1936–38

Special collar patches were introduced during the third pattern period. These were worn by Party Court Officials and Political Leaders retired from the active list. They had the same design of collar patch emblem but the patch colour of dark blue and black and piping colours were quite distinctive.

26 Reichsleiter of Party Courts.

27 Beisitzer of Party Courts.

28 Hauptstellenleiter retired of Ortsgruppen of Stützpunkt.

29 Stellvertr. Gauleiter retired.

4th Pattern 1938–45

The fourth and final series of collar patches was by far the most complex of all. In total, there were 97 separate ranks of appointment divided into four areas of responsibility: seventeen Ortsgruppen ranks, 22 Kreisleitung ranks, 27 Gauleitung ranks, and 28 Reichsleitung ranks, with the addition of three special collar patch designs for holders of special honorary commissions in the NSDAP Political Leadership Corps.

30 Oberhelfer in Ortsgruppen.

31 Bereitschaftsleiter in Gauleitung.

32 Haupteinsatzleiter in Reichsleitung.

33 Oberabschnittsleiter in Ortsgruppen.

34 Dienstleiter in Kreisleitung.

35 Gauleiter.

36 Reichsleiter.

37 Sonderbeauftrager der NSDAP.

The use of the fourth pattern series of collar patches were tied in with the special NSDAP Political Leaders arm bands (see Plate 32, nos 3, 4, 5 and 6).

11 Reichsorganisationsleiter Dr Robert Ley on board the flagship of the 'Strength through Joy' fleet, the *Robert Ley*, surrounded by young people in national costumes from Lithuania, Finland and Slovakia (24 July 1939). Ley is wearing the late pattern collar patches for a Reichsleiter.

Plate 4. SA Shoulder Straps and Collar Patches

The SA (Sturmabteilung) was the oldest of all the Nazi Party uniformed organisations, tracing its foundation back to 3 August 1921 when, as a fledgling formation, it was known as the 'Gymnastic and Sports Section' of the NSDAP under the command of Josef Klintsch.

From the time when the first SA Detachments were organised, the members received titles of rank that were deliberately chosen in order to be different from the then existing German military rank terms.

The evolution of SA insignia was closely associated with the development of the SA uniform. The Swastika arm band, known as a 'Kampfbinde' or 'Battle Band' (see also Plate 32, no. 1) was the first recognizable insignia worn by the membership of the SA. The year 1923 saw the introduction of the first brown shirt uniform, albeit of a fairly basic appearance.

In 1927, colour, which was to play an important part in the development of SA uniform items, was first used with the introduction of coloured collar patches. By 1933, with the issuing of specific dress regulations, shoulder straps and coloured tops to the SA képis were added to the existing collar patches and all were worn together both on the former 'tradition' uniform and the newly introduced, military style, SA brown, four-pocket tunic and breeches uniform.

There were two separate patterns of SA insignia, the first covering the period from 1933 to 1938, the second from 1938–39 to 1945. The first pattern shoulder straps were worn singly, on the right shoulder of the brown shirt uniform and the officers tunic and later the greatcoat. The Collar patches were worn in pairs, the left hand patch showing the wearer's service unit and the right hand patch the rank. Officers from the rank of Standartenführer and above wore patches in matching pairs, with their rank displayed on both patches.

Coloured material used as underlay to the first pattern shoulder straps and in the manufacture of the first pattern collar patches identified the wearer's SA district.

In 1931 the Nazis, in an effort to keep alive the former military traditions which the Weimar Republic had deliberately allowed to lapse, introduced a numbering system for their SA Regiments. These numbers, which were featured on their collar patches, corresponded with the enumeration of the pre-1918 German Army Regiments that had been garrisoned in the same area where the SA Standarten were raised. Where Jäger Battalions had been stationed the local SA Standarte was known as a Jägerstandarte.

1st pattern, 1933–38.

1 Shoulder strap for SA Medical personnel from SA-Sanitätsmann to SA-Sanitätsobertruppführer.

2 Shoulder strap for SA Administrative personnel from SA-Verwaltungsmann to SA-Verwaltungsobertruppführer.

3 Shoulder strap for SA-Mann to SA-Obertruppführer in the SA District Thüringen.

4 Shoulder strap for SA-Mann to SA-Obertruppführer in the SA District Niederrhein.

5 Shoulder strap for SA-Mann to SA-Obertruppführer in SA District Hessen.

6 Shoulder strap for SA-Sturmführer to SA-Sturmhauptführer in SA District of Thüringen.

7 Shoulder strap for SA-Sturmbannführer to SA-Standartenführer in the SA District of Franken.

8 Shoulder strap for SA-Oberführer to SA-Obergruppenführer in SA District Berlin-Brandenburg.

9 Shoulder strap for SA-Chef des Stabes

(Ernst Röhm).

10 Left hand rank collar patch for rank of SA-Obertruppführer for the SA District of Ostmark.

11 Right hand unit collar patch for ranks from SA-Mann to SA-Obertruppführer worn by members of 2nd SA Flying unit in the SA District of Südwest.

12 Right hand unit collar patch worn by members from ranks of SA-Mann to SA-Obertruppführer from 1st Sturm of 1st Jäger-Regiment in the SA District of Hochland.

13 Right hand unit collar patch worn by members from the ranks of SA-Sturmführer to SA-Sturmhauptführer from 15th Pionier Sturm of the 69th Regiment from the SA District of Westmark.

14 Right hand unit collar patch for ranks from SA-Mann to SA-Obertruppführer from 3rd Marinesturm of 43rd Marine-SA Regiment.

15 Right hand collar patch of a matching pair of collar patches for the SA-Chef des Stabes. These collar patches were only worn by Chief of Staff of the SA Ernst Röhm from 1933 until July 1934. The six-pointed star emblem used on both the collar patches as well as on the single shoulder strap (no. 9 above) was based on the rank insignia of a Bolivian Army General. Röhm designed these items for himself and he based his insignia on the rank insignia used by a General of the Bolivian Army, Röhm having been a Staff Officer Advisor to the Bolivian Army.

2nd pattern, 1938/39–45.

16 Shoulder strap for SA-Sturmmann to SA-Hauptruppführer from SA Foot units including the SA-Standarten 'Feldherrnhalle'.

17 Shoulder strap for SA-Sturmmann to SA-Hauptruppführer from SA Engineer units.

18 Shoulder strap for SA-Sturmmann to SA-Hauptruppführer from SA Cavalry units.

19 Shoulder strap for SA-Sturmführer to SA-

12 SA-Obergruppenführer Wilhelm Scheppmann who took over the position of Chief of Staff of the SA on the death in a motor car accident of Viktor Lutze. Scheppmann, shown here wearing the war-time insignia of an SA-Obergruppenführer (shoulder straps as well as collar patches worn in matching pairs), was the last SA Chief of Staff (19 August 1943).

Hauptsturmführer from SA Foot Units including the SA-Standarten 'Feldherrnhalle'.

20 Shoulder strap for SA-Sturmführer to SA-Hauptsturmführer from SA Cavalry units.

21 Shoulder strap for SA-Sturmbannführer to SA-Standartenführer from SA Engineer units.

22 Shoulder strap for SA-Oberführer to SA-Obergruppenführer.

23 Shoulder strap for the SA-Stabschef (Viktor Lutze and Wilhelm Scheppmann), c. 1934–45.

24 Right hand unit collar patch worn by pupils of the Reichsführerschule (State

Leaders School). The left hand patch is of the same design, with the Tyr-rune emblem pointing in the opposite direction.

25 Right hand unit collar patch worn by members of the Reich Medical School.

26 Right hand unit collar patch worn by members of the SA-Standarten 'Feldherrnhalle' from the rank of SA-Mann/SA-Sturmmann to SA-Obertruppführer.

27 Right hand unit collar patch worn by members of 3rd Sturm from 30th Standart from SA District Kurpfalz.

28 Right hand collar patch worn by ranks from SA-Sturmmann to SA-Haupttruppführer from 4th Sturm of Standart 70 from SA district Tannenberg.

29 Right hand collar patch of a matching pair for the rank of SA-Stabschef.

Plate 5. NSKK Shoulder Straps and Collar Patches

From the time when the NSKK became a separate branch of the Nazi Party and was removed from the control of the SA (23 August 1934), new insignia was issued.

NSKK Collar patches possessed two distinctive features. Almost all the patches were of black material, with just very limited exceptions, and the letters and numerals displayed on these patches were in metal, silver-white for normal NSKK personnel and gilt for Marine-NSKK units.

1 Right hand unit patch for the Motorsturm 11 from the Motorstandarte 29.

2 Right hand unit patch for personnel of Lehrsturm from Motorgruppe Hessen.

3 Right hand unit patch for personnel on the staff of Motorobergruppen 'Ost'; orange-red.

4 Right hand unit patch for the personnel on the staff of Motorgruppe Ostsee.

5 Right hand unit patch for staff of Motorboots Standarte 1, a Marine-NSKK unit.

6 Right hand patch for personnel on the staff of the NSKK-Korpsführer.

7 Right hand unit patch for personnel on the staff of Motorstandarte M51.

8 Right hand unit patch for personnel of the staff of the NSKK Technical Branch.

Whereas NSKK collar patches displayed the wearer's individual rank (left hand patch) and his unit designation (right hand patch) for all nineteen NSKK ranks, shoulder straps were shared by groups of ranks, there only being six straps for the nineteen different ranks. Colour was also used as a secondary piping to the black underlay of these straps. The various colours indicated the wearer's NSKK brigade or sub-division locality. NSKK shoulder straps were often worn singly, on the wearer's right shoulder, but certain war-raised NSKK units wore them on both shoulders.

9 Shoulder strap for ranks from NSKK-Mann to NSKK-Obertruppführer from the NSKK Motor-Brigade 'Westfalen'.

10 Shoulder strap for ranks from NSKK-Sturmführer to NSKK-Sturmhauptführer from the Motor-Brigade 'Franken'.

11 Shoulder strap for ranks from NSKK-Staffelführer to NSKK-Standartenführer from the Motor-Brigade 'Hochland'.

12 Shoulder strap for the rank of NSKK-Oberführer only from Motor sub-Division 'Ostland'.

13 Shoulder strap for ranks from NSKK-Brigadeführer to NSKK-Obergruppenführer. Carmine red piping indicated a member of the Korpsführung (NSKK High Command).

14 Shoulder strap for the NSKK-Korpsführer.

Stahlhelm Collar Patches, 1918–33/35

The Stahlhelm (Steel Helmets) was an organisation of former German servicemen. It was founded on Christmas day 1918 by Franz Seldte. It was organised along military lines, with its members wearing field-grey uniforms based on the field-service uniforms worn by

German Army troops during the Great War. The Stahlhelm rank system was of a semi-military nature with the use of collar patches, worn in matching pairs, as the principal indication of the wearer's rank and branch of service. The collar patches were made of cloth with cloth piping displaying metal oakleaves, pips, and sometimes bars.

15 Wehrmann, also worn by Oberwehrmann and Stabswehrmann, but in their case the distinction was made between ranks by the use of a single braided chevron (Oberwehrmann), and a double braided chevron (Stabswehrmann) worn on the left upper arm (not illustrated).

16 Wehrmann, cavalry branch.

17 Wehrmann, paymasters department.

18 Gruppenführer, motorised units.

19 Feldmeister.

20 Oberfeldmeister, leadership assistant.

21 Zugführer.

22 Oberzugführer, signals unit.

23 Kompanieführer.

24 Divisionsführer.

25 Bundesführer.

26 Collar patch for members of the Scharnhorst Jugend, the youth section of the Stahlhelm.

Stahlhelm branch colours are shown on Plate 5 and are indicated above.

Plate 6. Allgemeine-SS and Waffen-SS Shoulder Straps and Collar Patches

November 1925 saw the introduction of distinctive items of dress for wear by members of the newly formed SS. Like the membership of the SA, to which the SS were subordinate, the SS personnel of that period wore brown shirts and brown breeches. However, as a distinction, the SS wore black instead of brown ties, black képis in place of the SA brown ones, and their Swastika arm bands had black edging (see Plate 32, no. 9).

In July 1934, almost a month after the assassination of the SA Chief of Staff Ernst Röhm, control of the SS was taken from the SA, and, in recognition of the part the SS had played in the Röhm purge, the SS was elevated to the position of an independent organisation within the NSDAP.

While publication of the first SA and SS dress regulation had been made in 1932, and in May of the same year the SS had received new badges of rank, July 1934 saw the publication of new dress regulation separate from those of the SA. Shoulder straps of the Allgemeine-SS (General-SS) were worn singly on the right shoulder of the original brown shirt uniform (the 'Tradition Uniform' that was phased out of use between 1933 and the summer of 1935), the black service uniform universally worn from 1936, and the black greatcoat. Collar patches were worn in pairs, the right hand patch displaying unit designations or emblem up to the rank of SS-Standartenführer and the left hand patch displaying rank.

Allegemeine-SS Insignia, 1933–45

1 Shoulder strap for ranks from SS-Mann to SS-Stabsscharführer and SS-Sturmscharführer.

2 Shoulder strap for ranks from SS-Untersturmführer to SS-Hauptsturmführer.

3 Shoulder strap for ranks from SS-Sturmbannführer to SS-Standartenführer.

4 Shoulder strap for ranks from SS-Oberführer to SS-Obergruppenführer.

5 Shoulder strap for the Reichsführer-SS (Heinrich Himmler) introduced on 15 October 1934.

Collar patches nos 6 to 9 were worn c. May 1933 to September 1934.

6 Right hand rank collar patch for SS-Mann.

7 Right hand rank collar patch for SS-Oberscharführer.

8 Right hand rank collar patch for SS-

Obersturmbannführer.

9 Right hand rank collar patch for SS-Standartenführer.

Collar patches nos 10 to 13 were worn c. September 1934 to May 1945.

10 Right hand rank collar patch for SS-Mann.

11 Right hand rank collar patch for SS-Oberscharführer.

12 Right hand rank collar patch for SS-Sturmbannführer.

13 Right hand rank collar patch for SS-Standartenführer.

14 Left hand unit collar patch for non-commissioned ranks in 8th SS Signals Unit.

15 Left hand unit collar patch for commissioned ranks on the staff of SS-Sub District XXXVI.

16 Left hand unit collar patch for non-commissioned ranks in 2nd Cavalry Regiment.

17 Left hand unit collar patch for non-commissioned ranks in 12th SS Motorised unit.

18 Left hand unit collar patch for non-commissioned ranks in 82nd SS Foot Regiment.

19 Left hand unit collar patch for members of the Special Purpose Motorcycle Squadron of SS District East.

20 Left hand unit collar patch for commissioned ranks on the staff of SS-Sub District IX.

and Air Force, as arm-of-service colour.

21 Shoulder strap for SS-Kannonier (Gunner in the Armed-SS).

22 Collar patch for this rank (and others such as SS-Mann and SS-Sturmmann not listed here).

23 Shoulder strap for SS-Oberscharführer, signals section of SS Regiment Leibstandarte SS 'Adolf Hitler'.

24 Basic SS runic collar patch, worn on right side.

25 Rank collar patch for SS-Oberscharführer.

26 Shoulder strap for SS-Sturmbannführer, armoured units.

27 Rank collar patch for SS-Sturmbannführer.

28 Unit collar patch for an officer from the SS-Totenkopf Regiment, introduced in May 1940.

29 Shoulder strap for SS-Standartenführer from supply, administration and technical service branches.

30 Collar patch for SS-Standartenführer.

31 Shoulder strap for an SS-Brigadeführer und Generalmajor der Waffen-SS.

32 Collar patch for an SS-Brigadeführer und Generalmajor der Waffen-SS.

33 Shoulder strap for an SS-Oberstgruppenführer und Generaloberst der Waffen-SS.

34 Collar patch for an SS-Oberstgruppenführer und Generaloberst der Waffen-SS.

SS-VT Insignia 1933–39, and Waffen-SS Insignia, 1939–40, and 1942–45

Two issues of rank insignia (shoulder straps and collar patches) were introduced for wear by members of the SS-VT and Waffen-SS at different times. The first issue covered the period from 1939 to 1940, the second, below, covered from 1942 to 1945. However, it was common practice for earlier issue insignia to continue in use long after the new issues were made. Colour was introduced into these items, used on the same principle as that of the Army

Plate 7. Hitler-Jugend and Deutsche Jungvolk Shoulder Straps and Collar Patch

Two patterns of shoulder straps were used by the membership of the Hitler Youth (HJ) at different times. These straps were the main method that the Hitler Youth adopted in order to display the individual ranks of their members. The first pattern of straps was brought into service around 1933. The second pattern was in use from 1938 until 1945. Only

13 Reichsjugendführer Arthur Axmann (right) who took over the control of the Hitler Youth from Baulder von Schirach and held the position right up to the end of the war. He was with Hitler in the Bunker when Hitler committed suicide in 1945. The rank of Reich Youth Leader was the only Hitler Youth rank that made use of collar patches. Axmann is seen here in conversation with the Portuguese Youth Leader, Quintino da Costa.

one person, that of the Reichsjugendführer, wore collar patches (no. 23). The HJ also used lanyards for some ranks, in conjunction with shoulder strap ranks.

1st Pattern, 1933–38

The first pattern of HJ shoulder straps was more complicated than was the case with the second pattern. Not only did they show the wearer's individual rank, but, by the use of coloured piping and shoulder strap insignia, they also indicated his particular 'Oberbann.' This coloured piping was also used on the khaki peaked cap. The actual colour of the strap for the higher ranks from HJ-Bannführer upwards was tied in with the coloured cap bands as worn on the early pattern Hitler

Youth peaked caps, both of which indicated senior HJ ranks. This was a feature not found with the head-dress of the later Hitler Youth uniforms and did not feature on the second pattern shoulder straps.

The 'Oberbann' colours as used by the Hitler Youth (and by the DJ – see Plate 41, nos 1 to 6) were as follows:

Oberbann 1	red	Oberbann 4	blue
Oberbann 2	yellow	Oberbann 5	black
Oberbann 3	green	Oberbann 6	white

1 Shoulder strap for Hitlerjunge from Oberbann 1, Bann 80.
2 Shoulder strap for HJ-Kameradschaftsführer from Bann 124, Oberbann 5.
3 Shoulder strap for HJ-Unterbannführer from Bann 158, Oberbann 6.
4 Shoulder strap for HJ-Bannführer from Bann 129, Oberbann 1.
5 Shoulder strap for HJ-Oberbannführer.
6 Shoulder strap for Führer des Stabes der R.J.F. (Reichsjugendführer).

German youths living abroad – outside the borders of Germany – who were members of the Hitler Youth were distinguished by wearing special shoulder straps that were piped in a designated colour according to the area of the world where they were living. These colours were:

Red: Europe (other than Germany)
Yellow: North and South America
Green: Asia
Blue: Africa
White: Australia.

7 Shoulder straps for a member of the Foreign Hitler Youth from Japan.

All HJ shoulder straps of both first and second patterns were worn in pairs.

2nd Pattern, 1938–45

The second series of straps, as already stated, were of a less complicated system. The basic colour for the strap was black for all HJ personnel regardless of rank, and dark navy-

14 Members of the Hitler Youth and the DJ receiving instruction from a young Army officer in the use of a machine-gun. Clearly shown are the HJ shoulder straps and the single DJ strap worn by the youth at the top left of the picture.

blue for Marine-HJ personnel. Piping for the shoulder straps of the lower ranks together with the Bann numbers or special letters were in selected colours indicating particular branches of the Hitler Youth. Individual ranks were shown by a system of metal 'pips', braided bars, and oakleaves in white metal or gilt.

8 Shoulder strap for Hitlerjunge in the General-HJ (Allgemeine-HJ).

9 Shoulder strap for HJ-Oberrottenführer in signals branch (Nachrichten-HJ).

10 Shoulder strap for HJ-Kameradschaftsführer of the One Year's Land Service scheme (Landjahr).

11 Shoulder strap for HJ-Gefolgschaftsführer on the staff of his Gebiet (Gebietsstab).

12 Shoulder strap for HJ-Oberstammführer of the Reichsjugend führung.

13 Shoulder strap for HJ-Bannführer from Bann 123.

14 Shoulder strap for an HJ-Obergebietsführer.

Special shoulder straps were a feature of these second pattern straps.

15 Shoulder strap for blind members of the Hitler Youth organised into a special 'Blinde' or Blind Bann for boys.

16 Shoulder strap for HJ-Hauptstabsarzt (senior staff doctor).

17 Shoulder strap for an Oberzugführer (senior squad leader) from the war-time formation known as the 'Wachgefolgschaft

"Baldur von Schirach"' (Baldur von Schirach Guard Platoon).

18 Shoulder strap for Marine-Hitler Youth of the Binnenschiffahrt (Inland Navigation).

19 Shoulder strap for Mannschaften (other ranks) at the Adolf Hitler Schule (Adolf Hitler School).

20 Shoulder strap for HJ-Scharführer at the NPEA (Nat.Pol. Erziehungsanstalten).

Members of the Deutsche Jungvolk (DJ) wore only a single shoulder strap on the right shoulder. It was narrower than the second pattern Hitler Youth shoulder straps. It was all black with black piping. The DJ unit numbers that were displayed on these straps were positioned along the length of the strap and not, as was the case with the straps for the HJ, across the strap.

21 Shoulder strap for a DJ member from DJ unit 666.

22 Shoulder strap for DJ member attending the Adolf Hitler School.

Plate 8. Reichsarbeitsdienst Shoulder Straps and Collar Patches

Rank insignia for the RAD as displayed by the use of shoulder straps and collar patches underwent three changes during the period 1936 to 1945, the last two styles of RAD insignia, of 1940 and 1942, being very different in appearance to the initial RAD insignia of 1936.

1st Pattern National Socialist German Volunteer Labour Service Insignia, c. 1936

Collar patches were worn in matching mirror pairs. Shoulder straps were worn in matching pairs.

1 Obervormann.
2 Truppführer.
3 Obertruppführer.

These three ranks wore only collar patches and no shoulder straps.

15 Reichs Labour Leader Konstantin Hierl (right) taking leave of a Political Leader. Hierl wears first pattern collar patches and shoulder straps for the rank of Reichsarbeitsführer.

4 Shoulder strap for Musikzugführer.
5 Collar patch for Musikzugführer.
6 Shoulder strap for Oberfeldmeister.
7 Collar patch for Oberfeldmeister.
8 Shoulder strap for Arbeitsdienst-Inspekteur.
9 Collar patch for Arbeitsdienst-Inspekteur.

2nd Pattern Reichsarbeitsdienst Insignia, c. 1940

10 RAD-Arbeitsmann shoulder strap. The black and silver twisted cording around the edge of the shoulder strap indicates that the wearer had volunteered for at least one year's Labour service.

11 Collar patch for RAD-Arbeitsmann.
12 Shoulder strap for RAD-Obertruppführer.
13 Collar patch for RAD-Obertruppführer.

14 Shoulder strap for RAD-Unterfeldmeister.
15 Collar patch for RAD-Unterfeldmeister.
16 Shoulder strap for RAD-Hauptamtswalter of the RAD Administration branch.
17 Collar patch for RAD-Hauptamtswalter, RAD Administration branch.

17 Generalleutnant Specht, holder of the Knights Cross with Oak Leaves inspecting RAD personnel wearing 3rd and final pattern collar patches.

16 A member of the RAD wearing 2nd pattern collar patches for an RAD-Truppführer (19 February 1943).

3rd Pattern Reichsarbeitsdienst Insignia, c. 1942

18 Shoulder strap for RAD-Hauptvormann.
19 Collar patch for RAD-Hauptvormann.
20 Shoulder strap for RAD-Oberfeldmeister, Justice Department.
21 Collar patch for RAD-Oberfeldmeister, Justice Department.
22 Shoulder strap for RAD-Arbeitsführer.
23 Collar patch for RAD-Arbeitsführer.
24 Shoulder strap for the Reichsarbeitsführer. This insignia was introduced during September 1942 and was worn exclusively by Reichsarbeitsführer Konstantin Hierl. (See also Plate 32, no. 13.)

25 Collar patch for the Reichsarbeitsführer.

The collar patches of the second and third patterns for ranks from RAD-Vormann to RAD-Obertruppführer were normally machine-woven patches with white cotton designs for the second pattern and grey cotton designs for the third pattern on a backing of black. Collar patches for ranks from RAD-Unterfeldmeister to RAD-Oberstarbeitsführer were usually hand embroidered in silver-aluminium thread on to black velvet or black cloth. Examples of this latter type exist where the collar patch device has been pressed out of silver coloured metal to appear as hand worked embroidery and mounted on to black velvet patches.

Colours were used as collar patch colouring and as underlay and piping to shoulder straps at different times. Prior to the outbreak of World War II, dark blue (cornflower blue) was used to indicate RAD medical personnel, dark green was used for administration personnel, red for musicians, and light blue for

18 Generaloberst von Kleist (left) accompanied by Obergeneralarbeitsführer Dr Schmeidler, inspecting and presenting military decorations to 500 RAD troops who had been engaged in front line construction work (15 June 1942).

RAD Justice Department.

During the war Specialist Officers were employed in the RAD. They were distinguished by wearing narrow shoulder straps of a special design (not illustrated here), together with collar patches of a design similar to those worn by the regular RAD personnel. The background colouring to their collar patches was black for Leadership personnel, dark green for administration, and lemon yellow for war correspondents.

Plate 9. German Army Shoulder Straps and Collar Patches

The subject of German Army shoulder straps and, to a slightly lesser extent, collar patches is almost a study of its own. With their system of varied branch-of-service colours (Waffenfarbe), their rank insignia, and, especially, their complex and wide ranging system of shoulder strap motifs and metal mounts, they could easily fill a book. Illustrated here are

27

19 Army collar patches and shoulder straps worn by French Volunteers from the Infantry Regiment 638 'France'.

only a limited number of the items that were known to exist or were recorded as having been authorised. They have been primarily selected to show some of the more interesting shoulder strap mounts, without regard to trying to show the full range of ranks. German Army shoulder straps and collar patches were worn in matching pairs.

1 Shoulder strap worn by a private on the staff of the Military School at Dresden (Kriegsschule Dresden). White Waffenfarbe.
2 Shoulder strap worn by a private on the staff of a Military Medical Academy (Militärarztliche Akademie). Cornflower blue Waffenfarbe.
3 Shoulder strap worn by a private as part of the Frontier Force Headquarters Staff at Eifel (Stäbe der Generalkommandos der Grenz-

truppen, Eifel). White Waffenfarbe.
4 Shoulder strap worn by a private of the Signals Translator Replacement Battalion (Nachrichtendolmetscher Ersatzabteilung) introduced on 26 May 1941. Lemon yellow Waffenfarbe.
5 Shoulder strap worn by a lance-sergeant (Unteroffizier) from the Fusilier Regiment 'Greater Germany' (Füsilier-Regiment-Grossdeutschland), introduced on 1 June 1943. White Waffenfarbe.
6 Shoulder strap for a lance-sergeant (Unteroffizier) from the Führer-Grenadier-Batallion, introduced on 16 September 1943. White Waffenfarbe.
7 Shoulder strap for a sergeant-major (Wachtmeister) from the 11th Army Anti-Aircraft Artillery Regiment. White Waffenfarbe.

20 Oberst d. R. Hyazinth Graf Strachwitz, the eleventh soldier of the German Armed Forces to receive the Diamonds to his Oakleaves with Swords of the Knights Cross. He wears the special black uniform worn by German Army Panzer troops with its distinctive deaths-head collar patches (21 April 1944).

21 Collar patches and shoulder straps for an Army General: Generalleutnant Karl, RKT (3 October 1940).

8 Shoulder strap for a regimental sergeant-major (Oberfeldwebel) on the staff of the NCO School (Unteroffizierschule) at Biebrich. Bright red Waffenfarbe.

9 Shoulder strap for second lieutenant bandmaster (Musikmeister) from Artillery Regiment 33. Bright red Waffenfarbe.

10 Shoulder strap for field post officer (Feldpost Sekretär). Lemon yellow Nebenfarbe on dark green underlay.

11 Shoulder strap for Secret Field Police second lieutenant (Feldpolizei-Sekretär). Light blue Nebenfarbe on dark green underlay. (See also Plate 25, no. 2.)

12 Shoulder strap for second lieutenant (Leutnant) from the 60th Panzer-Grenadier-Regiment 'Feldherrnhalle'. Grass-green Waffenfarbe.

13 Shoulder strap for second lieutenant (Leutnant) as a member of the junior staff of the Military Commander in the occupied territory of Poland (Militärbefehlshaber im Generalgouvernementunterstab), introduced on 18 February 1941. White Waffenfarbe.

14 Shoulder strap for a second lieutenant (Leutnant) as a member at an Engineer Officers Academy. Orange Waffenfarbe.

15 Shoulder strap for a lieutenant (Oberleut-

22 Sonderführer (specialist officer) Josef Arens. The special shoulder straps with their fine design of small red, white and black chevrons are not illustrated in the colour plates.

23 The pattern of shoulder straps as worn by the Army rank of Major: Major Fritsche, Knights Cross Holder with Oakleaves (14 November 1943).

nant) from the Grenadier-Regiment 'Hoch- und Deutschmeister'. White Waffenfarbe. (See also Plate 61, no. 5.)

16 Shoulder strap for a lieutenant (Oberleutnant) of the Guard Regiment Berlin (Wachregiment Berlin). White Waffenfarbe.

17 Shoulder strap for a captain (Rittmeister) of 5th Cavalry Regiment. Gold Yellow Waffenfarbe.

18 Shoulder strap for a captain (Hauptmann) from an Army Anti-Aircraft Artillery unit (Heeresflak), introduced on 18 July 1941. Bright red Waffenfarbe.

19 Shoulder strap for a major of the Guard

Battalion Vienna (Wachbatallion Wien), introduced on 7 September 1938. White Waffenfarbe.

20 Collar patch for student at an Army NCO Preparatory School (Jungschütze der Heeres-Unteroffiziersvorschule).

21 Collar patch as worn by all ranks of the Panzer Pionier Company, introduced on 10 May 1940 and in use for a limited period.

22 Collar patch as worn by German Army clergy with the status of a Field Bishop. Military clergy wore no shoulder straps. Introduced at the time of the new uniforms on 10 April 1937.

23 Collar patch (right hand side) as worn by an administrative official with the rank equivalent to that of an Army general (Wehrmachtbeamte im Generalsrang).

Plate 10. German Navy and Marine-Artillery Shoulder Straps and Collar Patches

In the German Navy shoulder cords and shoulder straps were only worn by midshipmen (no. 9), warrant officers (nos 1 to 5), Naval musicians (no. 8), and officers and administration officials (nos 6 and 7). Collar patches were only worn by Naval clergy (nos 11, 12, 14 and 15), and seamen, petty officers and chief

petty officers (nos 10 and 13), but even then only on certain tunics. Shoulder straps and collar patches, when they were worn, were worn in matching pairs.

1 Shoulder strap for boatswain (Bootsmann).
2 Shoulder strap for gunnery NCO (Geschütz Feldwebel).
3 Shoulder strap for chief signals boatswain (Signal Oberfeldwebel).
4 Shoulder strap for chief machinist (Stabsobermaschinist).
5 Shoulder strap for chief ordnance NCO (Stabsfeuerwerker). This quality of strap in khaki tan material with dark blue silk braiding was for tropical use, not for summer wear.

24 German Naval Kriegsberichter (war reporter) interviewing machine room personnel of a German E-Boat. Naval War Reporters wore small gilt metal anchor insignia fastened directly into the collar of their tunics.

25 Two German naval warrant officers examine an enemy mine. Both can be identified as belonging to the naval defence ordnance branch by the small mine crossed with an anchor mounted on their shoulder straps (9 June 1944).

26 A clear example of the collar patches worn by a naval Maate: Bootsmannsmaat Karl Jörss, Knights Cross Holder (1 March 1943).

6 Shoulder strap for Legal Branch administration official with the rank of lieutenant.

7 Shoulder strap for administrative officials, pharmacists and non-technical instructors with the rank of sub-lieutenant.

8 Shoulder strap for Naval sub-lieutenant bandsman (Musikmeister).

9 Shoulder strap for senior engineer midshipman (Oberfähnrich-Ing.).

10 Collar patch for Maat – petty officer.

11 Collar patch for Obermaat – chief petty officer. Both these patterns of collar patches together with the plain patch worn by ratings were worn on the Pea Jacket (Überzieher).

12 Collar patch (first type) for German Naval

padre (Marine-pfarrer), 1938–42.

13 Collar patch (second type) for German Naval padre of one year's service (Marine-Kriegspfarrer im ersten Jahr), 1942–45.

14 Collar patch (second type) for German Naval padre of over two years service as Marine padre or senior marine padre (Marine-Kriegspfarrer v.2 Jahr ab Marine-pfarrer, Marine-Oberpfarrer).

15 Collar patch (second type) for senior German Naval deacon (Dienstälteste Marine Dekane).

27 A Marinehelferin receiving advice from a naval Machinist.

Marine-Artillery Insignia, 1933–45

16 Shoulder strap for lower rating personnel of the Marine-Artillery.

17 Early pattern shoulder strap for lower rating of the Coastal Artillery, 4th Regiment.

18 Early pattern shoulder strap for petty officer aspirant in the 1st Naval NCO Instruc-

tion Battalion (1.Marine-Unteroffizier-Lehrabteilungen).

19 Shoulder strap for petty officer of the 1st Manning Division (Schiffsstammabteilung 1).

20 Shoulder strap Marine-Artillery lieutenant. The short cross bar at the base of the shoulder strap allowed for this strap to be fitted

into two small holes set in the shoulder seam of leather coats or thick material top coats.

21 Shoulder strap for female auxiliary of the Naval Air Raid Warning Service (Weiblichenflugmeldedienst).

22 Gilded metal insignia worn by Naval war correspondents directly into the cloth of their tunic collar. Worn in matching pairs.

23 Lower ratings collar patch for Marine-Artillery personnel.

24 Collar patch for officers of the Marine-Artillery.

25 Collar patch for Marine-Artillery admiral, c. 1944.

28 This photograph of a Marine-Artillerie range-taker clearly shows the dark blue-green shoulder strap with its crossed anchors worked in yellow threads as well as the collar patch (5 September 1942).

Plate 11. NSFK and DLV Shoulder Straps and Collar Patches

The choice of blue-grey and yellow as the colours used for the NSFK insignia was an apposite one. The blue-grey, also used as the colour for their uniforms, reflected the close affiliation the Flying Corps had with the Luftwaffe, while the yellow used as piping and underlay to their collar patches and shoulder straps was the same yellow Waffenfarbe as used by the flying branch personnel of the Luftwaffe.

The NSFK uniforms and their insignia were introduced in 1937. Collar patches were worn in pairs, the right hand patch showing the wearer's unit for those ranks up to NSFK-Obersturmbannführer, and the left hand patch for ranks. Before the war shoulder straps were worn singly on the right shoulder, but during the war were worn in matching pairs.

1 Shoulder strap as worn by ranks from NSFK-Mann to NSFK-Obertruppführer.

2 Shoulder strap as worn by ranks from NSFK-Sturmführer to NSFK-Hauptsturmführer.

3 Shoulder strap as worn by ranks from NSFK-Sturmbannführer to NSFK-Standartenführer.

4 Shoulder strap as worn by ranks from NSFK-Oberführer to NSFK-Obergruppenführer. The shoulder strap as worn by the most senior NSFK rank of Korpsführer (not illustrated) was of the same construction as no. 4 but with its interwoven design in gold in place of silver.

5 Right hand unit collar patch for any rank from NSFK-Mann to NSFK-Obertruppführer. Patch shows wearer to be from 7th Sturm in the 91st Standarte.

6 Left hand rank collar patch for the rank of NSFK-Sturmmann.

7 Right hand unit patch for any rank from

NSFK-Mann to NSFK-Obertruppführer. Patch shows the wearer to be on the staff of Group 2.

8 Left hand rank collar patch for the rank of NSFK-Truppführer.

9/10 Pair of collar patches for an NSFK-Sturmbannführer on the staff of Standarte 94.

11/12 Pair of collar patches for an NSFK-Obersturmbannführer on the staff of the Korpsführer.

13 The left hand patch of a matching pair of collar patches worn by the rank of an NSFK-Standartenführer.

14 The left hand patch of a matching pair of collar patches worn by the rank of an NSFK-Obergruppenführer.

15 The left hand patch of a matching pair of collar patches worn by the most senior rank of NSFK-Korpsführer.

16 The left hand patch of a matching pair of collar patches worn by the pre-war appointment of NSFK-Ehrenführer, an Honour Leader or a person holding an Honorary Commission in the NSFK. This appointment was dropped prior to, or at the beginning of World War II.

DLV Shoulder Straps and Collar Patches

The rank insignia – shoulder straps and collar patches introduced in 1933 and used by the personnel of the Deutscher Luftsport-Verband (DLV) was the forerunner of the insignia that the Luftwaffe adopted three years later. The DLV also chose to use four basic colours to indicate the four branches of the Air Sports Association, similar to the colours used by the Luftwaffe when, in 1935, Hermann Göring revealed the existence of a German air force. These branch-of-service colours were: blue for personnel of the Deutscher Luftsport-Verband; gold-yellow for personnel of the Deutsche Verkehrfliegerschule; black for personnel of the Reichsluftfahrtministerium; and white for DLV ministers. All collar patches were worn in matching pairs. Shoulder straps were originally worn on the right shoulder only, but were later worn (at least by lower ranks) in matching pairs.

17 Collar patch for DLV-Flieger.

18 Collar patch for DLV-Oberflieger.

19 Collar patch for DLV-Flugmeister, Bordfunkmeister or Meister.

20 Collar patch for DLV-Oberflugmeister, Bordoberfunkmeister or Obermeister.

21 Shoulder strap for all DLV ranks from DLV-Flieger to DLV-Oberflugmeister.

22/23 Collar patch and shoulder strap for DLV-Kettenführer.

24/25 Collar patch and shoulder strap for DLV-Flieger-Vizekommodore.

26/27 Collar patch and shoulder strap for DLV-Minister also referred to as Reichsminister der Luftfahrt.

Plate 12. Luftwaffe Shoulder Straps and Collar Patches

The rank insignia in the form of shoulder straps and collar patches brought into use by the German Air Force in March 1935 was a development of the insignia previously in use with the DLV from 1933 to 1935. Like those items in use by the German Army the Luftwaffe items grew into a complex system which not only showed the wearer's rank status but also his branch-of-service as well as his unit, school or special formation. Shoulder straps and collar patches worn in the Luftwaffe and all its affiliated formations were worn in matching pairs.

1 Shoulder strap for the lowest Luftwaffe rank of Kanonier. Red Waffenfarbe is for Flak Artillerie (Anti-Aircraft Artillery); 'L' indicates an Instruction Unit which, being in red chain stitching, signifies a Kanonier from a Flak Artillerie Instruction Unit.

29 Luftwaffe Flugzeugführer drafted into the fighting during the Allied combined forces landings at Dieppe (21 August 1942).

2 Shoulder strap for the rank of Unteroffizier on the staff of an Aerial Warfare School (Kriegsschule).

3 Shoulder strap for the rank of Wachtmeister on the staff of a Flak Artillerie Schule (Anti-Aircraft Artillery School).

4 Shoulder strap for tropical use for the rank of Feldwebel, Flying branch.

5 Shoulder strap for Leutnant on the staff of a an Air Signals School (Nachrichtenschule), light brown Waffenfarbe.

6 Shoulder strap for Flieger Nautiker (the equivalent of a Leutnant). The original Nebenfarbe (secondary branch-of-service colour) for the Luftwaffe Navigation Corps personnel was gold-yellow on dark green underlay up to early 1940. It was then changed to lemon-yellow on dark green and on 8 October 1941 changed yet again to the colour combination shown here of light blue on pink.

7 Shoulder strap for a specialist officer from the Administrative Service of the Luftwaffe (Sonderführer der Wehrmachtbeamte der Luftwaffe) with the rank of Wehrmachtbeamter a.Kr. (auf Kriegsdauer – for the duration of the war).

8 Shoulder strap for a Flieger-Hauptnautiker for the period 1940 to October 1941. The Nebenfarbe is lemon-yellow on dark green underlay.

9 Shoulder strap for a major of reserve on the staff of the Reich Air Ministry.

10 Shoulder strap for a major on the staff of the Reich Air Ministry, early pattern.

11 Shoulder strap for a General der Flieger (general of flying personnel), General der Flakartillerie (general of anti-aircraft artillery), General der Luftnachrichtentruppe (general of air signals troops) and General der Fallschirmtruppen (general of paratroops).

12 The special shoulder strap for Hermann Göring as Reichsmarschall des Grossdeutschen Reiches, introduced in August 1940.

13 Collar patch for the lowest Luftwaffe rank of Flieger.

14 Collar patch for Gefreiter.

15 Collar patch for Obergefreiter from the Flak-Abteilung of Regiment 'General Göring'.

16 Collar patch for a Stabsfeldwebel as worn on the greatcoat. All NCO ranks wore collar patches with silver-grey braiding along two sides of the patch on the collar of the greatcoat only. On the tunic collar they wore plain collar patches with the appropriate number of 'wings' with the silver-grey braiding stitched around the edge of the collar. During the war years the first type of collar patches as described above were discontinued for economy reasons.

17 Collar patch for Leutnant of the Medical Branch, dark blue Waffenfarbe.

18 Collar patch for an Oberleutnant either on the staff of the Reichsluftfahrtministerium or from the Luftwaffe Construction Engineers. Officers, NCOs and men in the RLM wore black as their branch-of-service colour up to 30 June 1939. After 22 December 1939 the colour black was appointed to Luftwaffe Construction Engineers as their Waffenfarbe.
19 Collar patch for a Hauptmann (captain) from Regiment 'General Göring'.
20 Collar patch for a major of the Anti-Aircraft Artillery.
21 Collar patch for a Reserve Leutnant, the light blue inner border indicates the officer's Reserve status and the yellow patch shows him to belong to the Flying Branch.
22 Collar patch for a Flieger-Oberingenieur (equivalent to an Oberleutnant). Officers who wore pink collar patches with a design of a two, three or four bladed propeller were members of the Engineer Corps of the Luftwaffe.
23 Collar patch as worn by a Luftwaffe Administrative official with the equivalent Air Force rank of Hauptmann (captain).
24 Collar patch as worn by Luftwaffe Sonderführer with the equivalent Air Force rank of both Major and Oberst.

Plate 13. German Police Formation Shoulder Straps and Collar Patches

The reorganisation of the German police began in January 1934 when the sovereign right to exercise police power was transferred from the Länder to the Reich. By July 1936 new uniforms were introduced together with a number of their related insignia. The opportunity was taken to standardise the shoulder straps and collar patches worn by the personnel of the various police formations. The design of the shoulder straps and to a certain extent the rank terms used for the new German Police ranks were modelled on those in use by the German Army.

Certain colours, known as Truppenfarbe, were allocated for the various branches of the Police. These were: police green for the Schutzpolizei des Reiches; orange for the Gendarmerie; bright yellow for the Wasserschutzpolizei; carmine (karmesinrot) for the Feuerschutzpolizei; cornflower blue for the Polizei Medizinal Beamte; light grey for the Polizei Verwaltungs Beamte and black for Polizei Veterinar Beamte; and wine red for the Schutzpolizei des Gemeinden (during the war years this separate branch colour was replaced and merged with the Schutzpolizei des Reiches, both branches wearing police green). White was used by personnel of the Motorised Gendarmerie Emergency Units whose task it was to patrol the German Autobahn system.

Shoulder straps and collar patches in the German Police were worn in matching pairs.

1 Shoulder strap for an Unterwachtmeister der Wasserschutzpolizei. Waterways police did not wear collar patches.
2 Shoulder strap for Unterwachtmeister der Motorisierten Gendarmerie Bereitschaft.
3 Shoulder strap for a Wachtmeister der Gendarmerie with over four years service.
4 Shoulder strap for a Wachtmeister of the Verkehrskompanien (Mot.) z.b.V. of the Motorisierte Gendarmerie. Bright red truppenfarbe.
5 Shoulder strap for an Oberwachtmeister der Schutzpolizei d. Reiches. This pattern of shoulder strap with the 'bar' across the base of the strap is a war-time introduction.
6 Shoulder strap for a Revieroberwacht-meister of the Gendarmerie.
7 Shoulder strap for a Hauptwachtmeister and Oberjunker from the Schutzpolizei d.Gemeinden.
8 Shoulder strap for a Meister of the Feuerschutzpolizei.
9 Shoulder strap for a Meister of the Wasserschutzpolizei.

10 Shoulder strap for a Revier-Leutnant (Ward Lieutenant) of the Feuerschutzpolizei.

11 Shoulder strap for a Revier-Hauptmann (Police Ward Captain) of the Schutzpolizei d.Reiches.

12 Shoulder strap for a Stabszahnarzt der Polizei.

13 Shoulder strap for an Oberstabsapotheker der Polizei.

14 Shoulder strap for a General der Polizei but which was worn after the autumn of 1942 by an SS-Obergruppenführer und General der Polizei.

15 Shoulder strap for an SS-Oberstgruppen-führer und Generaloberst der Polizei.

16 Collar patch for men and NCOs (Unter-wachtmeister to Meister) of the Reich Protection Police.

17 Collar patch for men and NCOs of the Rural Police (Gendarmerie).

18 Collar patch for the pre-war ranks of Wachtmeister and Oberwachtmeister of the Schutzpolizei d.Gemeinden.

19 Collar patch for veterinarian men and NCOs in the Police.

20 Collar patch for men and NCOs of the Administration Police.

21 Collar patch for Police medical men and NCOs.

22 Collar patch for men and NCOs of the Reich Autobahn Police.

23 Collar patch for police generals with the ranks of Generalmajor, Generalleutnant and General der Polizei (pre war ranks).

24 Collar patch for Administration officials with the rank of General (Verwaltungsbeamte im Generalsrang).

25 Collar patch for an officer of the Fire Protection Police.

26 Collar patch for an officer of the Rural Police.

27 Collar patch for a Wachtmeister and Ober-wachtmeister of the Reich Autobahn Police.

28 Collar patch for the war-time rank of SS-Oberstgruppenführer und Generaloberst der Polizei.

Plate 14. Railway Protection Police (Bahnschutzpolizei) Shoulder Straps and Collar Patches

The insignia used by the personnel of the Bahnschutzpolizei as the main method of indicating rank consisted of shoulder straps and collar patches. Cuff-titles to a lesser extent reflected the wearer's rank but the six titles introduced in 1941 were shared by the five groups of ranks which in turn consisted of four-teen separate ranks (see Plate 27, nos 2 to 5). Two types of collar patches were worn. The types illustrated here were used on the closed-neck tunics. The other pattern of patches were of an upright shape and were used on the open-neck tunics (not illustrated). Both types of collar patches were worn in matching pairs. Shoulder straps were also worn in pairs.

1 Shoulder strap for the lowest rank of Bzp-Anwärter.

2 Shoulder strap for Bzp-Mann.

3 Shoulder strap for Stellv.Bzp-Gruppen-führer.

4 Collar patch worn by all three above ranks.

5 Shoulder strap for Bzp-Zugführer.

6 Collar patch for Bzp-Zugführer.

The same basic shoulder strap and collar patch with just one metal pip would have been worn by the rank of Bzp-Unterzugführer, and without any pips was for the rank of Bzp-Gruppenführer.

7 Shoulder cord for the rank of Bzp-Ober-zugführer.

8 Collar patch for the rank of Bzp-Ober-zugführer. This rank, although part of the second group of ranks was special insofar as it was distinguished by having a quite different style of shoulder cord and a separate cuff-title (see Plate 27, no. 3).

9 Shoulder cord for a musician with the rank of Bzp-Musikzugführer.

10 Collar patch for Bzp-Musikzugführer.

11 Shoulder cord for Bzp-Abteilungsführer.

12 Collar patch for Bzp-Abteilungshauptführer.

Nos 9 to 12 were in the third group of ranks. The next most senior musicians rank of Bzp-Obermusikzugführer wore the same basic shoulder cord as no. 9 but with the addition of a small four-pointed star, and had collar patches of the same design and colouring as no. 10 but with an extra 'pip'. The collar patch for a Bzp-Abteilungsführer was as no. 10 except it was in black velvet and not red cloth. The shoulder strap is as shown, no. 11. The ranks of Bzp-Oberabteilungsführer and Bzp-Abteilungshauptführer had the addition of one and two 'stars' and 'pips' on their respective shoulder cords and collar patches, the patch for Bzp-Abteilungshauptführer shown under no. 12.

13 Shoulder cord for Bzp-Bezirksführer.

14 Collar patch for Bzp-Bezirksführer.

15 Shoulder cord for Bzp-Arzt (doctor).

16 Collar patch for Bzp-Arzt.

Nos 13 to 16 were part of the fourth rank group. The rank of Bzp-Bezirkshauptführer (not illustrated) had the addition of a single 'star' to the shoulder cord and a 'pip' to the collar patch. The shoulder cord for the penultimate rank of Stabsführer der Bzp was as shown by no. 13, the collar patch for this rank is illustrated by no. 18. The Stabsführer der Bzp was part of the fourth group of ranks.

17 Shoulder cord for the most senior Bahnschutzpolizei rank of Chef der Bzp. The collar patch for this rank was as for no. 18 but with the addition of a small gilt 'pip' set in the lower right corner of the design.

18 Collar patch for the rank of Stabsführer der Bzp.

19/20/21 Examples of shoulder straps of the pre-1941 Bahnschutzpolizei issue insignia. Precise ranks are not established as yet.

Plate 15. Customs, DAF, and Government Officials Shoulder Straps and Collar Patches

German Customs Officials were divided into two main branches: the Landzollbeamte (Zollgrenzschutz), which also included the Wasserzollbeamte, and the Zollbeamte. This division between the Land Customs Officials (Customs Frontier Protection Service), including the Water Customs Officials and the remaining Customs Officials, was indicated on their uniform insignia by the slight difference in the colouring of their silver braiding. Personnel of the first group used insignia of dark bottle-green and dull grey, whereas the insignia used by the second group personnel was of dark bottle-green and bright silver-aluminium. The Water Customs Service, however, despite their being part of the first group personnel, had their insignia of dark bottle-green with bright silver-aluminium. They were distinguished further, however, by the use of gilt buttons bearing a fouled anchor design, underlay to their shoulder straps in dark navy-blue cloth, and the fact that they wore no collar patches. A common feature of German Customs Officials shoulder strap was the shoulder strap mount consisting of the Gothic-styled initial letters of RFV. This stood for 'Reichsfinanzverwaltung' (National Finance Administration). All shoulder straps were worn in matching pairs.

German Customs Officials

1 Shoulder strap for Zollanwärter.

2 Shoulder strap for Zollwachtmeister.

3 Shoulder strap for Zollbetriebs-Assistent.

4 Shoulder strap for Oberzollschiffer, Waterways Customs official.

5 Shoulder strap for Bezirkszoll Kommissar, Oberzollinspektor and rank of Regierungs-assistent.

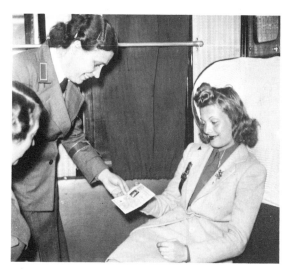

30 A female Customs official checking the papers of a traveller passing between German occupied and Vichy France (2 March 1943). In this comparatively rare photograph can be seen the most junior grade of Customs collar patch as well as the Customs cuff-title.

6 Shoulder strap for Zollamtmann and Zollfinanzrat.

7 Shoulder strap for the rank of Oberfinanzpräsident (worn in conjunction with collar patch illustrated as no. 13 but without the small gilt 'pip'). Shoulder strap also worn by the rank of Generalinspekteur der Zollgrenzschutzes, Ministerialdirektor, worn in conjunction with the collar patch illustrated as no. 13.

Collar patches were worn by all personnel except Waterways Customs officials.

8 Basic, lowest rank collar patch worn by Zollgrenzangestelter, Zollanwärter, and Finanzanwärter Z from both groups of Customs officials.

9 Collar patch worn by first group Landzollbeamten ranks of Zollwachtmeister and Zollbetriebsassistent. Also worn by second group Zollbeamten ranks of Zollwachtmeister, Zolloberwachtmeister and Zollbetriebsassistent.

10 Collar patch for Zollbeamten second group rank of Oberzollsekretär.

11 Collar patch for Zollbeamten second group rank of Zollfinanzrat. (*The illustration should only show the two end pips.*)

12 Collar patch for Zollbeamten second group rank of Zollrat.

13 Collar patch for Generalinspekteur der Zollgrenzschutzes, Ministerialdirektor (Landzollbeamten). Also worn by Zollbeamten ranks of Reichsminister der Finanzen, Staatssekretär and Generalinspekteur der Zollgrenzschutzes, Ministerialdirektor.

Deutsche Arbeitsfront shoulder straps

14 DAF-Ortswerkscharführer shoulder strap, with light blue piping. The same strap with a gilt cog-wheel emblem and shoulder strap button was worn by a DAF-Ortsobmann (Oberwerkscharstammführer) (not illustrated).

15 Shoulder strap for DAF-Kreiswerkscharführer (Werkscharbannführer), with black piping. The same strap with a gilt cog-wheel and button was worn by a DAF-Kreisobmann (Kreiswerkscharstammführer).

16 Shoulder strap for DAF-Gauwerkscharführer (Oberwerkscharführer) with bright red piping. The same strap with a gilt cog-wheel emblem and strap button was worn by a DAF-Gauobmann (Gauwerkscharstammführer).

17 Shoulder strap for DAF-Oberstwerkscharführer with bright yellow piping. The same strap with a gilt coloured cog-wheel metal emblem and shoulder strap button was worn by the rank of Der Reichsorganisationsleiter der NSDAP (Der Oberste Werkscharführer).

Shoulder straps for Government Administration Officials

Government Administration officials were distinguished by wearing very distinctive sleeve badges consisting of an eagle and Swastika surmounting a 'horse-shoe' shaped badge edged by lines of silver-aluminium twisted cording or

31 Reichsminister Albert Speer (back to camera) presenting awards to members of the DAF in the 'Haus der Flieger' in Berlin (16 November 1942). An example of the DAF shoulder strap with its metal cog-wheel device can be seen in the centre of the picture.

by embroidered oak leaves. These are illustrated on Plate 52, nos 4 to 12. These sleeve badges, together with a series of four shoulder straps, were based on the four pay group structures. The coloured underlay to the shoulder straps indicated the wearer's administrative service, as follows: light grey was used by General Administration officials, Internal Administration officials, Financial Administration officials and Special Administration officials, light red by Transport Administration officials, orange-red by Postal Administration officials, and wine-red by Justice Administration officials.

18 Shoulder strap for Group IV officials of pay groups B3 to B9, General, Internal, Financial and Special Administration officials, who wore arm badge pattern as Plate 52, no. 9, plus various 'stars'.

19 Shoulder strap for Group III officials of pay groups A1a, Transportation officials, who wore arm badge pattern as Plate 52, no. 8 in grey, plus various 'stars'.

20 Shoulder strap for Group II officials of pay groups A1b to A2d, Postal Administration officials, who wore arm badge pattern as Plate 52, no. 6, plus various 'stars'.

21 Shoulder strap for most senior group, Group I officials of pay groups A3b, A4b1 and A4c2, Justice Administration officials who wore arm badge pattern as Plate 52, no. 4, plus various 'stars'.

41

Plate 16. Shoulder Straps and Collar Patches for the Technical Stud Service in Prussia, 'Ostgebeit' and 'Ostbeamte'

These shoulder straps and collar patches were introduced in March 1942 as a 'new set of insignia' for personnel of the Technical Stud Service on the State stud farms situated in Prussia and at Stargard (east of Stettin) and Marienwerder (south of Danzig in West Prussia).

The shoulder straps were worn in pairs and the collar patches in mirror pairs on the dark blue, closed-neck uniform tunic only. They were not worn on the greatcoat.

Technical Stud Service in Prussia Insignia, 1942–44

1 Shoulder strap for a Gestütwärter or Stud Attendant.

2 Shoulder strap for a Gestütoberwärter or Senior Stud Attendant.

3 Collar patch (worn in pairs) worn by Stud and Senior Stud Attendants.

4 Collar patch (worn in pairs) worn by personnel in senior positions on the stud farms listed below for items 5 and 6.

5 Shoulder strap worn by a Sattelmeister and Futtermeister, (Saddle Master and Fodder Master).

6 Shoulder strap for Obersattelmeister and Oberstütmeister, (Senior Saddle Master and Senior Stud Master).

Collar Patches of the Labour Operations Executive in the 'Ostgebiet'

The Labour Operations Executive referred to as the 'Arbeitseinsatzverwaltung' operated within the Eastern Occupied Territories – the 'Ostgebiet'. The personnel of the Executive wore uniforms of Erdbraun (earth brown) colour and their only system of displaying their rank was by the means of collar patches. These patches were worn in matching mirror pairs

and they were positioned within the corner points of their tunic and greatcoat collars.

7 Verwaltungsarbeiter (administrative worker).

8 Amtsgehilfe (office assistant/clerk).

9 Assistent (assistant).

10 Sekretär (secretary).

11 Reg.Inspektor (administrative inspector).

12 Reg.Oberinspektor (senior administration inspector).

13 Regierungsrat (governmental councillor).

14 Oberregierungsrat (senior governmental councillor).

15 Ministerialrat (ministerial councillor).

16 Präsident (President).

Collar Patches of the 'Ostbeamte', Eastern Officials

When Germany attacked the Soviet Union on 22 June 1941 German forces rapidly overran vast areas of territory. Four weeks after the invasion had begun, Hitler appointed Alfred Rosenberg to head the civil administration for these occupied areas. His appointment was given the title 'Reichsministerium für die besetzen Ostgebiete' (Reich Ministry for the Occupied Eastern Territories), officially abbreviated to RMBO, but more frequently referred to as the 'Ostministerium'.

The headquarters of the Ostministerium was in Berlin. Its personnel were organised into a special 'Leadership Corps East' (Führerkorps Ost). The occupied eastern areas administered by the RMBO were each governed by a Reichskommissariate headed by a Reichskommissar (Reich Commissar). Each Reich Commissariate was subdivided into at least six General Commissariats (Generalbezirke) each headed by a Generalkommissar, a German official responsible to the Reich Commissar. These General Commissariats were in turn comprised of several districts (Kreisgebiete) intended to be twenty in number, administered by a District Commissar (Gebietskommissar), the lowest ranking official of the German administrative hierarchy. (Below the Gebiet the next unit was the Rayon or group of villages and here the Rayon-Chefs were native Ukrainians. Still lower were the village headmen and small-town Starosts and the Council of Elders.)

Most members of the RMBO were uniformed according to the special designs introduced for them. Ranks were indicated by the use of collar patches and cuff designs (the latter not illustrated here). Four basic colours were used to show different levels of responsibility which, combined with collar patch piping, edging, oakleaves and stars gave a total of 24 different sets of patches.

The four basic levels of responsibility colours were as follows:

Dark red: Gebietskommissariate
Orange: Hauptkommissariate
Carmine: Reichskommissariate
Bright red: Ministry Officials.

17 Landes, Bezirks and Gebietsbetriebassisten (Regional, District, and Territorial Management Assistant).

18 Regierungs, Landes, Bezirks and Gebietssekretär (Governmental, Regional, District, and Territorial Secretary).

19 Amtsrat, Landesamtsrat, Bezirksamtsrat (Office Councillor, Regional Office Councillor, District Office Councillor).

20 Landes, and Bezirksdirigent (Regional, and District Manager).

21 Ministerialdirektor, Landesverwaltungspräsident and Generalkommissar (Ministerial Director, Regional Administration President, and General Commissar).

22 Vertreter des Ministers und Reichskommissar (Representative of the Minister and Reich Commissar).

23 Reichsminister (Reich Minister).

Plate 17. RLB, SHD and LSW Shoulder Straps and Collar Patches

In addition to the Luftwaffe and the Fire Police, Germany possessed three civilian uniformed formations organised to protect people and property against enemy air attacks.

Reichsluftschutzbund Insignia, 1940–45

The Reichsluftschutzbund (RLB) – National Air Defence League – was formed on 28 April 1933. Its purpose was to instruct the German population in all matters related to civil defence. They were issued with, or purchased, uniforms of blue-grey. The facing colour chosen for their collar patches and shoulder strap underlay was lilac. Shoulder straps were worn singly on the right shoulder. Collar patches were worn in matching pairs. The series illustrated here was introduced in July 1940.

1 Shoulder strap for all RLB ranks from LS-Truppmann (no. 2) through the ranks (not illustrated) of LS-Obertruppwart and LS-Truppmeister to the rank of LS-Obertruppmeister (no. 5).

2 Collar patch for rank of LS-Truppmann.

3 Collar patch for the rank of LS-Obertruppmann.

4 Collar patch for the rank of LS-Truppwart.

5 Collar patch for the rank of LS-Obertruppmeister.

6/7 Shoulder strap and collar patch for rank of Luftschutz-Führer.

8/9 Shoulder strap and collar patch for the rank of Hauptluftschutz-Führer.

10/11 Shoulder strap and collar patch for the rank of Stabsluftschutz-Führer.

12/13 Shoulder strap and collar patch for the rank of Oberstluftschutz-Führer.

14/15 Shoulder strap and collar patch for the rank of General-Luftschutz-Führer.

16/17 Shoulder strap and collar patch for the

rank of General-Haupt-Luftschutz-Führer (Chef des Stabes).

18/19 Shoulder strap and collar patch for the rank of RLB Präsident.

SHD-LSW Insignia, 1940–45

The Sicherheits und Hilfsdienst (SHD) – the Security and Assistance Service – together with the Luftschutz Warndienst (LSW) – Air Raid Warning Service – were the other two important arms of the civilian air defence system created to help minimize the effects of enemy air attacks on the German Reich. Their personnel were clothed in uniforms of blue-grey but they wore collar patches of dark green cloth and shoulder straps with underlays of dark green. Both collar patches and shoulder straps were worn in matching pairs.

20 Shoulder strap for rank of SHD/LSW-Mann.

21 Shoulder strap for rank of SHD/LSW-Hauptgruppenführer.

22 Shoulder strap for the rank of SHD/LSW-Oberzugführer (Arzt).

23 Shoulder strap for rank of SHD/LSW-Bereitschaftsführer.

24 Shoulder strap for rank of SHD/LSW-Abteilungsführer.

25 Collar patch for lower ranks of the Luftschutz Warndienst.

26 Collar patch for officer classes of the Luftschutz Warndienst.

27 Collar patch for officer classes of the Sicherheits und Hilfsdienst.

Plate 18. DRK and Waterways Air Protection Service Shoulder Straps and Collar Patches

German Red Cross Insignia

The German Red Cross service provided separate sets of shoulder straps for the rank insignia of the male members of the DRK.

32 German Red Cross doctors, orderlies and a nurse, part of a Berlin Red Cross unit. Note that the collar patches are the same for all ranks of the DRK.

Female nurses displayed their rank insignia by a system of dark blue embroidered 'stars' worked into the corners of the collar of their nursing uniforms or as small white metal or gilt coloured 'pips' or oak leaves mounted on to the corners of the service uniform collar.

1 Shoulder strap for DRK-Anwärter and DRK-Helfer.
2 Shoulder strap for DRK-Vorhelfer with Group Leader examination.
3 Shoulder strap for DRK-Haupthelfer.
4 Shoulder strap for DRK-Hauptführer.
5 Shoulder strap for DRK-Oberstführer.
6 Shoulder strap for DRK-Generalhauptführer.
7 Collar patch worn as a matching pair for all ranks up to DRK-Generalführer and DRK-Generalhauptführer. Their collar patch was edged in gold-coloured twisted cording.

Waterways Air Protection Service Insignia, 1942–45

The Wasserstrassenluftschutz (Waterways Air Protection Service) was created in 1942 to meet the need to protect and supervise the inland waterways and harbours of Germany against enemy air attacks. They operated in much the same way as the Luftschutzdienst, the land-based Air Protection Service. In June 1942 details were published of their rank insignia which took the form of twelve separate shoulder straps worn with four sets of collar patches shared between these twelve ranks.

Shoulder straps were worn in matching pairs. Rosettes were used in place of the normal 'pip' when increasing ranks on ascending shoulder strap ranks. Collar patches were worn in matching pairs.
8 Shoulder strap for LS-Mann.
9 Shoulder strap for LS-Vormann.
10 Shoulder strap for LS-Obertruppführer.
11 Shoulder strap for LS-Gruppenführer.
12 Shoulder strap for LS-Zugführer.
13 Shoulder strap for LS-Bereitschaftsführer.

14 Shoulder strap for LS-Abschnittsführer.
15 Shoulder strap for LS-Reichswasserstrassenluftschutzführer.
16 Collar patch worn by the following ranks: LS-Mann, LS-Vormann, LS-Truppführer and LS-Obertruppführer.
17 Collar patch worn by the following ranks: LS-Gruppenführer and LS-Hauptgruppenführer.
18 Collar patch worn by the following ranks: LS-Zugführer, LS-Hauptzugführer and LS-Bereitschaftsführer.
19 Collar patch worn by the following ranks: LS-Abschnittsführer, LS-Gruppenluftschutzleiter and LS-Reichswasserstrassenluftschutzführer.

Plate 19. Organisation Todt Shoulder Straps and Collar Patches

From June 1938 to just prior to the outbreak of war in September 1939 the Organisation Todt workforce was provided by civilian contractors under the direct command of Dr Fritz Todt. Members wore civilian working clothes. Senior members of the OT would have been uniformed personnel of the SA, RAD, Army, Luftwaffe, etc., including specialist officials (Sonder-Führer). Once war broke out it was necessary to uniform these men.

The first type of rank insignia introduced in 1940 for wear by uniformed members of the Organisation Todt was a series of arm bands. Some of these arm bands are featured on Plate 36, nos 10–13.

The second pattern of rank insignia, introduced in 1942 to replace the earlier arm bands system, were arm chevrons and shoulder straps. Coloured piping was used on the straps to identify the wearer's branch of service. Shoulder straps were worn in pairs.

2nd Pattern, 1942–43

1 OT-Meister of the Medical Branch (dark

blue piping), worn in conjunction with a three bar, silver chevrons on a black backing worn on the right upper arm (not illustrated). This same shoulder strap – and regardless of the wearer's branch of service – was also used by the Organisation Todt rank of OT-Rotten-führer, together with a single silver chevron worn on the right upper arm, and for the rank of OT-Kameradschaftsführer, with a double silver chevron also worn on the right upper arm.

2 OT-Truppführer from Construction and Accommodation Control (black piping – the commonest form of branch colour).

3 OT-Obertruppführer, Equipment, Provisions, and Messing Sections (white piping).

4 OT-Haupttruppführer, Propaganda Wing (brown piping).

5 OT-Frontführer, Signals Section (lemon-yellow piping).

6 OT-Hauptfrontführer, Administration (green piping).

7 OT-Gruppenleiter, musicians, and Musical Detachments (carmine piping).

Gilt pips were used on the shoulder straps by leadership personnel of Construction units, Front Direction, Medical Service, Communication units, Equipment, Furnishing, Personnel and Fortification Troops. Silver or white metal pips were only worn by leaders of Propaganda and Administration units.

3rd Pattern, 1943–45

In 1943 a third and final series of rank insignia was issued for wear by all ranks of the Organisation Todt which did away with shoulder straps and in their place arm chevrons (see Plate 54, nos 9, 10, 11), collar patches and arm bands (see Plate 36, nos 5, 6, 7) were used to indicate ranks.

OT Workers

8 Collar patch for the ranks of OT-Arbeiter, OT-Sanitäter, and OT-Stammarbeiter. These collar patches were worn in matching pairs on the open-neck tunics. They were the only indication of rank used for the above three rank grades.

OT Under Leaders

8 The same plain OT collar patches were also worn by OT-Vorarbeiter and OT-Stamm-sanitäter. These two ranks were distinguished by wearing a single rank chevron of red braid on a khaki background (see Plate 54, no. 9) worn on the upper right arm. The OT ranks of OT-Meister and OT-Obersanitäter wore the basic plain OT collar patches but with two red chevrons (see Plate 54, no. 10) worn on the upper right arm. For the final two OT ranks of OT-Obermeister and OT-Hauptsanitäter in the Under-Leaders group of ranks the same blank OT collar patches were worn but with three red chevrons worn on the right upper arm (see Plate 54, no. 11).

9 OT-Truppführer and OT-Sanitäts-Truppführer.

10 OT-Obertruppführer and OT-Sanitäts-Obertruppführer.

11 OT-Haupttruppführer and OT-Sanitäts-Haupttruppführer.

OT Leaders

These machine-woven silver zig-zag emblems were worn as matching collar insignia and were known as 'Wehrbau-Abzeichen' (Defence Construction Badges).

12 Worn by OT-Bauführer, OT-Frontführer, and OT-Arzt.

13 Worn by OT-Oberbauführer, OT-Oberfrontführer, and OT-Oberarzt.

14 Worn by OT-Hauptbauführer, OT-Hauptfrontführer, and OT-Stabsarzt.

OT Staff Leaders

15 Collar patch (worn in matching pairs) for OT-Bauleiter, OT-Stabsfrontführer, and OT-Oberstabsarzt.

16 OT-Oberbauleiter, OT-Oberstabsfront-führer, and OT-Oberfeldarzt.

17 OT-Hauptbauleiter, OT-Oberstfront-führer, and OT-Oberstarzt.

OT Higher Leaders

18 OT-Einsatzleiter.

19 OT-Einsatzgruppenleiter II.

20 OT-Einsatzgruppenleiter I.

21 Chef des Amtes Bau OT.

(*Patches 18–21 are yellowish-brown not grey; the OT on 18 is gold not silver.*)

Plate 20. Technische Nothilfe Collar Patches and Shoulder Straps

The Technische Nothilfe (TeNo), or Technical Emergency Service, adopted three changes of rank insignia over the period from 1937 to 1945. During the period 1937–43 rank was displayed by the use of shoulder straps and collar patches, and the collar patches themselves were used – below the three most senior ranks – to show the wearer's TeNo unit number. From 1943 the existing TeNo collar patches were changed to a style almost identical to that used by its then parent body, the SS. Even the rank terms were changed. During the earlier period, 1937–43, the rank insignia underwent a major change with minor modifications to the then existing system.

1 Right hand unit collar patch used by the majority of the 1937–40 and the 1941–43 TeNo ranks from TN-Anwärter/TN-Noth-elfer/TN-Mann right up to the rank of TN-Bezirksführer. The combination of Roman numerals and Arabic numerals differed according to the number of the wearer's TeNo unit and detachment.

2 Left hand rank collar patch here shown for the 1937–40 period rank of TN-Anwärter.

3 Shoulder strap for the 1937–40 ranks of TN-Anwärter and TN-Nothelfer, the 1941–42 rank of TN-Nothelfer, and the 1942–43 ranks of TN-Anwärter and TN-Mann. TeNo shoulder straps were worn in matching pairs.

4 Collar patch (left hand rank patch) as used by the 1937–40 ranks of TN-Nothelfer and TN-Vormann, the 1941–42 ranks of TN-Nothelfer and TN-Vormann and the 1942–43 ranks of TN-Mann, TN-Vormann, and TN-Obervormann.

5 Shoulder strap for the rank of TN-Vormann for all three periods, 1937–43.

6 Left hand rank collar patch for the ranks of TN-Scharführer to TN-Gefolgschaftsführer for the period 1937–43.

7 Shoulder strap for TN-Musikzugführer, period 1942–43.

8 Shoulder strap for TN-Scharführer, period 1937–43.

9 Shoulder strap for TN-Oberscharführer, period 1937–43.

10 Collar patch as for no. 1 above.

11 Left hand rank collar patch for the ranks of TN-Bereitschaftsführer to TN-Bezirksführer for the period 1937–40 and 1941–42, and for the ranks of TN-Kameradschaftsführer to TN-Bezirksführer for the period 1942–43.

12 Shoulder strap for the 1942–43 rank of TN-Gefolgschaftsführer.

13 Right hand unit collar patch as already described under no. 1 above.

14 Left hand rank patch as already described under no. 11 above.

15 Shoulder strap for TN-Hauptbereitschafts-führer of the period 1937–43.

16/17 Collar patches for the 1937–41 period rank of TN-Landesführer. This senior rank wore only rank patches in matching pairs.

18 Shoulder strap for the 1937–41 period rank of TN-Landesführer.

19 Collar patch, worn in matching pairs, for the 1941–42 period rank of TN-Landesführer and also the 1942–43 period rank of TN-Landesführer.

20 Shoulder strap for the 1941–42 and 1942–

43 period ranks of TN-Landesführer.

21/22 Collar patch, worn in matching pairs, and shoulder strap for the 1937–40 period rank of Stellv. Reichsführer.

23/24 Collar patch, worn in matching pairs, and shoulder strap for the 1941–42 period rank of TeNo-Reichsführer and the 1942–43 period rank of Chef der TN.

As already mentioned, from the year 1943 to the end of the war in May 1945, SS-style collar patches were introduced for wear by all personnel of the TeNo. Presumably the membership continued to wear their existing shoulder straps.

25 Collar patch for Anwärter der TN.

26 Collar patch for Hauptwachtmeister der TN with less than twelve year's service.

27 Collar patch for Zugführer der TN.

28 Collar patch for Bereitschaftsführer der TN.

29 Collar patch for TN-Landesführer.

Plate 21. Shoulder Straps, Collar Patches and 'Passants'

Transportflotte Speer Insignia, 1943–45

The Transportflotte Speer was a waterborne transportation formation formed early in 1943. Its uniforms and insignia were designed by the Berlin artist and designer Egon Jantke and were strongly influenced by the uniforms worn by personnel of the German Navy.

The rank insignia for the lower ratings consisted of a series of red-coloured chevrons only (see Plate 55, nos 9, 10, 11). The 'Unterführer' ranks, the equivalent of petty officers and chief petty officers, wore both collar patches and arm chevrons (see Plate 55, nos 12, 13, 14).

Collar patches were worn in matching pairs on the open-neck jackets.

1 Collar patch for Unterbootsmann (Fourier, geh.Buchhalter) worn in conjunction with single arm chevron on upper left arm as shown in Plate 55, no. 12.

2 Collar patch for Bootsmann (geh.Fourier) worn in conjunction with double arm chevron on upper left arm as shown in Plate 55, no. 13.

3 Collar patch for Oberbootsmann (Verwaltungsführer, Inspektoren) and worn in conjunction with a triple arm chevron on the upper left arm as shown in Plate 55, no. 14.

4 Collar patch for Hauptbootsmann (Hauptverwaltungsführer, Oberinspektoren) worn in conjunction with a silver arm eagle on the upper left arm (not illustrated).

The rank insignia worn by officers of the 'Transportflotte Speer' were collar patches only.

5 Collar patch for Schiffsführer (Dienststellenleiter).

6 Collar patch for Oberschiffsführer (Dienststellenleiter von grösserer Dienststelle).

7 Collar patch for Hauptschiffsführer (Einsatzleiter).

8 Collar patch for Kapitän.

Other collar patches existed for the remaining three senior ranks of Stabskapitän, Kommodore and Generalkapitän (not illustrated).

Shoulder Straps and Collar Patches of the Transportkorps Speer

With the re-organisation late in 1944 of the former Transport Groups and Brigades Speer and Todt into one Transportkorps Speer a new series of uniforms and rank insignia was produced and issued. All former items of insignia, including the various cuff-titles worn at different times by the various Transport formations (see Plate 30, nos 1 and 2) were done away with.

The new series of collar patches for the personnel of Transportkorps Speer displayed the stylised letters 'S' and 'P' on a coloured patch of cloth in the colour of the wearer's branch. These items were worn in matching pairs. Shoulder straps which displayed the wearer's individual rank were very closely based on those types of straps found in use with the Armed Forces. These, too, were worn in pairs.

9 Collar patch worn by those ranks classed as Unterführer (equivalent of NCOs) and Mannschaften (men), black being the 'branch' colour appointed for their use.

10 Collar patch worn by Troop Supply personnel, officers.

11 Collar patch worn by Technical personnel, officers.

12 Collar patch worn by High Leaders, represented by the gold-embroidered 'SP' and the twisted gold cording, of the Medical branch, (Generalarzt).

13 Shoulder strap worn by Kraftfahrer (drivers), the lowest rank grade.

14 Shoulder strap worn by Oberfeldkornett.

15 Shoulder strap worn by Oberstabsingenieur.

16 Shoulder strap worn by Generalarzt.

The colours appointed for other Transportkorps Speer branches were: wine-red for Judicial Services; green for Administrative personnel; and pale violet-grey for specialist officials (Sonderführer). The colours were also encountered on this formation's shoulder straps and collar patches.

Passants for the Reichsautobahnen-Strassenmeister

As part of the issue of new uniforms in 1942 to personnel responsible for the maintenance, repair and administration of the German Autobahn system, a series of 'Passants' were introduced. These shoulder insignia which, unlike shoulder straps that were attached to the shoulder seam of the tunic and buttoned next to the wearer's collar, were positioned on the shoulder of the tunic lying approximately along the line of the shoulder seam. The German Railway authorities also issued passants to their uniformed personnel in the summer of 1941 (see Plate 23, nos 20 to 29).

Passants were worn in pairs, one to each shoulder.

17 Passant for Reg.-Assistant.

18 Passant for Reg.-Sekretär.

19 Passant for Reg.-Obersekretär.

20 Passant for Reg.-Bauinspektor.

21 Passant for Reg.-Oberbauinspektor.

22 Passant for Amtmann.

Plate 22. Deutschen Falkenorden and Deutscher Jägerschaft and various Forestry Services Collar Patches, Collar Insignia and Shoulder Straps

Individual ranks in the German Falconry Order and the German Hunting Association were displayed on the collar of the uniform jackets. They did not use collar patches: instead, the rank insignia emblems were hand-embroidered directly into the cloth of the collar. These emblems were worn in matching pairs on both collars. One pattern of silver braided shoulder strap was used for all ranks up to the most senior persons who wore the same pattern but in gold-coloured braiding. In 1934 to 1936 these straps were worn singly on the right shoulder only; from 1936 onwards the straps were worn in matching pairs.

1 Falconry Order collar insignia for the rank of Kreismeister des Deutschen Falkenordens.

2 Collar insignia for the rank of DFO-Gaumeister.

3 Collar insignia for the rank of Stabsleiter des Ordensmeister.

4 Collar insignia for the most senior rank of Ordensmeister des Deutschen Falkenordens.

The DFO was brought into being during 1938. Their special arm badge is illustrated on Plate 54, no. 6.

5 The 1934 period collar insignia for the rank of Kreisjägermeister.

6 The 1934 period collar insignia for the rank of Gaujägermeister.

7 The 1934 period collar insignia for the rank of Oberjägermeister.

8 The 1934 period collar insignia for the rank of Reichsjägermeister.

In 1936 minor changes were brought about. The uniform remained unchanged with certain modifications and new introductions to the rank insignia.

9 The 1936 period collar insignia for the rank of Jagdräte beim Gaujägermeister. This and the next item represented pine branches.

10 The 1936 period collar insignia for the rank of Jagdräte beim Reichsjägermeister.

In 1938 more minor alterations were introduced for the collar insignia.

11 The 1938 period collar insignia for the rank of Jagdräte beim Gaujägermeister.

12 The 1938 period collar insignia for the rank of Jagdräte beim Reichsjägermeister.

13 Shoulder strap introduced in 1934 and used continuously through the various uniform changes. The green button was that used on the service dress, white metal for ceremonial dress, and gold for most senior rank of Reichsjägermeister. The shoulder strap shown here is for all ranks from Hegeringsführer (local surveyor) to Stabsleiter beim Reichsjägermeister (Chief of Staff to the National Hunting Master). The same pattern and colour shoulder strap was also worn by members of the Deutschen Falkenordens from the rank of Kreismeister des DFO to Ordensmeister des DFO.

14 Shoulder strap for the most senior rank of Reichsjägermeister. This rank wore two shoulder straps.

Forestry Services existed in Germany, each operating under the supervision of its parent body. The State Forestry service was divided into the Gemeinde Forst Dienst (General Forestry Service) and the Privat Forst Dienst, (Private Forestry Service). The first was responsible for the upkeep of tracts of forest under State ownership, whilst the second forestry service covered those forests in private hands.

Both the German Army and the German Air Force had forestry services, mainly responsible for development, conservation and maintenance of areas of woodland and forest belonging to their respective services. The personnel of these forestry services were clothed in the uniform of the State Forestry Service, with different emblems and selected colours used for their collar patches to distinguish one service from another.

15 Collar patch for the rank of Forstaufseher in the Private Forestry Service.

16 Collar patch for the rank of Revierförster in Army Forestry Service.

17 Collar patch for an unestablished rank in the Luftwaffe Forestry Service. It may be possible that this collar patch was worn by a Forestry 'Sonderführer', specialist official.

18 Collar patch for the rank of Landforstmeister in the General State Forestry Service.

19 Shoulder strap for the rank of Oberforstmeister in the Private Forestry Service.

Plate 23. German National Railways Shoulder Straps, Collar Patches and Passants

Shoulder straps first began to be worn on railway uniforms with the introduction of new uniforms and rank insignia in June 1936. The 21 different shoulder straps were worn by railway personnel of different pay groups. The collar patches worn with these straps were the same as those that had been in use prior to the introduction in June 1936 of the series of shoulder straps. These collar patches, which are shown under items 12 and 13 below, were worn either for the closed-neck or open-neck tunics.

On 13 February 1942 the existing collar patches were abolished and a new series, nos 14 to 19 below, were introduced which were worn together with the shoulder straps first

33 On the 'Day of the German Railways' held on 7 December 1943 in the Mosaic Hall in the new Reichs Chancellory, Berlin members of the German Railways were presented with the Iron Cross, 2nd class. The three railway men seated in the foreground, all of whom seem to be disabled to some degree, are all wearing the 1942 pattern collar patches, whilst the man at the far end of the row is still wearing the early pre-war collar patches, a typical pictorial example of the mixing of old and new insignia.

introduced back in June 1936, except for the most senior pay groups which were replaced by shoulder straps of a new design (nos 8 and 9).

In September 1941 details were published that explained about a completely new system of wearing and displaying rank insignia on the shoulder. These 'Passants' were to be worn by all pay group levels of the Reichsbahn and where intended to be introduced over a staggered period of time. The end result of all these changes was that the use of these different styles of insignia became hopelessly mixed up, especially amongst the lower pay group levels.

1 Shoulder strap for Dienstkleidungs-pflichtige u.-berechtigte, Arbeiter, Beamtenanwärter.
2 Shoulder strap for Beamte der Besoldungs-gruppe 17a and 17 (officials of pay group 17a and 17).
3 Shoulder strap for officials of pay groups 13 and 12.
4 Shoulder strap for aspirant officials of pay group 11.
5 Shoulder strap for established officials of

pay groups 8 and 7a and aspirant officials of pay group 7.

6 Shoulder strap for officials of pay group 5.

7 Shoulder strap for officials of pay groups 4a and 4 and aspirant officials for pay group 3.

8 Shoulder strap introduced in February 1942 to replace senior pay group shoulder straps from previous issues, for officials of pay group 5 and aspirant officials for pay group 3.

9 Shoulder strap c. February 1942 for most senior pay group grade 1.

10 Unestablished Reichsbahn shoulder strap.

11 Unestablished Reichsbahn shoulder strap.

12 Pair of collar patches, c. 1933–42 for wear on the closed-neck tunic.

13 Pair of collar patches, c. 1933–42 for wear on the open-neck jacket.

14 Collar patch introduced in 1942 for Railway Workers, closed-neck tunic.

15 Collar patch for pay group officials 17a to 12, open-neck jacket.

16 Collar patch for pay group officials 11 to 8 and 7a, open-neck jacket.

17 Collar patch for pay group officials 7 and 6, closed-neck tunic.

18 Collar patch for pay group officials 7 and 6, open-neck jacket.

19 Collar patch for pay group officials 5 and upwards, open-neck jacket.

The collar patches of the 1942 series were in three qualities. The most common was the silk machine-woven variety (as in nos 14, 15 and 16) with the type with metal insignia mounted on to black cloth patches being a close second (nos 17 and 19). Gold-coloured threads hand-embroidered on to black velvet patches, almost certainly a private purchase and not a common item, came third as illustrated by no. 18. The metal insignia mounted on to these patches, consisting of a winged wheel, a small Swastika and sprays of oak leaves of varying size, were normally produced in a gilded metal. However, the gilding was easily worn away and it left the metal insignia having the appearance of gun-metal grey, as shown in no. 17.

The Reichsbahn Passants introduced from September 1941 onwards were worn on both shoulders of the Railway tunics and greatcoats. They were set across the shoulders following the line of the shoulder seam.

20/21 Reichsbahn Candidate Functionaries.

22 Reichsbahn Candidate for higher service.

23 Reichsbahn Worker.

24 Passant for officials of pay groups 17 and 16.

25 Passant for officials of pay groups 15 to 12.

26 Passant for officials of pay groups 11 to 9.

27 Passant for officials of pay group 8 to 6.

28 Passant for officials of pay group 5.

29 Passant for highest officials of pay groups 1 to 4.

Cuff-Titles

Cuff-titles (Armelstreifen) were a common feature of German uniform insignia. Many uniformed formations, military, para-military, political, and ancillary, wore such items, as will be seen from Plates 24 to 31.

Cuff-titles can be divided into a number of main categories:

1 Campaign awards
2 Cuff-titles bearing emblems, numerals, and initial letters
3 Dated titles
4 Special functions
5 Areas and districts
6 Schools and training establishments
7 Formations using:
   Own title
   Name of unit or formation commander, past or present
   Commemorative title bearing the name of a (former) military hero, or a Nazi Party personality, or a special or commemorative place.

However, the dividing line between some of these categories and sub-categories is somewhat ill-defined.

Regulations were laid down for the manufacture and issue of all types of cuff-titles. Definite rules were set out regarding the wearing of these items, although these rules were occasionally bent or even ignored. Most cuff titles were of a standard width, which was usually 33 mm, although there were a number which were much wider and others narrower than this. Quite a number of the formations that wore cuff-titles on their uniforms made a distinction between those items worn by other ranks and those worn by officers. This distinction usually took the form of the quality of the material used in the inscription, either white or grey cotton threads, usually machine-stitched, for their lower ranks, and in silver-aluminium, hand-embroidered threads for officers.

Some of the cuff-titles had edging, whilst others had none. Those that had edging were of two types. Either the edging was woven into the fabric of the band – as on many of the SS cuff-titles – or the edging was laid on to the band as part of the manufacture, such as the russa braid on the late pattern army cuff-titles for 'Grossdeutschland'.

Plate 24. Cuff-Titles

Military Campaign Cuff-Titles

The cuff-titles illustrated as nos 1 to 4 are regarded as 'Campaign Awards'. That is they were awarded to be worn by German personnel of whatever branch of the Armed Forces that had been involved in a particular campaign and had fulfilled certain requirements. Other forms of campaign awards existed and these consisted either of medals or Campaign Arm Shields (see Plate 60). Unlike other cuff-titles there was no distinction made with these campaign cuff-titles between those awarded to officers and those for the other ranks. The quality was the same for all.

1 The '1936 Spanien 1939' cuff-title was instituted on 21 June 1939 to commemorate the participation of those German troops who had served in Spain during the Civil War with

34 Field Marshal Rommel accompanied by Army and Air Force Paratroop officers in France in 1944. The use of two campaign cuff-titles worn together are clearly shown in this picture, the Afrika with Palms worn over the Kreta cuff-title.

the Armoured Instruction Regiment and the Signals Instruction Detachments, part of the Tradition Units of the Imker-Verbände of the Legion Condor. The title was a 3.2 cm wide band of deep red material with gold-coloured, metallic thread Gothic lettering flanked by the dates '1936' and '1939', the dates for the beginning and end of the Spanish Civil War. The colours of red and gold were those of the Nationalist Forces of Spain and were to become the State colours of Spain under Franco. The cuff-title was worn on the right forearm of all uniform tunics and greatcoats.

2 The 'Afrika' cuff-title was instituted on 15 January 1943 by order of the Chief of the German Army General Staff. It was intended to replace the earlier Afrikakorps cuff-title (see no. 5 below). The cuff-title was awarded to those German personnel who had served for at least six months in the North African theatre, a time restriction dispensed with if the combatant was wounded, or became incapacitated as a result of contracting a tropical disease after serving in the theatre for a minimum of three months.

The title was also awarded to any person who received a German decoration whilst serving in North Africa regardless of length of service spent in that theatre. It was announced in March 1943 that German personnel who had served honourably in the North African campaign and had been eligible for the award of either the 'Kreta' or 'Afrika' cuff-titles, or both, but were serving in another uniformed organisation other than the Army, Navy, or Air Force were also permitted to wear the appropriate cuff-title on their present uniform.

The title was of the same quality and colour-

35 Grand Admiral Karl Dönitz greeting senior officers of the Party, the SA and the Wehrmacht. The NSDAP Political Leader on the far right of the picture is wearing the campaign cuff-title awarded for service in North Africa.

ing for all ranks and all branches of the Armed Forces. It was a soft khaki-green-coloured cloth band 3.3 cm wide with the title 'Afrika' in Roman lettering flanked by palm trees worked in silver-grey cotton threads. The edging was of silver-grey cotton russa braiding. The title was worn on the left cuff of all uniform tunics, including the greatcoat.

3 The 'Kreta' cuff-title was instituted on 16 October 1942 for wear by those German troops who had taken part in the successful battle for the Mediterranean island of Crete. Persons permitted to wear the title had to have fulfilled any of the following requirements:

(a) to have made a parachute or gliderborne landing on the island of Crete between 20 and 27 May 1941 (this applied mainly to Luftwaffe Parachute and Army troops);

(b) to have taken part in the air operations over Crete (mostly aircrew);

(c) to have been on active service at sea in the Cretan theatre of operations up to 27 May 1941 (predominately naval personnel).

The white cloth cuff-title was 33 mm wide with yellow 'Latin' lettering 'Kreta' flanked by yellow-coloured stylized acanthus leaf motifs. The edging of the title had yellow russa braiding. There was no quality distinction made for those titles worn by the troops or those worn by officers. It was worn on the left forearm.

4 The 'Kurland' cuff-title was instituted on 12 March 1945, less than two months before the end of the war in Europe. It proved, therefore, to be the last cuff-title instituted in the Wehrmacht. It was intended to be awarded to those German forces surrounded and under siege by the Soviet Army in the Kurland region of Latvia. The 'Kurland' cuff-title was manufactured locally within the area of Army Group Kurland and, although considerable numbers of the title were produced and awarded before the Army Group capitulated in May 1945, there was quite a degree of variations during the manufacture. The 4 cm wide sleeve band was made from silvery-grey to grey-white cloth edged in black. The wording of Kurland and the two emblems – on the left appeared the shield of the Grand Masters of the Order of Teutonic Knights, and on the right a shield bearing an elk's head, which were taken from the arms of Mitau, the principal town in Kurland – were also worked in black threads. For those troops that actually received the cuff-title it was worn on the left forearm.

It was not uncommon for an individual to have been authorised to wear more than one campaign cuff-title. When this occurred the titles were worn on the left sleeve with the earliest awarded title worn above and taking precedence over the other title.

German Army Cuff-Titles

5 The Afrikakorps cuff-title was introduced on 18 July 1941. It was authorised to be worn by personnel of the Deutsches Afrika Korps – DAK (German Africa Corps) fighting in North Africa. The 33 mm wide title was completely machine-woven in two shades of green and silver aluminium threads. The cuff-title was worn on the right forearm of the Service, Field-Service, and Uniform Tunic as well as

36 Reichsminister Dr Goebbels inspecting gifts presented to him by members of the 'Grossdeutschland' Division, with Oberleutnant Gerhard Konopka, who was awarded four 'Tank Destruction Badges', to his right and Generalleutnant von Hase, State Commandant of Berlin behind him (19 November 1942).

the greatcoat. This item was superseded by the campaign cuff-title 'Afrika' with palms.

6 The Grossdeutschland (Greater Germany) cuff-title was introduced on 15 September 1939. It was worn by all ranks of Infanterie-Regiment 'Grossdeutschland' on the right forearm.

7 The Grossdeutschland cuff-title was introduced during November 1944. It was worn by all ranks of Panzer-Division 'Grossdeutschland' on the right forearm.

8 The Grossdeutschland cuff-title was introduced on 7 October 1940 to replace the previous green and silver Inf Regt 'Grossdeutschland' cuff-title which had been issued six months earlier in May 1940 (not illustrated). Both this and the first green and silver Grossdeutschland cuff-title (no. 6, above) were much despised, their colouring not being considered 'military' and the issue of this black and silver title was very welcome. It was worn by all ranks of Infanterie-Regiment 'Grossdeutsch-

land', as well as by the Grossdeutschland personnel of the 'Führer-Begleit-Bataillon' (the Führer's Escort Battalion). It was worn on the right forearm.

9 The first pattern Führerhauptquartier cuff-title was in use during 1939. It was of a colour and quality of manufacture very similar to the Reichsbahn cuff-titles (see Plate 29, nos 3 to 6). It was worn on the left forearm of all ranks of Army personnel entrusted with the personal safety of the Führer, Adolf Hitler, and the security of all the personnel at, and visitors to the Führer's Headquarters. The title was 4 cm wide, machine-woven as a single piece, and was worn on the left forearm of the army tunic and greatcoat, including the black Panzer uniform for armoured personnel.

10 The second pattern Führerhauptquartier (Führer Headquarters) cuff-title was introduced into service on 15 January 1941. It replaced the previous black and yellow version and its use was extended to personnel of the

37 The 'Grossdeutschland' cuff-title worn by a member of the division's administration unit (6 January 1944).

38 Ritterkreuzträger Generalmajor Conrath (holding maps), the Commander of Panzer-Grenadier-Division 'Hermann Göring', with other divisional officers. Clearly seen are the 'General Göring' cuff-titles, the white collar patches, and the special Luftwaffe/Hermann Göring Division Panzer collar patches – black patches with white metal deaths heads and white piping.

'General Göring' Regiment, who undertook guard duty at the Headquarters as well as the contingents of army personnel from the 'Grossdeutschland' Infantry Regiment. This too was worn on the left forearm and, where appropriate, was worn in conjunction with either the black and silver 'Grossdeutschland' cuff-title worn on the right forearm or the blue and white or blue and silver 'General Göring' cuff-title worn by the Air Force personnel – also on their right forearm. (See plate 25, no. 9).

11 All ranks of the Grenadier-Regiment 199 (from the 57th Infantry Division) and the Replacement Battalion were honoured during the winter of 1944 by having bestowed on them the 'Infanterie-Regiment List' cuff-title. This title commomorated the Imperial German Army regiment, 16th Bavarian Reserve Infantry Regt 'List', the predecessor of Grenadier-Regiment 199, in which Adolf Hitler had served as a Gefreiter (corporal) in World War I. The dark green cuff-title was worn on the left forearm.

12 The Feldmarschall v. Mackensen cuff-title was introduced on 6 December 1944 to be worn by all ranks of 5. Kavallerie-Regiment. It is thought to have been worn on the left cuff.

13 The Feldherrnhalle cuff-title which was already in use by the elite SA Regiments bearing the title 'Feldherrnhalle' was extended on 4 September 1942 for wear by members of Infanterie-Regiment 271 and its Replacement Battalions, also known as Infanterie-Regiment 'Feldherrnhalle'.

The 27 mm wide brown band was worn on the left forearm of the army tunic and greatcoat. Examples of this title exist where the edging is in grey cotton with the lettering machine-woven in silver-aluminium threads. Other titles have both the edging and the lettering in silver-aluminium metallic threads, as illustrated here. These are thought to have been used by other ranks and for officers respectively.

58

Plate 25. Cuff-Titles

German Army Cuff-Titles (Continued)

1 Machine-woven cuff-title for wear by other ranks of Army Field Police units. Worn on the left forearm in conjunction with the Feldgendarmerie arm eagle (see Plate 44, no. 8). Officers quality cuff-titles existed, hand embroidered in silver-aluminium threads on a chocolate brown cloth band.

2 Cuff-title for uniformed personnel of the German Army Secret Field Police. A very rare cuff-title manufactured in exactly the same way and in the same quality as the Propagandakompanie and Feldpost cuff-titles, nos 3 and 4 below.

3 Army Propaganda Company cuff-title worn on the left forearm by personnel of Army units (companies) employed in war reporting, filming, and taking photographs.

4 Army Field Post cuff-title for wear by Army postal officials.

5 Unteroffiziervorschule. Cuff-title worn by staff personnel of Army NCOs preparatory schools.

6 Cuff-title worn by senior female staff assistants in the German Army.

7 Cuff-title worn by junior female staff assistants in the German Army.

German Air Force Cuff-Titles

8 The Luftwaffe version of the 'Afrika' cuff-title was instituted on the 6 March 1942. It was authorised to be worn by members of all Luftwaffe units and formations which were actually stationed in North Africa, by those who had been wounded in North Africa and had been removed to European military hospitals, and those on leave in Europe. The cuff-title had to be removed when an individual's unit was transferred out of the African theatre. It was worn 16 cm above the lower edge to the right sleeve on the tropical tunic, and just above the cuff of the blue-grey service tunic.

The German Air Force introduced a third class of cuff-title, whereas the majority of cuff-titles used within the German Armed Forces were either of one standard quality and design for all ranks of a particular unit, or had a separate quality for ranks below officer and another quality, usually somewhat superior, for wear by ranks from junior officer upwards. In the case of cuff-titles issued to personnel of the 'General Göring' and 'Hermann Göring' Regiments, those issued to the other Ranks were embroidered in grey cotton threads on blue material bands without edging. NCOs received cuff-titles also embroidered in grey cotton threads but with an edging of grey russa braid and officers of all ranks wore cuff-titles where the lettering was hand-embroidered in silver-aluminium threads and had silver-aluminium russa braid edging.

9 Cuff-title as worn by other ranks of the Regiment 'General Göring'. Instituted 1 April 1936, worn on right forearm.

10 Cuff-title as worn by other ranks of the 'Hermann Göring' Brigade, introduced between May and August 1942.

11 Cuff-title as worn by officers of the Division 'Hermann Göring'.

12 Cuff-title as worn by officers of the 1st Parachute Regiment (Fallschirm-Jäger Rgt 1).

13 Cuff-title as worn by officers of the Parachute Division, that is, by all Fallschirmjäger and remaining troops of the 7th Flieger (Fallschirm) Division including the Fallschirmschule with the exception of the 1st and 2nd Fallschirmjäger Regiments. This cuff-title was worn without edging. Officers had the lettering hand-embroidered in silver-aluminium threads – as shown here – whilst all other ranks were in grey cotton threads. The two parachute unit cuff-titles together with the Fallschirm-Jäger Rgt 2 cuff-title (not illustrated) were supposed to have been withdrawn during the war years, although photographic evidence points to the contrary.

14 Cuff-title as worn by officers of Flieger Gruppe Schwerin which became Sturzkampfgeschwader 163 and finally Sturzkampfgeschwader 2. Title was instituted on 3 April 1935. It was worn on the right forearm.

39 A German Luftwaffe officer (left) wearing the Air Force 'War Commemorative cuff-title' as illustrated on colour Plate 26, no. 1, with two Rumanian air force officers.

Plate 26. Cuff-Titles

Luftwaffe Cuff-Titles (Continued)

1 This cuff-title together with the Jagdstaffel Boelcke Nr. 2 1916–18 cuff-title (not illustrated) were considered as War Commemorative cuff-titles. Both were introduced in October 1935. These cuff-titles were permitted to be worn by those persons serving in the new Luftwaffe provided they could prove that they had been members of the original World War I squadrons for at least one year or more, less if they had been wounded. Either cuff-title could only be worn if the person eligible was not already entitled to wear any other commemorative cuff-title. In January 1939 the privilege of being able to wear either of these cuff-titles was extended to members of the NSFK for wear on the NSFK service uniform. The cuff-titles were worn on the right forearm.

2 Special commemorative cuff-titles worn by officers of the new Luftwaffe Flieger Gruppe Fassberg who had originally served in the World War I Geschwader Boelcke. The addition of the 3 mm wide silver-aluminium russa braiding along the top and bottom edge of this cuff-title was a very short lived feature, having been authorised on 25 March 1935 and withdrawn on 23 April 1935. In place of this commemorative cuff-title those eligible persons were issued with the War Commemorative cuff-title as described above under no. 1. The second type of Geschwader Boelcke cuff-title without edging worn by officers, in silver-aluminium lettering, and NCOs and men, in grey cotton lettering, and introduced on 23 April 1935, was worn by all personnel of Flieger Gruppe Fassberg, which became Kampfgeschwader 154, then KG 157, and finally KG 27. Both types of title were worn on the right forearm.

3 Instituted on 24 March 1936 for wear by all ranks of the Zerstörergeschwader 'Horst Wessel' (here shown for NCOs and men) of the Fliegergeschwader Dortmund, which later became ZG 142, and, finally, on the forty-sixth birthday of SA Stabschef Viktor Lutze was renamed ZG 26 'Horst Wessel'. Worn on the right forearm.

4 The Jagdgeschwader 'Mölders' cuff-title (here shown for wear by officers) was instituted on 20 December 1941 for all ranks of the Jagdgeschwader 51. The title was adopted after the death of Oberstleutnant Werner Mölders, who died on 22 November 1941 and who had served as Commanding Officer of JG 51 from 27 July 1940 until his death. (It is

40 The 'Hans E Maikowski' SA cuff-title, whose lettering is in German sutterlin script (31 August 1943).

of interest to note that in the West German Bundesluftwaffe there is a squadron permitted to wear the new cuff-title bearing the legend 'Geschwader Mölders'.)

5 Instituted on 20 November 1940 for Luftwaffe personnel and Luftwaffe Administrative personnel acting as war reporters. The title for NCOs and men, as shown here, was in matt grey cotton yarn lettering without edging. Officers and war reporters with officer status had the lettering of their cuff-title in hand-embroidered, silver-aluminium thread with silver-aluminium russa braid edging. It was worn on the right forearm.

SA Cuff-Titles

Early SA Staff Guard cuff-titles were first introduced sometime during 1933 and continued in use until March 1934. All three categories of these titles were worn on the left cuff of the SA Service Tunic and the greatcoat along the upper edge of the turn back cuff. On the SA brown shirt they were worn 15 cm from the lower edge of the cuff. The cuff-titles were 3 cm wide in the colour of the wearer's collar patch. All bore the word 'Stabswache'.

A For Staff Guard personnel of the Obersten SA-Führung, the Supreme SA Leader (Ernst Röhm), a carmine band with yellow lettering 'Stabswache' (not illustrated).

B For Staff Guards for SA-Obergruppen und SA-Gruppen in bright red bands with white lettering 'Stabswache' (not illustrated).

C For Staff Guards of other SA units in bands of colour corresponding to individual collar patch colour with lettering in colour of collar patch number bearing the legend 'Stabswache' (no. 8 below).

In March 1934 the above regulations were changed to:

A For Staff Guard personnel for the Supreme SA Leader (Ernst Röhm), a carmine red band with gold lettering and edging with title 'Stabschef Röhm' (no. 7 below).

B For Staff Guards for SA-Obergruppen und SA-Gruppen cuff bands in colour of wearer's collar patch (bright red) with white lettering 'Stabswache'.

C This category abolished.

D For Staff Guards for Hermann Göring bright red band with silver edging and lettering 'Stabswache Göring', (no. 6 below).

E For Regiment 'Adolf Hitler' a black band with grey edging and lettering 'Adolf Hitler' (see Plate 31, no. 2).

6 Cuff-title instituted March 1934 for personnel of Hermann Göring's own Staff Guard. Worn on left forearm.

7 Cuff-title instituted March 1934 for personnel of Ernst Röhm's own Staff Guard. Worn on left forearm.

8 Cuff-title for personnel of SA Staff Guard

from the SA District of Südwest.

Other cuff-titles worn by the membership of the Sturmabteilung very often carried the name of an important Nazi personality or a person who was considered by the Nazis worthy of commemorating.

Such cuff-titles included: Albert Leo Schlageter; Curt Kreth; Daniel Sauer; Emil Müller; Hallermann; Hans E. Maikowski; Hans von Manteuffel (no. 10 below); Hermann Förg; Hermann Pantföder; Horst Wessel (no. 9 below); Karl Frenburger; Karl Roos, Knickmann; Kuetermeyer; and Wilhelm Gustloff. Almost all these cuff-titles had their lettering machine-embroidered on to black edged black bands. The style of the lettering varied from block capital letters through Gothic style upper and lower case lettering to German handwritten Suterlin script. All were approximately 33 mm wide and all were worn on the right forearm.

9 Cuff-title worn by the personnel of the 5th SA Standart 'Horst Wessel', a Berlin-based unit.

10 Cuff-title worn by personnel of the 'Hans von Manteuffel' SA Regiment.

German Police Formation Cuff-Titles

11 Cuff-title instituted on 22 December 1933 for officers of the Landpolizeigruppe 'General Göring'. Men of the LPG 'General Göring' wore a plain dark green cuff-band with the lettering machine-embroidered in white cotton threads. NCOs had the same quality of band and lettering but with the addition of white russa braiding along top and bottom edges (not illustrated). Officer's cuff-titles as shown here were hand-embroidered in silver-aluminium threads with silver-aluminium edging. The titles were worn on the left forearm of the green police tunic and greatcoat.

12 The 'Motorisierte Gendarmerie' (Motorised Gendarmerie) cuff-title as shown was worn on the left forearm of all officer personnel and

41 A Police Oberwachtmeister wearing the 'Deutsche Wehrmacht' cuff-title.

inspectors of the Motorised Gendarmerie. For NCOs and men the same cuff-title was worn but without the edging.

13 Cuff-title worn on the left forearm by German Police personnel operating alongside units of the German Armed Forces outside the Reich Borders. This cuff-title was worn for the same reason as the black and yellow 'Deutsche Wehrmacht' arm band (see Plate 33, no. 3).

Plate 27. Cuff-Titles

German Police Formation Cuff-Titles (Continued)

1 SS-Polizei-Regiment Todt. This has proved to be a very rare cuff-title with only very few examples of this title known to have survived from World War II. The introduction of the cuff-title probably dates from the formation of the SS Police Regiment no. 28 in 1942. From examining a surviving example, it can clearly be seen that the silver-aluminium runic SS has been added to the silver-grey cotton embroidered lettering, implying that at some previous time the legend on the title was only that of 'Polizei-Regiment-Todt', but that after a particular date the SS runes were added for some reason as yet unexplained. The title was worn on the left forearm.

The introduction of new uniforms, insignia and dress regulations for members of the Bahnschutzpolizei in 1941 included a series of six separate cuff-titles.

2 Cuff-title for first, and most junior, group of ranks from Bzp-Anwärter to Stellv. Bzp-Gruppenführer.

The cuff-title for the second group of ranks, excluding the rank of Bzp-Oberzugführer, which had a separate cuff-title (see no. 3 below) but which are not illustrated here, had a black band with machine-woven silver-aluminium lettering and wide silver-aluminium edging. The ranks were Bzp-Gruppenführer to Bzp-Zugführer.

3 Cuff-title for the separate rank of Bzp-Oberzugführer.

4 Cuff-title for the third group of Railway Protection Police ranks from Bzp-Abteilungsführer to Bzp-Abteilungshauptführer.

The fourth group of ranks from Bzp-Bezirksführer to Stabsführer der Bzp. wore cuff-titles of silver-aluminium woven metallic cloth with gold-coloured lettering and white edging (not illustrated).

5 Cuff-title for the most senior rank of Chef der Bahnschutz.

6 The personnel of the Coastal Protection Police wore a very narrow, dark blue cuff-title bearing the legend 'Marine-Küstenpolizei' in yellow Gothic-style lettering with yellow russa braid edging. It was worn on the left forearm.

7 The Grenz-Polizei cuff-title was worn on the left forearm of the field-grey service uniform of the Security Police responsible for the control of Germany's frontiers. Introduced in 1937, the title was worn by personnel of the Frontier Police under the supervision of the Chief of the Security Police. These units are believed to have ceased to function, and they were disbanded altogether by October 1941.

Naval, Customs Officials, and TeNo Cuff-Titles

8 Cuff-title worn by female German auxiliaries attached to the Germany Navy. It was worn on the left cuff. It also exists with yellow lettering on a green backing.

9 Cuff-title worn by male German auxiliaries attached to the Germany Navy. It was worn on the left forearm.

10 Cuff-title worn by senior male auxiliaries attached to the German Navy and serving at shore-based establishments. These were also worn on the left forearm.

11 Cuff-title as worn by all senior personnel with the rank status of a 'General' in the German Customs Service – Landzollbeamten (Zollgrenzschutz) and Zollbeamte. For the cuff-title as worn by all other Customs Service ranks including the Water Customs Officials see Plate 2, no. 11.

12 The Technische Nothilfe (TeNo) cuff-title, illustrated here as the bright silver-aluminium threads on black band type, worn on the field-grey uniform worn by TeNo personnel serving with, or assisting units of the German Armed Forces. The other, more common, TeNo cuff-title very often encountered in collections is of the same design but with the lettering in dull grey cotton machine-woven on to a black band. This pattern was used on the work and fatigue uniforms. There was no rank difference intended by the use of the silver-aluminium lettered band and that of the dull grey lettered cuff-title.

13 A series of cuff-titles were brought into use by the TeNo whereby the wearer's date of entry into the TeNo was displayed on the cuff-title. Known as 'Jahresband der TN', they displayed the dates 1919, 1920, 1921, 1922, and 1923. All were of the same design colouring and quality with only the date being different. Shown here is the Year Band of the TeNo for 1919.

42 The Technische Nothilfe cuff-title worn on the work and fatigue TeNo uniform.

43 The Technische Nothilfe cuff-title worn on the field-grey TeNo uniform.

Plate 28. Cuff-Title

Hitler-Jugend and Bund Deutsche Mädel Cuff-Titles
1 Landdienst der HJ. Cuff-title worn by HJ personnel who undertook to serve for one year's voluntary agricultural labour service on the land. (See also Plate 40, no. 19.) Worn on

45 Members of the Hitler Youth between the ages of 16 and 18 underwent pre-military training first begun in October 1939. This member of the HJ Patrol Service training to use a rifle is wearing the HJ-Streifendienst cuff-title.

left cuff, it was introduced c. 1934.
2 HJ-Streifendienst. Cuff-title worn on the left forearm by HJ personnel of the Hitler Youth Patrol Service.
3 Almost nothing is known about this cuff-title, other than that it must have been for use by BDM officials working in the eastern territories.
4 Cuff-title for wear by personnel on the staff of the Reich Youth Leader. It was worn by senior members of the BDM on the left forearm. It is unique in that it has a single edging along the base line of the cuff-title.
5 BDM cuff-title for Southeast Salzburg.

Reichsarbeitsdienst Cuff-Titles
6 Cuff-title worn by RAD personnel of the Staff Guard for the Reichsarbeitsführer.

44 A young member of the 'Landdienst der Hitler-Jugend', the one year's land service.

65

7 The RAD 'Anhalt' commemorative cuff-title, worn by officers from the Arbeitsgaues XIII and RAD members from RAD Group 135. The green cloth band with red silk, machine-stitched edging and white cotton machine-stitched lettering was worn on the left forearm. It commemorated the state of Anhalt, the colours of red, white, and green being the state colours, where state-wide labour service was first introduced under the Nazis.

The three versions of the Emsland cuff-titles illustrated here were worn by RAD personnel on their left forearms. These titles are thought to represent a district in Germany and acted as a commemorative emblem. They were known to be in use in 1937.

8 Emsland worn by RAD Group personnel.

9 Emsland cuff-title also worn by RAD Group personnel from Gruppe IV.

10 Emsland cuff-title machine-woven in white cotton threads on black band worn by RAD personnel from Abteilung 4.

The general rule was that those cuff-titles manufactured with silver-aluminium machine-woven letters and Roman numerals were for Group personnel, and those with white cotton letters and Arabic numerals were for Detachment personnel.

The Reichsarbeitsdienst cuff-titles bearing just an initial letter and flanked on either side by a horizontal line remain something of a mystery. They were in use during the pre-war years. The gold-coloured emblem cuff-titles were definitely associated with the senior ranks of the RAD. It may be that the silver-aluminium-coloured titles were for officers of the RAD whilst the white cotton cuff-titles were for use by the lower ranks.

11 Unestablished RAD cuff-title, 'O' probably standing for Ost.

12 Unestablished RAD cuff-title, 'N' probably standing for Nord.

13 Unestablished RAD cuff-title, 'W' prob-ably standing for West.

14 Unestablished RAD cuff-title, 'S' probably standing for Süd.

15 Unestablished RAD cuff-title, 'R' probably standing for Reich.

Plate 29. Cuff-Titles

Postal Protection, and Brigade Ehrhardt Cuff-Titles

1 The Postschutz, or Postal Protection cuff-title. Little is known about this item other than its colouring. It is fairly certain that this item would have been in use up to 1942, when the Postschutz came under the control of the Reich Ministry of Post and Telegraph. After March 1942 the Postal Protection service was incorporated into the Allgemeine-SS and the service was then referred to as the SS-Post-schutz.

2 The Brigade Ehrhardt cuff-title, c. 1920, worn by all ranks on the left forearm. The Brigade Ehrhardt were using the double 'S' rune emblem before its adoption by the Nazi Party's own Schutzstaffel.

German National Railways Cuff-Titles

German Railway cuff-titles were introduced on 13 February 1941 to be worn in conjunction with the arm eagle badge already described (see Plate 1, no. 9). However, after only seven months these items were withdrawn and replaced by the more familiar and much more numerous named arm badges (see Plate 56, nos 1 to 6). Of all these cuff-titles – and not many are known to have been produced – the one that is often encountered in advanced collections is the 'Wehrmacht-Verkehrsdirektion Brüssel' title (not illustrated) which is the same as no. 5 but has the name Brüssel in place of Paris.

3 Cuff-titles worn on the left forearm by Railway personnel of the State Railway Directorate based on Berlin.

4 Cuff-title worn by personnel of the State

Railway Directorate based on Cologne, also worn on the left forearm.

5 Cuff-title worn by personnel of the Armed Forces Traffic Directorate based on Paris, France.

6 Cuff-title worn on the left forearm by Railway personnel in the eastern occupied territories of the 'Generalgovernment' (Poland) and based on Cracow. (See Plate 56, no. 3.)

NSDAP Political Leadership Cuff-Titles

7 Early NSDAP Political Leaders cuff-title showing the wearer's date of entry into the Nazi Party, referred to as a 'Verdienstabzeichen'. (See also Plate 37, no. 3a.)

8 Commemorative cuff-title worn on the right forearm by former members of the 1923 Stosstrupp 'Adolf Hitler'.

9 Cuff-title worn by staff and students at the NSDAP Political Leaders Training School (Ordensburg) Vogelsang. It was worn on the left cuff of the Political Leaders uniform.

10 Cuff-title worn by staff and students at the NSDAP Political Leaders Training School at Krössinsee (*it is rendered incorrectly on the plate*), also worn on the left cuff.

Other cuff-titles for other schools existed: these were 'Sonthofen' and 'Ordensburgen', the latter probably a universal title to cover those schools without a separate designation.

NS-Reichskriegerbund Cuff-Titles

Cuff-titles were a feature of the uniforms worn by all members of the NS-Reichskriegerbund. They were in three levels of importance and each bore the name appointed to a particular NS-RKB administrative area. Those cuff-titles with gold-coloured metallic thread design and edging were worn by NS-RKB members in a leadership position. Those in silver-aluminium thread were for NS-RKB members belonging to the staff and the members of the Kameradschaft Advisory Groups. Cuff-titles with grey cotton edging and emblem details were for all remaining Association members. The NS-RKB districts were as follows: Alpenland, Donau, Elbe, Fulda-Werra, Main, Mitte, Nord, Nordost, Nordwest, Rhein, Spree, Süd (Hochland), Sudetenland, Südost, Südwest, Warthe, Weichsel and West. All these district names appear on the cuff-titles of the NS-Reichskriegerbund.

11 Cuff-title for Leadership personnel from the NS-RKB district of Alpenland, worn on left forearm.

12 Cuff-title for members and staff members of the NS-RKB Kameradschafts Advisory Group from the district of Süd (Hochland), also worn on left forearm.

13 Cuff-title for members, other than those shown above, of the NS-RKB district of West. It was worn on left forearm.

Plate 30. Cuff-Titles

Nationalsozialistische Kraftfahr Korps Cuff-Titles

During the first months of World War II NSKK transport units were attached to the German Army and Air Force to help supplement their regular front-line transport units. These NSKK transport units were initially organised into regiments. Later, they were expanded into transport groups and brigades and finally, in 1944, they were all brought together and re-titled as a transport corps, with individual regiments from the corps being farmed out to both the Air Force and the Army.

1 Cuff-title for wear by NSKK members of the NSKK Brigade 'Luftwaffe'.

2 Early cuff-title for use by NSKK members of the 1st NSKK Transport Regiment 'Luftwaffe'.

Other cuff-titles are known to have existed, amongst them are NSKK-Transportbrigade-Todt which despite its name was not connected with the Organisation Todt, the name 'Todt' commemorating Dr Fritz Todt.

46 The NSKK Honour Leader cuff-title worn here by NSKK-Obergruppenführer Herzog von Coburg in conversation with the British Ambassador Sir Nevile Henderson. In the background stands Reichsleiter Alfred Rosenberg.

3 The practice of creating Honorary Leaders was carried out in the SS, the NSDAP Political Leadership, the NSFK, and the SA, amongst others. In some cases (the NSDAP Political Leadership, the NSFK, the SA, etc.), these honorary members were distinguished by wearing specially designed collar patches (see Plate 11, no. 16 and Plate 3, no. 37). With other formations, including the NSKK, these members wore cuff-titles, as shown here.

4 Cuff-title for NSKK members of Emergency Squads.

Air Raid Warning Service and General-SS Cuff-Titles

5 Cuff-title worn on the left forearm by mem-bers of the Luftschutz Warndienst (Air Raid Warning Service).

6 Silver-aluminium with black silk design cuff-title worn by a Hauptabteilungsleiter on the staff of the Reichsführer-SS and the three SS main offices. It was worn on the left fore-arm.

7 Cuff-title worn by all personnel of the 1st SS-Regiment of Foot (Munich). Introduced on 25 August 1936 after the death of Julius Schreck, Hitler's personal driver and long time body-guard, as a commemorative item.

8 Cuff-title worn by SS personnel from the 2nd Company of the 1st Battalion of 1st SS Regiment. The cuff-title with its name 'Casella' commemorated one of the Nazis that fell at the Feldherrnhalle in Munich on 9 November 1923. It was introduced in December 1934.

9 Cuff-title worn by SS personnel from the 10th Company of the 3rd Battalion from 1st SS Regiment, also introduced in December 1934. Karl Laforce was another of those Nazis that died in front of the Munich Feldherrnhalle during the unsuccesful putsch of 9 November 1923.

10 Cuff-title worn by personnel on the staff of SS-Abschnitte (SS Sub-district) XXXIII.

11 Cuff-title for SS men and non-commis-sioned ranks of the 6th Company of the 2nd Battalion of an SS Regiment of Foot.

12 Cuff-title for SS men and non-commis-sioned ranks of the 5th Company of an SS Cavalry Regiment.

13 Cuff-title for the staff of an SS Reserve battalion.

Plate 31. Cuff-Titles

General-SS (Continued), SS-Verfügungstruppe, and Waffen-SS Cuff-Titles

1 San.-Abt.Ost cuff-title for all ranks in an SS Medical Company under the command of SS District East. It was worn on the left forearm.

2 Adolf Hitler cuff-title worn by all ranks in the SS-Leibstandarte 'Adolf Hitler'. Cuff-title shown here was for wear by officers, and has an embroidered inscription and machine-woven silver edging.

3 Brandenburg cuff-title introduced in March 1936 for all ranks (here shown for SS other ranks) from 2nd SS-Totenkopf-Standarte Brandenburg.

4 SS-Schule Tölz cuff-title introduced in 1934 for all ranks (here shown for SS officers) on the staff of the SS-Junkerschule Tölz (SS officers training school situated at Bad Tölz in southern Bavaria, now known as 'Flint Barracks' accommodating the US Special Forces [Air borne]).

5 SS-Polizei-Division cuff-title introduced in 1943. BeVo quality manufacture as worn by all ranks of the 4th SS-Polizei-Panzer-Grenadier-Division.

6 Theodor Eicke cuff-title for all ranks, in-

47 Foreign Minister Joachim von Ribbentrop (4 February 1938).

48 Reichsminister Dr Joseph Goebbels greeting Army and Waffen-SS officers who had taken part in the fighting at Demjansk (4 May 1943). The officer shaking hands with Goebbels is from the SS-Totenkopf Division and wears the 'Totenkopf' cuff-title.

49 Members of the Waffen-SS in Greece, the NCO on the right is wearing the SS-War Correspondent Company cuff-title (11 December 1942).

50 Cadet pupils of the SS School of Music at Brunswick, all are wearing the 'Musikschule Braunschweig' cuff-title.

cluding officers, of the 3rd SS Totenkopf Regiment. BeVo quality title introduced sometime after 2 March 1943.

7 SS-Heimwehr Danzig cuff-title introduced in September 1938 for use by all ranks of the Danzig SS Home Defence unit.

8 Der Führer cuff-title as worn by personnel from the 3rd SS Regiment. Their name 'Der Führer' was bestowed on 8 April 1938.

9 Cuff-title for officers of the SS Regiment 'Deutschland'.

10 SS-Feldgendarmerie cuff-title introduced 1 August 1942 for wear by all ranks (shown here is officer's quality title) in the SS Feldgendarmerie. This cuff-title was abolished on 15 November 1944 after which date all mem-

bers of the SS-Feldgendarmerie reverted to wearing the cuff-title of their division.

11 SS-Kriegsberichter-Kp. cuff-title introduced in 1939 for all ranks (here shown as for other ranks) in the SS-War Correspondent Company. It was of unusual manufacture in that it had machine-embroidered German Suterlin inscription in thin chain stitching with chain stitching edging to the black cloth band. It was very probably a semi-official item.

12 Cuff-title introduced sometime after August 1941 for all ranks (here shown for other ranks) of an SS War Correspondent Battalion.

13 Cuff-title worn by all ranks at the SS School of Music at Brunswick, including cadet pupils.

Arm Bands

Arm bands were an important aspect of German uniform dress and served a necessary function when worn with civilian clothing.

A very large number of arm bands are known to have existed during the Third Reich period, many of them being introduced during the years of World War II.

Generally speaking German arm bands can be divided into two main types:

1. Those that were an integral part of the uniform dress.
2. Those that were worn on German uniform dress, civilian clothing or non-German uniform dress, usually being worn on a temporary basis.

These two main categories can themselves be sub-divided into three further types:

(i) Those arm bands worn to indicate rank or level of responsibility, sometimes using a combination of the Party or a formation emblem with rank insignia of whatever type, examples being NSDAP Political Leaders, Org.Todt, etc.

(ii) Those worn on uniform dress of any type or with civilian clothing to show that the wearer was carrying out a particular function or held a particular office of responsibility for a limited period of time which, without this visual aid, was not apparent to an observer, examples being Stretcher Bearer, Railway Station Officer, etc.

(iii) Arm bands worn on uniform dress, civilian clothing or foreign military attire in order to show that the wearer belonged to a particular German formation, examples being Volkssturm, RAD-Kriegsberichter,

Feld-Polizei, Deutsche Wehrmacht, etc.

The colours used for the arm bands, the size of the bands themselves, the emblems they displayed, and the style of the lettering or the numerals used varied considerably. Many arm bands were manufactured to precise specifications, whilst others were more of a makeshift variety, often being produced during times of emergency.

The manufacturing qualities can be classified as follows:

1. Machine-woven;
2. Emblems or lettering, etc. hand-embroidered on to a cloth band;
3. Silk screen printed;
4. Hand-stencilled in paint or waterproof inks;
5. Appliqué work;
6. Hand-written or hand-painted directly on to a cloth band;
7. Cloth bands with a metal item attached, usually an emblem or device.

Most arm bands, with the obvious exception of those that formed an integral part of the uniform, were not the property of the individual. They were issued out to both uniformed and non-uniformed personnel as and when it was necessary and were returned to the issuing authority when they were no longer required.

In some cases arm bands were, for security reasons, marked with an indelible ink-stamp of the issuing office or unit. The cashette details on the arm band were intended to correspond with details entered on the official papers normally carried by the individual wearing the arm band. This simple procedure re-inforced the security aspect of the wearer if stopped and questioned by civil or military police patrols. This was the same procedure as that employed on military vehicle number plates and the papers, movement orders, etc. carried by the drivers of these military vehicles.

Plate 32. Arm Bands

NSDAP and NSDAP Political Leaders

1 The 'Kampfbinde', the standard pattern arm band worn by members of the NSDAP with or without uniforms. Worn on the left upper arm, it was the earliest arm band in use by the Nazi Party. It was in use in 1920 even before the introduction of the brown uniform.

The Swastika emblem and the arm band are claimed to have been designed by Adolf Hitler himself, although the emblem was in use by an Austrian right-wing political party before Hitler became involved in German politics. Various qualities of this band are often encountered from a fine melton cloth with appliquéd white silk disc and black silk tape forming the Swastika to thin cotton printed with the Swastika design. All are correct, quality depending on how much a Party Member could afford to pay for his or her arm band.

2 An early version of the NSDAP Leaders arm band. An unspecified system of bands was used as a form of rank. These bands of braid varied in number and in width. According to contemporary photographic evidence the more bands

51 The Chief of the Carabinieri in Rome, Luigi Corenei, being greeted by SD, Army, Police and Political Leaders on his arrival in Berlin on an official visit (29 October 1942). On the far right is Gaupropagandaleiter Böker.

of braid the more senior the wearer's rank.

In 1938–39 the Nazi Party introduced new forms of uniform clothing and related insignia for the members of its Political Leadership. Amongst these new items was a range of new style arm bands which were worn on the left upper arm and were used to indicate the wearer's level of responsibility and political district. In all there were 38 separate arm bands for various levels of responsibility within the four political groupings, Orts, Kreis, Gau, and Reich.

3 Arm band for an NSDAP Blockhelfer-Betriebsobmann (A) in an Ortsgruppe.

4 Arm band for a Leiter eines Hauptamtes in a Kreisleitung.

5 Arm band for a Gauleiter.

6 Arm band for a Leiter eines Ob.Amtes in the Reichsleitung.

The 'new' uniform regulations for the NSDAP Political Leaders allocated four colours as facing colours and four colours as piping colours for various items of insignia in order to distinguish between members of various political levels. These were: light brown facing cloth with pale blue piping for members of Local Group levels (Ortsgruppen); dark brown facing cloth with white piping for members at District level (Kreisleitung); bright red facing cloth with dark red piping for members at Regional level (Gauleitung); and for members at National level (Reichsleitung) carmine red facing cloth with gold-yellow piping. This coloured piping appears along the top and bottom edge of each arm band indicating the political level of the wearer. The white disc and the black Swastika is edged with a fine gold-coloured cording on all arm bands for Political Leaders with the exception of the very lowest level, that of Candidate Political Leader (Politische Leiter Anwärter – not illustrated). The gold-coloured oak-leaves, where they appear on these arm bands, are meant to 'point' upwards.

SA and SS

7 Arm bands as worn by the membership of the SA were those as illustrated above under item 1. Another arm band, fairly common, and obviously associated with the SA, having a silk-woven representation of the SA Sport-Abzeichen (SA Sports Badge) as its central motif existed, although its precise purpose is not wholly established. In all probability it was worn by sports umpires, time keepers and track officials of the SA judging at the official sports events for members of the SA and other NSDAP formations who were competing for the SA Sports Badge.

8 Arm band worn by uniformed members of the SA and the SS acting as assistants to Town Police. Other examples are known to have existed and they were generally worn on the forearm.

9 The SS-Kampfbinde. Introduced in November 1925, it was worn on the upper left arm of all SS black service uniforms.

52 Dr Goebbels wearing the standard pattern NSDAP Swastika arm band, congratulating a Railway official who has just been awarded the Knights Cross of the War Merit Cross on the 'Day of the German Railways' (7 December 1943).

HJ, DJ and NS-Studentenbund

The distinctive Hitler Youth arm bands were first seen in July 1924 at a youth rally held at Plauen (a small town – now in East Germany –

on the river Elster between Leipzig and Nürnberg). Prior to this date, and up to the time of the abortive putsch of 9 November 1923, there had existed a 'Youth League of the National Socialist Workers' Party' founded on 13 May 1922, and, later, a sub-division of this organisation for sixteen to eighteen year old youths entitled 'Jungsturm Adolf Hitler', brought into being on 28 January 1923. Members of the Youth League and the Jungsturm Adolf Hitler came under the direct command of the SA. Their uniforms and insignia were very similar to those worn by the SA, the result of which caused resentment amongst the SA and problems for the youth members, many of whom were attacked, beaten up, and, in some instances, killed by their political opponents who mistook them for SA.

With the re-organisation of a Nazi Youth movement in 1924 the opportunity was taken to introduce new uniforms, insignia – amongst which was the new distinctive arm band – and new flags.

10 The Hitler Youth arm band, especially designed to avoid any confusion with the earlier SA and Party Swastika arm band (no. 1 above.).

11 Arm band, in all probability of an early pattern, for members of the Deutsche Jungvolk.

12 Arm band for members of the NS-Studentenbund (National Socialist Students League).

Reichsarbeitsdienst

The Swastika arm band was worn on all RAD Service Uniforms as an integral part of the uniform. Other types of arm bands were used in the RAD one of the most common being the 'Deutsche Wehrmacht' band, worn by RAD members when serving with the German Armed Forces during the war (see Plate 33, no. 3).

13 An obvious RAD arm band but the purpose of which is, as yet, unestablished. The motif is identical to the shoulder strap mount as used on the late pattern shoulder strap for

53 Hitler, accompanied by the Reichs Youth Leader Baldur von Schirach (behind and to right without cap) and Joseph Goebbels (behind von Schirach) talking with young women of the BDM (1 May 1937).

the Reichsarbeitsführer Konstantin Hierl (see Plate 8, no. 24). It is probably safe to assume that this arm band was introduced on or after the introduction date of the RAD shoulder strap, September 1942. It is also probable that this arm band was worn by members of the staff of the Reichsarbeitsführer.

14 RAD War Reporter arm band, introduced in 1941 and worn on the left upper arm.

NSKK, SA Reserve and NS-Frauenschaft-Deutsches Frauenwerk

15 Members of all ranks of the National Socialist Kraftfahr Korps (NSKK) wore the standard Swastika arm band as an integral part of their uniform. The arm band illustrated here was probably worn by NSKK officials participating in the numerous motor sports events held by the NSKK in pre-war Germany.

16 Traffic Control arm band, available to be worn by those persons of any branch of service or para-military formations including the NSKK who were appointed to control and direct civilian – and probably military traffic.

17 Arm band worn by SA reserve personnel.

18 Arm band worn by non-uniformed personnel of the war-time organisation which combined the membership of the Female Political Leaders of the NSDAP and the German Women's Welfare Work. The central device on this arm band was also used as a cloth emblem sown directly on to the working coats of these women.

Plate 33. Arm Bands

Army

1 Army personnel acting as stretcher bearers, usually worn on the right upper arm.

2 'In the Service of the German Armed Forces'. One type of arm band worn by German non-military personnel and non-German

volunteers working for and under the jurisdiction of the German Armed Forces. The Belgian national colours shown here on this band indicates that the wearer is a Belgian national. Other national colours are known to have been used in this manner.

3 An arm band similar in purpose to the above band, no. 2. This 'German Armed Forces' arm band tended to be used by German personnel, civilian and non-military uniformed persons, who were attached to, or were working closely with any of the branches of the German Armed Forces. The green and black cloth strip has been added as a form of rank insignia. (For further information on these items see Plate 44.)

4 Introduced during 1937 this distinctive band was worn by all ranks of German Army clergy of all denominations on their Field and Service uniforms and their greatcoats. It was worn on the upper left arm.

5 Military umpire arm band worn by members of the German Army, Air Force, Navy,

54 A German Army Chaplain conducting an open air religious service somewhere in Russia (20 July 1941). Army Chaplains and Field Bishops wore a white and purple distinguishing arm band on the left upper arm, as shown here.

and Waffen-SS when observing and umpiring at military exercises. These personnel were further distinguished by wearing a plain white cap band worn on their peaked caps or the side-caps.

6 Black cloth mourning arm band for use by any personnel of the German uniformed organisations. It was usually worn on the upper left sleeve, just above the elbow or on the left cuff. It was used by parading groups of uniformed personnel at times of national mourning or by individuals at the time of a funeral service for a family member. At the completion of the period of state mourning or at the end of a family burial service these arm bands were removed.

7 Basic Red Cross arm band. Worn by medical personnel of any formation whether uniformed or not. (See also Plate 37, nos 13 and 14.) The use of this insignia was intended to afford protection to the wearer under the terms of the Geneva Convention, provided the medical personnel did not carry or use military weapons.

8 Worn by personnel of Army Officer Cadet Schools.

9 Arm band worn by German Armed Forces personnel, usually Army troops, acting as Field Police supplementing the existing Feldgendarmerie forces.

10 Railway Station Guard. Usually formed from members of the Armed Forces including the Waffen-SS to patrol and control troop movement on railway stations of importance especially at main line terminals.

11 Railway Station Officer number 231. Worn by officers of the Armed Forces appointed to main-line railway stations charged with the task of the control, discipline, and welfare of troops passing through their area of responsibility. The number 231 probably referred to the station appointed to carry this number.

12 Auxiliary police arm band.

13 Arm band for a war blinded military person. Worn on the upper left arm, it was introduced in May 1941. A similar arm band but without the Iron Cross emblem was, and still is, used by blind civilian Germans.

14 Armed Forces patrol service.

15 Armed Forces personnel acting as stewards at military parades, especially the pre-war celebrations held in Berlin and other major cities.

DLV and German Air Force

16 Arm band worn by members of the Deutsche Luftsports Verband.

17 Worn as an identification arm band by crews of German aircraft who were shot down or bailed-out over German held territory. In trying to make their way to military units they could have been, and often were mistaken for advancing enemy troops. This band was introduced in December 1944 to overcome this problem.

18 Air Force officers assigned to railway station security duty. In February 1937 this yellow arm band was superseded by a white band with exactly the same style lettering.

Plate 34. Arm Bands

German Air Force (Continued)

1 Arm band worn by early volunteers of the German 'Legion Condor' serving in Spain. The band displayed the Spanish Nationalist colours.

2 Armed Forces interpreter, as worn during the Spanish Civil War.

3 Graduate at a Luftwaffe Officer Cadet School.

4 Other ranks Luftwaffe personnel assigned to fire-fighting duty on airfields. These arm bands were worn in pairs, one to each upper sleeve.

5 Air Force Property Assessing Personnel arm band worn on upper left sleeve. Troops were responsible for selecting, and commandering land intended for German air force installations.

SS and SD

By the late summer of 1943 events all along the Eastern Front were definitely turning in favour of the Red Army. The need to stiffen crumbling German resistance in the face of the enemy brought about desperate measures. One of these measures was the establishment, on 9 January 1944, of 'Feldjäger' units.

Consisting of experienced combat soldiers, NCOs, and officers, these Feldjäger units, who were answerable only to the OKW, were charged with the task of hunting down deserters, arresting insubordinates, looters, and general malingerers, combing through rear echelon areas for troops who were fit enough for front line duty and, through the use of fear, generally stiffening the will of the German soldier to stand and fight the enemy. These units were empowered to arrest and fling back into the front line any one they caught who could not account for their absence from active service. Unit Commanders had the power to conduct drum-head courts-material and when necessary have the defendants executed on the spot. The power of the Feldjäger units most definitely came out of the barrel of a gun, backed up by the authority of the High Command of the German Armed Forces.

6 Members of Feldjäger units wore two items which distinguished them from ordinary Army or Waffen-SS troops. When on duty they wore a special Feldjäger duty gorget (not illustrated) and a red arm band.

7 Arm band worn by personnel attached to and working with the Waffen-SS.

8 Auxiliary Police formations known as 'Landwacht' were created in January 1942 on the orders of the Reichsführer-SS, Himmler. Their task was that of guarding Prisoners of War when being used for labouring work within the confines of the German Reich. Personnel wore Gendarmerie Police uniforms and were further distinguished by a special 'Landwacht' cap badge (see Plate 1, no. 14) and the

55 An SS member of a Feldjäger unit on traffic control duty, Milan, Italy.

wearing of a white arm band bearing the word 'Landwacht'.

9 In the service of the Security Police. Non-German foreign auxiliaries from the Eastern territories attached to service offices of the German Security Police were, when used as guards, provided with field-grey uniforms devoid of all insignia and badges of rank but wore an arm band 'Im Dienste der Sicherheitspolizei' on the upper right arm. These arm bands were brought into use in the autumn of 1944. The colouring of the bands was appropriate in that it mirrored the green on black of the SD shoulder straps, the particular shade of green sometimes being referred to as 'Gift-Grün' or toxic-green.

Navy, National Militia, State Service, Air Defence League and Air Protection Service

10 Navy graduate at Naval Officers Training School.

11 Official issue Deutscher Volkssturm arm band. The German Volkssturm was established on 18 October 1944. Its membership consisted of all able-bodied men from sixteen to 60 years of age who were able to bear arms and who were not already in the Armed Forces. Volkssturm personnel were expected to furnish their own uniforms or to wear civilian clothing. In an effort to distinguish these militiamen as officially belonging to the Wehrmacht every man was issued with an arm band. The official issue band illustrated here used a combination of the German National colours of black, white, and red. Other examples, some of them produced by individual units, existed with different colourings, but all carried the legend 'Deutscher Volkssturm Wehrmacht'.

12 A variation of the Volkssturm arm band.

13 Arm band worn by personnel attached to the Department of the General Air Supply Master.

14 Arm band worn by persons in State Service.

15 First pattern Reichsluftschutzbund (National Air Defence League) arm band. The silver braiding along the top and bottom edges of the band indicates a level of rank as yet unestablished.

16 Second pattern RLB arm band for ordinary member.

17 NSDAP Political Leadership Air Defence arm band. Usually worn on the left upper arm or left forearm.

18 A variation of the Luftschutz arm band.

Plate 35. Arm Bands

National Air Defence League, Security and Assistance Service, German Red Cross, Factory Air Protection Service

1 Unestablished arm band, but probably that worn by a guard or watchman of the RLB.

2 Worn by members of the Security and Assistance Services. It was introduced during December 1941.

56 A member of one of the first National Militia units raised in Germany. This 55 year old textile salesman is wearing a variation of the 'Deutscher Volkssturm' arm band, of which there were quite a number in addition to the official design (23 October 1944).

57 German Red Cross arm band, worn by male orderlies and female nurses alike.

3 German Red Cross arm band for wear by members of the town of Recklinghausen.

4 Basic pattern German Red Cross arm band, worn on upper left arm.

5 Factory Air Protection Service medical staff personnel arm band, introduced in January 1940.

6 Werkluftschutz veterinary service personnel.

7 Werkluftschutz (Factory Air Protection Service) medical troop leader, also introduced in January 1940.

8 Luftschutz telephone operator.

9 Luftschutz arm band probably worn by special purpose personnel.

10 A Luftschutz arm band of undetermined purpose.

Labour Operations Executive, DAF, TeNo, Postal Service and Falconry Service

11 Basic Labour Operations Executive arm band.

12 Senior Camp Leader of the DAF.

13 Arm band as worn by Technishe Nothilfe personnel.

14 German Postal Service arm band as worn

before 1940 by German women and girls acting as postal auxiliaries but who were not entitled to wear the Postal Service uniform.

15 Deutsche Falkenorden arm band worn by Falconry personnel when wearing civilian clothing. Introduced in 1938 for wear on the left upper arm, the arm band motif was in fact the German Falconry Order arm badge as worn on the uniform (see Plate 54, no. 6).

War Veterans Associations

16 Nationalsozialistisches Kriegs-Opfer-Versorgung arm band as worn by the members of the National Socialist Disabled War Veterans Support Association from the district of Munich, Upper Bavaria. The NSKOV emblem in the centre of the dark blue cloth band is a small metal insignia sewn on to the cloth.

17 Old style pre-Nazi Kyffhauserbund (War Veterans Support Association) arm band for ordinary member.

18 New style Nazi-sponsored Kyffhauserbund arm band, also for use by ordinary members.

Plates 36. Arm Bands

War Veterans, Organisation Todt and German National Railways

On 4 March 1938 the Nazi Party created the Nationalsozialistisches Reichskriegerbund, the NS-RKB, which was the only War Veterans organisation permitted to exist and into which were absorbed the membership of all the former War Veterans Associations. A whole new series of arm bands known as 'Dienststellenabzeichen' were produced to reflect the range of ranks in this organisation. (See also the section on cuff-titles Plate 29, nos 11, 12 and 13.)

1 NS-RKB Member. The lowest rank arm band in the organisation, this and all other NS-RKB arm bands were worn on the right cuff of the uniform jacket 10 cm above the

58 Troops of the General-SS receiving instruction in firing a rifle. All the black uniformed personnel wear the black-edged SS arm band on the left upper arm.

lower edge of the sleeve.

2 NS-RKB Gaukriegerführer, Provincial Leader.

3 NS-RKB Stellvertr. d. Reichskriegerführer und Stellvertr. Präsident d. D. Krieger-Wohlf.-Gemeinschaft. Arm band for the Deputy to the Reichskriegerführer and Deputy President of the War Welfare Organisation.

4 Arm band for the most senior NS-RKB rank of Reichskriegerführer.

5 Organisation Todt arm band worn on upper left arm, introduced during 1943 as part of a whole range of new (and final) Org. Todt insignia. (See also Plate 19, nos 8–21). This was the basic OT arm band as worn by Organisation Todt personnel: OT-Mannschaften and OT-Unterführer (men and NCOs).

6 Arm band as worn by OT-Stabsführer (Staff Leaders).

7 Arm band as worn by the Chef des Amtes Bau-OT (Chief of Organisation Todt Construction Office).

8 OT arm band of the 1940 period worn by non-uniformed OT worker. The small number probably represented the OT unit number.

9 OT arm band also of the 1940 vintage supposed to have been for use by members of the Organisation Todt protection troops.

10 Arm band worn by the lowest grade of uniformed OT workers OT-Frontarbeiter, c. 1940.

11 Arm band as worn by an OT-Ober-Truppführer in Org. Todt Construction Units, c. 1940.

12 Arm band as worn by an OT-Ober-Kolonnenführer in the OT Transport branch, c. 1940.

13 Arm band for an OT-Haupt-Truppführer in the OT Construction branch, c. 1940.

The last four arm bands described above, nos 10 to 13, were all introduced during 1940 as part of the issue of new uniforms and insignia, albeit of a somewhat restricted nature.

59 An Organisation Todt sentry on guard at the entrance to an OT camp.

The arm bands at this time were the only method of displaying rank (with the single exception of the use of shoulder straps for the rank of Haupttruppführer) and the distinction was made between those bands worn by Construction services (Bau) and Transport branch (Transport), the latter employing small black outlined triangles on all their bands in order to distinguish them from those worn by OT Construction troops.

14 The basic pattern German National Railways arm band.

15 German Railways medical doctor.

16 German Railways signals personnel.

17 Train escort personnel.

18 Arm band worn by railway personnel from Wehrmacht Verkehrs Direktion, unit no. 446.

1

2

3

6

4

5

9

7

8

10

11

12

13

14

15

16

17

18

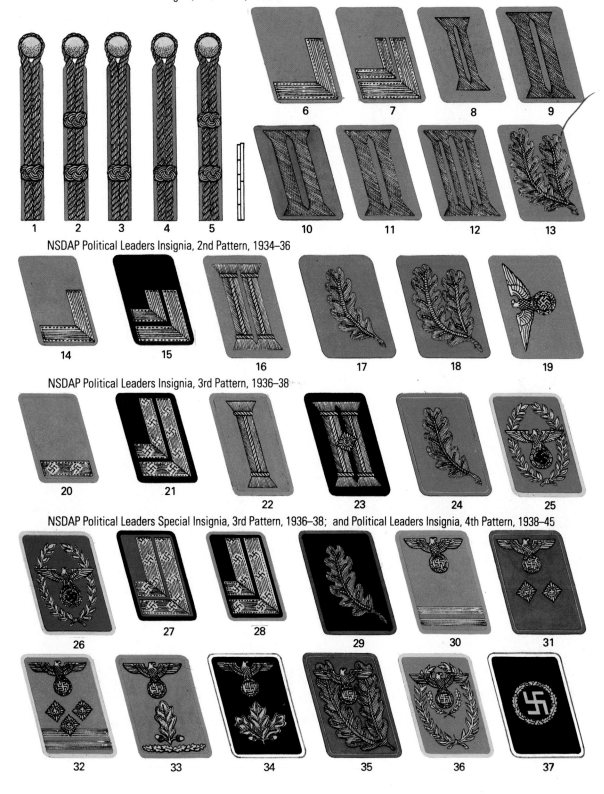

NSDAP Political Leaders Insignia, 1st Pattern, 1933–34

NSDAP Political Leaders Insignia, 2nd Pattern, 1934–36

NSDAP Political Leaders Insignia, 3rd Pattern, 1936–38

NSDAP Political Leaders Special Insignia, 3rd Pattern, 1936–38; and Political Leaders Insignia, 4th Pattern, 1938–45

Sturm-Abteilung Insignia, 1st Pattern, 1933–38

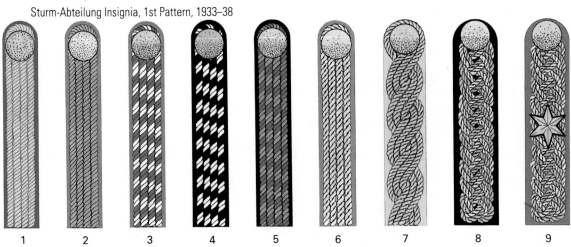

1 2 3 4 5 6 7 8 9

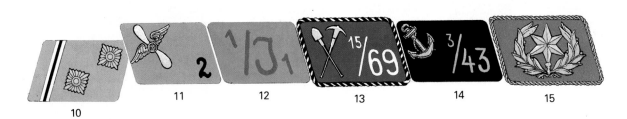

10 11 12 13 14 15

Sturm-Abteilung Insignia, 2nd Pattern, 1938/39–45

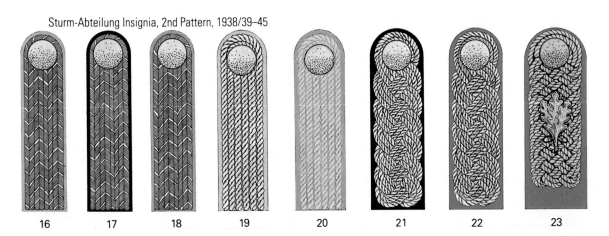

16 17 18 19 20 21 22 23

24 25 26 27 28 29

Nationalsozialistischen Kraftfahr Korps Insignia, 1934–45

Stahlhelm Insignia, 1918–33/35

Allgemeine-SS Insignia, 1933–45

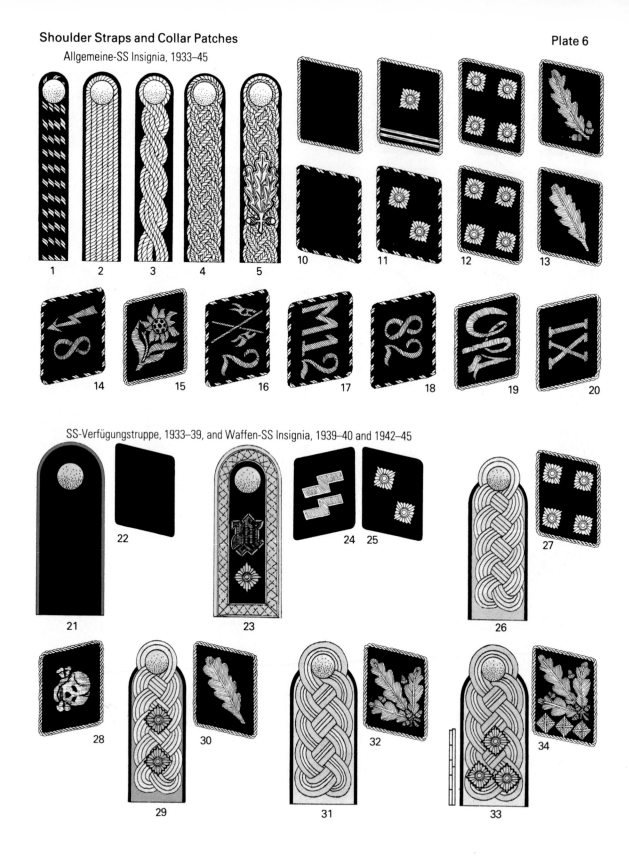

SS-Verfügungstruppe, 1933–39, and Waffen-SS Insignia, 1939–40 and 1942–45

Shoulder Straps and Collar Patches

Plate 7

Hitler-Jugend Shoulder Straps, 1st Pattern, 1933–38

1 2 3 4 5 6 7

Hitler-Jugend Shoulder Straps, 2nd Pattern, 1938–45

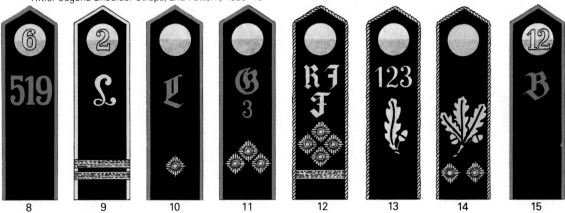

8 9 10 11 12 13 14 15

Hitler-Jugend Special Shoulder Straps, 2nd Pattern, RJF Collar Patches, and Deutsche Jungvolk Shoulder Straps, 1938–45

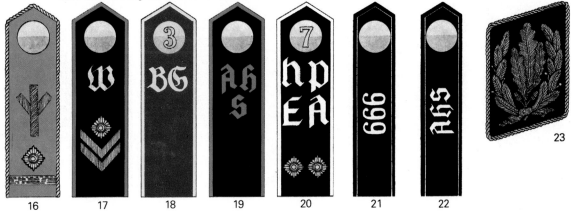

16 17 18 19 20 21 22 23

Freiwilligearbeitsdienst Insignia, 1st Pattern, 1936

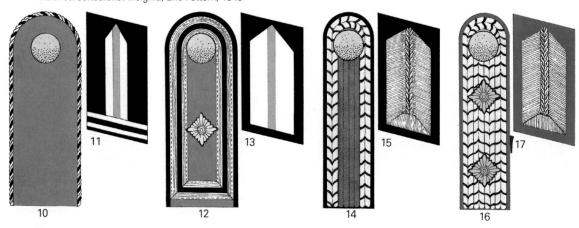

Reichsarbeitsdienst Insignia, 2nd Pattern, 1940

Reichsarbeitsdienst Insignia, 3rd Pattern, 1942

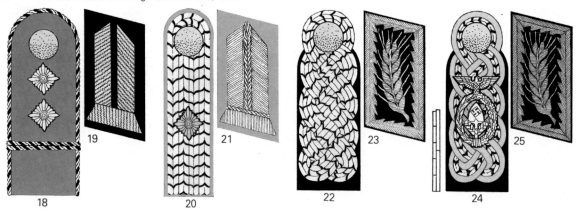

Plate 9

Shoulder Straps and Collar Patches

German Army Insignia, 1935–45

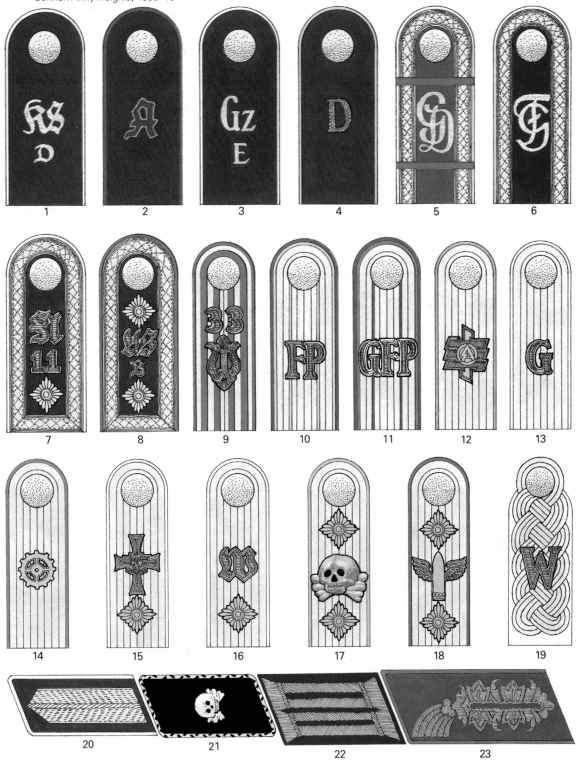

German Naval and Administration Branch Insignia, 1933–45

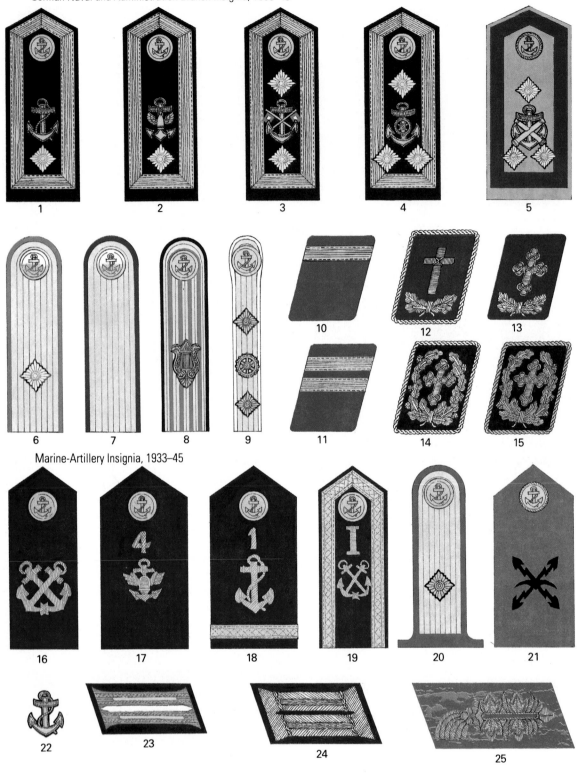

Marine-Artillery Insignia, 1933–45

Nationalsozialistisches Flieger Korps Insignia, 1937–45

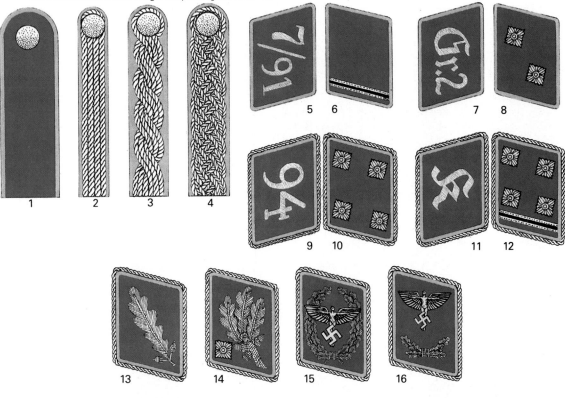

Deutsche Luftsports Verband Insignia, 1933–35

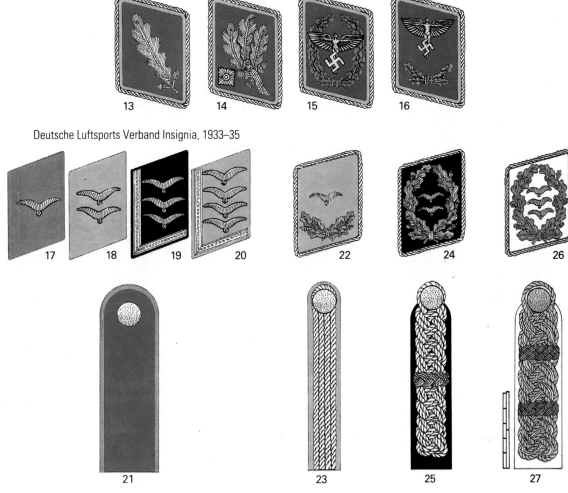

Plate 12

Shoulder Straps and Collar Patches

Luftwaffe Insignia, 1935–45

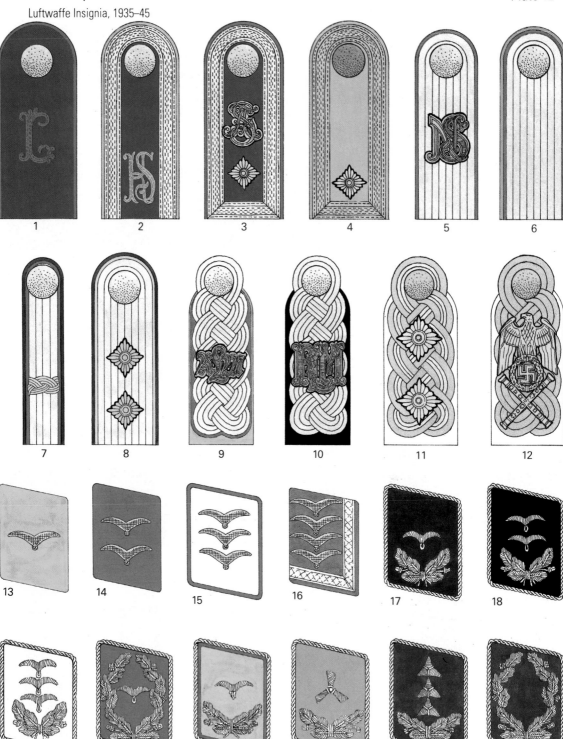

1 2 3 4 5 6
7 8 9 10 11 12
13 14 15 16 17 18
19 20 21 22 23 24

Plate 13

Shoulder Straps and Collar Patches

German Police Formation Insignia, 1936–45

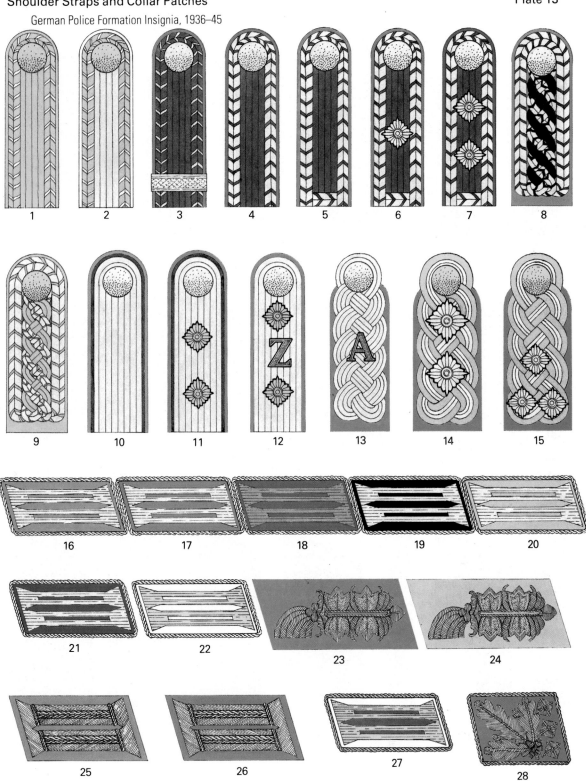

Railway Protection Police Insignia, 1941–45

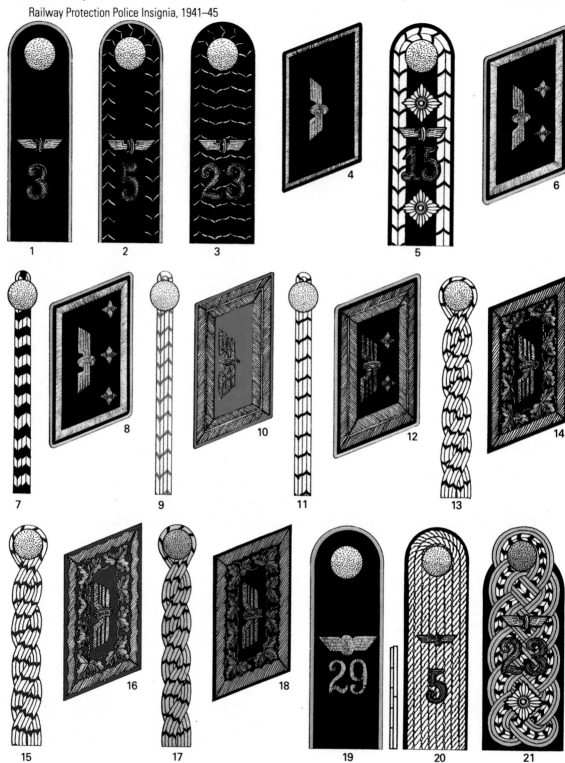

Plate 15

Shoulder Straps and Collar Patches

German Customs Officials, Landbased and Waterborne, Insignia

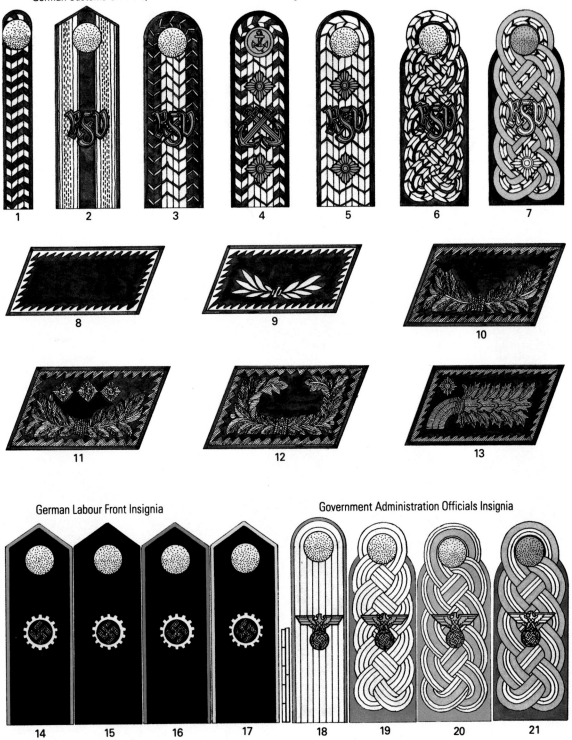

German Labour Front Insignia

Government Administration Officials Insignia

Shoulder Straps and Collar Patches

Plate 16

Technical Stud Service in Prussia Insignia, 1942–44

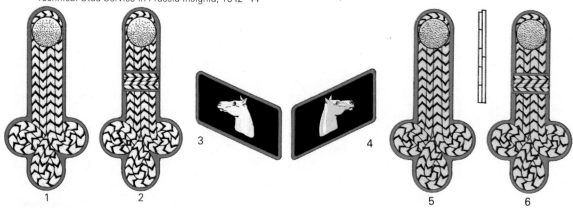

1 2 3 4 5 6

Labour Operations Executive Insignia

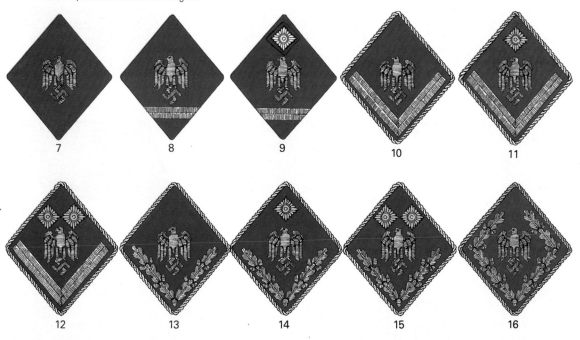

7 8 9 10 11 12 13 14 15 16

'Ostbeamte' Insignia

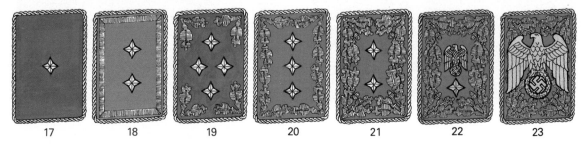

17 18 19 20 21 22 23

Reichs Luftschutze Bund Insignia, 1940–45

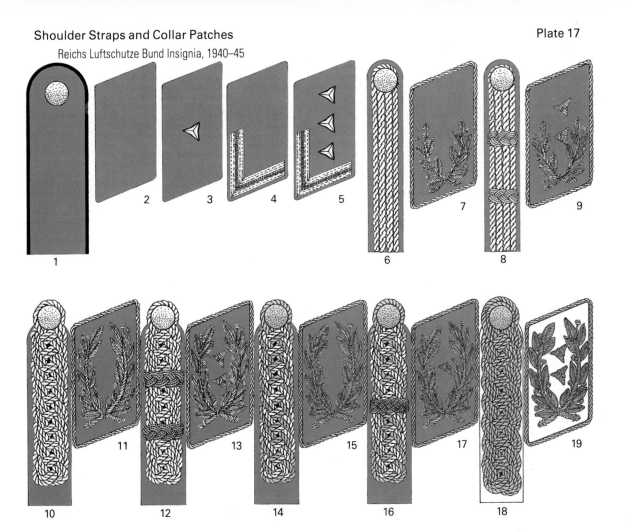

Sicherheits und Hilfsdienst and Luftschutz Warndienst Insignia, 1940–45

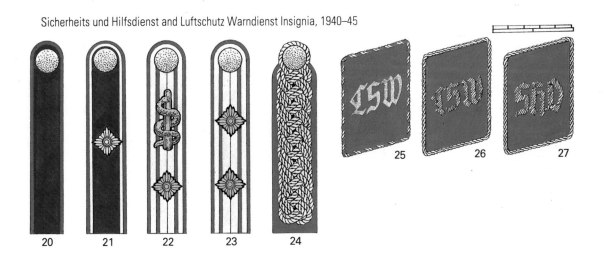

Plate 18

Shoulder Straps and Collar Patches

German Deutsche Rote Kreuz

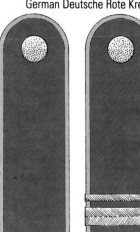

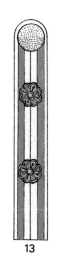

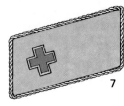

1   2   3   4   5   6   7

Waterways Air Protection Service Insignia, 1942–45

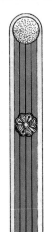
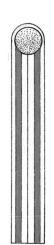
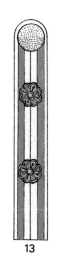
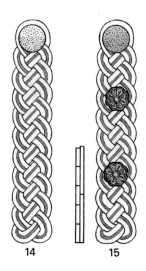

8   9   10   11   12   13   14   15

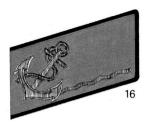

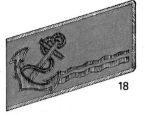

16   17   18   19

Plate 19

Shoulder Straps and Collar Patches

Organisation Todt Insignia, 2nd Pattern, 1942–43

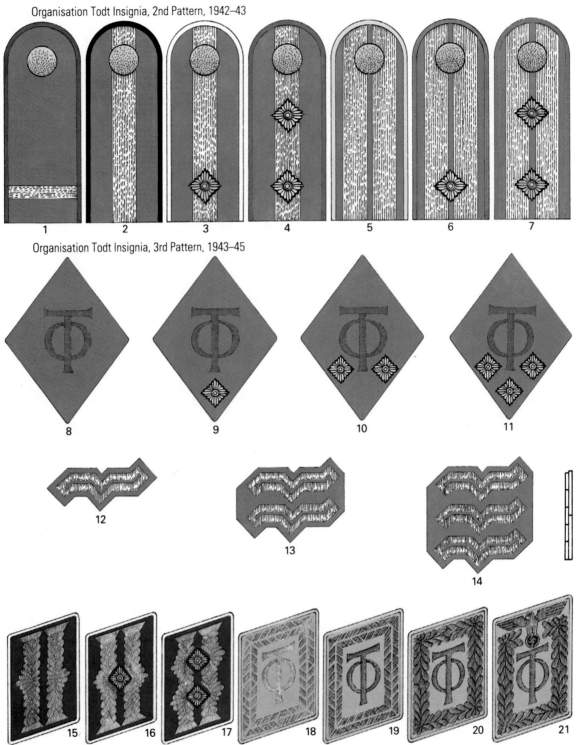

Organisation Todt Insignia, 3rd Pattern, 1943–45

Technical Emergency Service Insignia, 1937–40, 1941–42, 1942–43

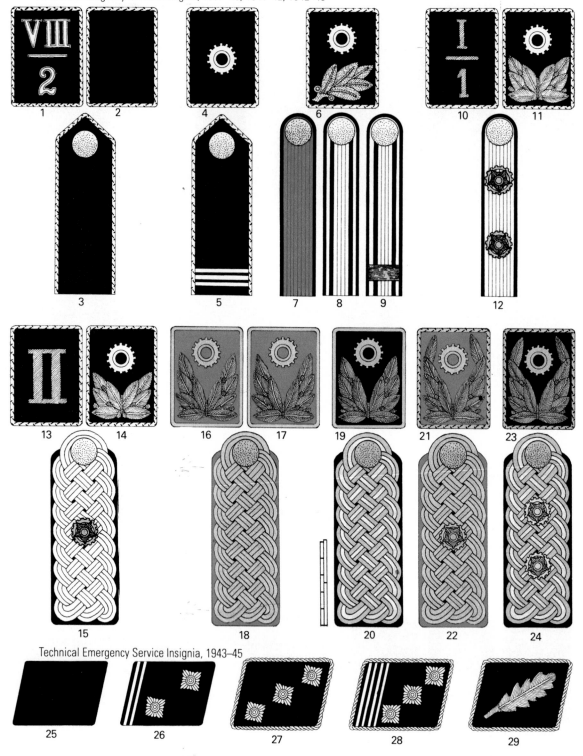

Technical Emergency Service Insignia, 1943–45

Plate 21

Shoulder Straps, Collar Patches, and 'Passants'

Transportflotte Speer Insignia, 1943–45

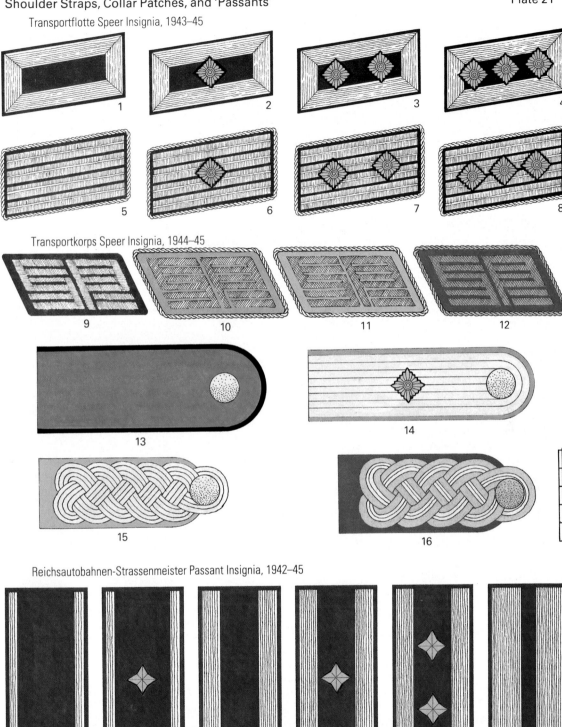

Transportkorps Speer Insignia, 1944–45

Reichsautobahnen-Strassenmeister Passant Insignia, 1942–45

Deutschen Falkenorden Insignia, 1938

1   2   3   4

Deutschen Jägerschaft Insignia, 1934, 1936 and 1938

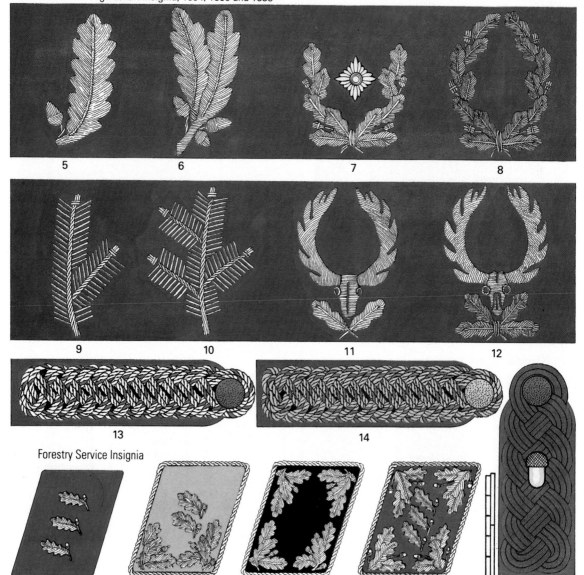

5   6   7   8

9   10   11   12

13   14

Forestry Service Insignia

15   16   17   18   19

Plate 23

Shoulder Straps, Collar Patches, and 'Passants'

German National Railway Insignia, 1936–45

1   2   3   4   5   6   7

8   9   10   11   12   13

14   15   16   17   18   19

20   21   22   23   24   25   26   27   28   29

Military Campaign Cuff-Titles

German Army Cuff-Titles

German Army Cuff-Titles (continued)

1. Feldgendarmerie

2. Geheime Feldpolizei

3. Propagandakompanie

4. Feldpost

5. Unteroffiziervorschule

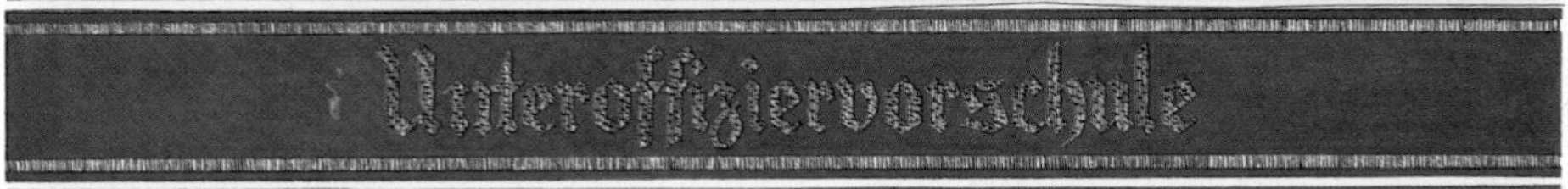

6. Stabshelferin des Heeres

7. Stabshelferin des Heeres

Luftwaffe Cuff-Titles

8. AFRIKA

9. General Göring

10. Hermann Göring

11. HERMANN GÖRING

12. Fallschirm-Jäger Rgt. 1

13. Fallschirm-Division

14. Geschwader Immelmann

Luftwaffe Cuff-Titles (continued)

1. Jagdgeschwader Frhr. v. Richthofen Nr.1 1917/18

2. Geschwader Boelcke

3. Geschwader Horst Wessel

4. Jagdgeschwader Mölders

5. Kriegsberichter der Luftwaffe

Sturm-Abteilung Cuff-Titles

6. Stabswache Göring

7. Stabschef Röhm

8. Stabswache

9. Horst Wessel

10. Hans von Manteuffel

German Police Formation Cuff-Titles

11. L.P.G. General Göring

12. Motorisierte Gendarmerie

13. Deutsche Wehrmacht

German Police Formations Cuff-Titles (continued)

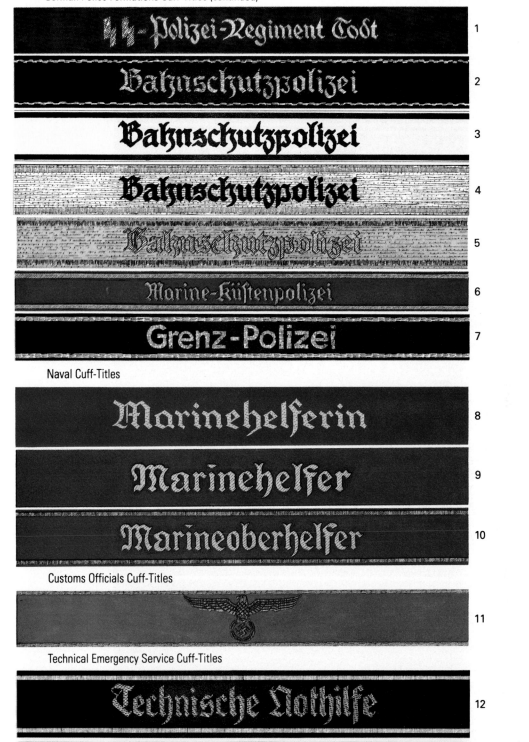

1. SS-Polizei-Regiment Todt

2. Bahnschutzpolizei

3. Bahnschutzpolizei

4. Bahnschutzpolizei

5. Bahnschutzpolizei

6. Marine-Küstenpolizei

7. Grenz-Polizei

Naval Cuff-Titles

8. Marinehelferin

9. Marinehelfer

10. Marineoberhelfer

Customs Officials Cuff-Titles

11.

Technical Emergency Service Cuff-Titles

12. Technische Nothilfe

13. 1919

Hitler-Jugend and Bund Deutsche Mädel Cuff-Titles

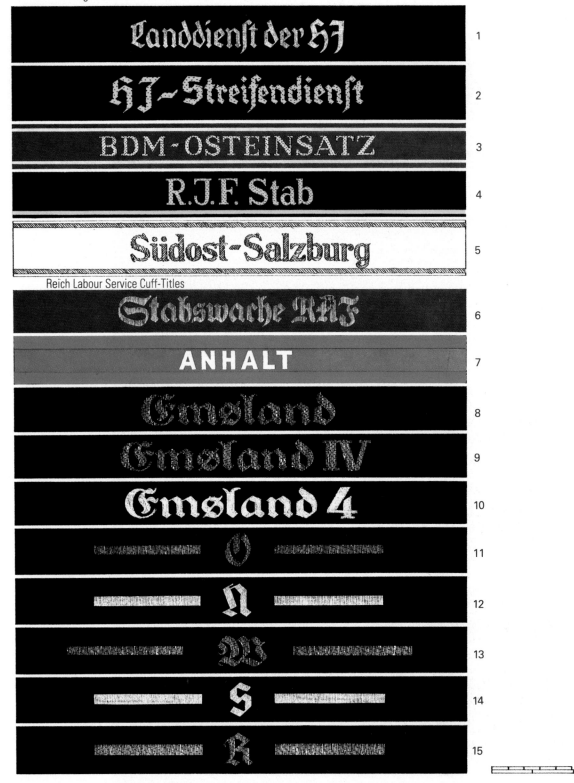

1 Landdienst der HJ

2 HJ-Streifendienst

3 BDM-OSTEINSATZ

4 R.J.F. Stab

5 Südost-Salzburg

Reich Labour Service Cuff-Titles

6 Stabswache RAF

7 ANHALT

8 Emsland

9 Emsland IV

10 Emsland 4

11

12

13

14

15

Postal Protection Cuff-Title

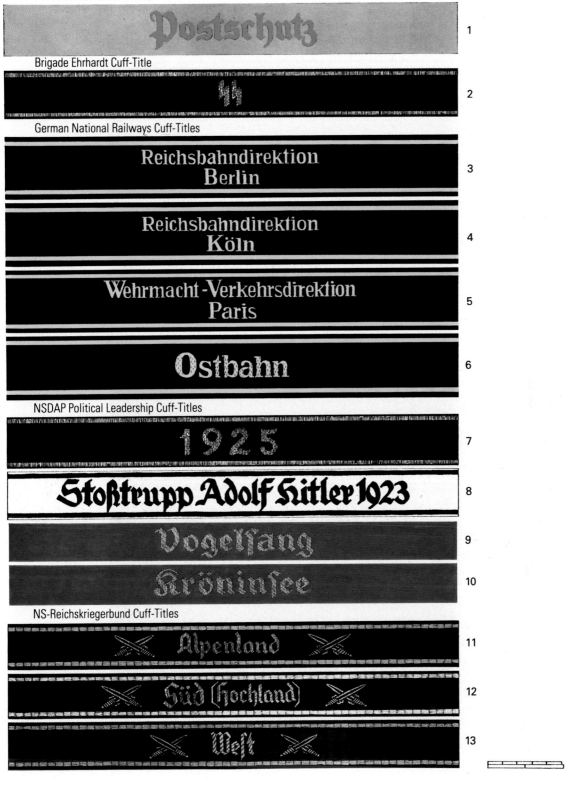

1

Brigade Ehrhardt Cuff-Title

2

German National Railways Cuff-Titles

Reichsbahndirektion
Berlin

3

Reichsbahndirektion
Köln

4

Wehrmacht-Verkehrsdirektion
Paris

5

Ostbahn

6

NSDAP Political Leadership Cuff-Titles

1925

7

Stoßtrupp Adolf Hitler 1923

8

Vogelsang

9

Kröninsee

10

NS-Reichskriegerbund Cuff-Titles

Alpenland

11

Süd (Hochland)

12

West

13

Nationalsozialistische Kraftfahr Korps Cuff-Titles

NSKK-Brigade Luftwaffe — 1

1.NSKK Transport-Regiment Luftwaffe — 2

NSKK Ehrenführer — 3

Einsatzbereitschaft — 4

Air Raid Warning Service Cuff-Title

L.S. Warndienst — 5

General-SS Cuff-Titles

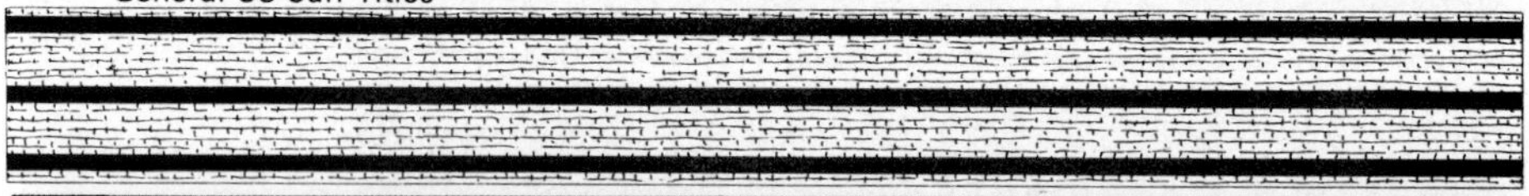

— 6

Julius Schreck — 7

2 Casella — 8

10 Karl Laforce — 9

XXXIII — 10

6 — 11

5 — 12

Reserve — 13

General-SS, SS-Verfügungstruppe, and Waffen-SS Cuff-Titles

1. San.-Abt. Ost

2. Adolf Hitler

3. Brandenburg

4. SS-Schule Tölz

5. SS-Polizei-Division

6. Theodor Eicke

7. SS-heimwehr Danzig

8. Der Führer

9. Deutschland

10. SS-Feldgendarmerie

11. SS-Remontereiter-Rgt.

12. SS-KB-Abt

13. SS-Musikschule Braunschweig

8 Der Standortführer Blankenburg a.H.

14 R.A.D. Kriegsberichter

16 Verkehrs-Aufsicht

18 N·S·K·K

Hilfs-Krankenträger

1

Im Dienst der DeutschenWehrmacht

2

Deutsche Wehrmacht

3

4

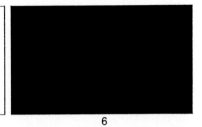

5

6

7

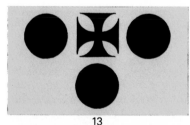

8

Feld-Gendarmerie

9

Bahnhofswache

10

Bhf. O. 231

11

Hilfsgendarmerie

12

13

Wehrmacht Streifendienst

14

15

16

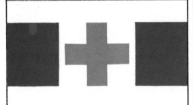

DEUTSCHE LUFTWAFFE

17

Bahnhofs-Offizier

18

1

Wehrmacht-Dolmetscher

2

3

4

5

**Oberkommando der Wehrmacht
–Feldjäger–**

6

Waffen-SS

7

Landwacht

8

Im Dienste der Sicherheitspolizei

9

10

**DEUTSCHER VOLKSSTURM
WEHRMACHT**

11

**Deutscher Volkssturm
Wehrmacht**

12

General-luftzeugmeister

13

14

15

16

**Luftschutz
NSDAP.**

17

18

Plate 35

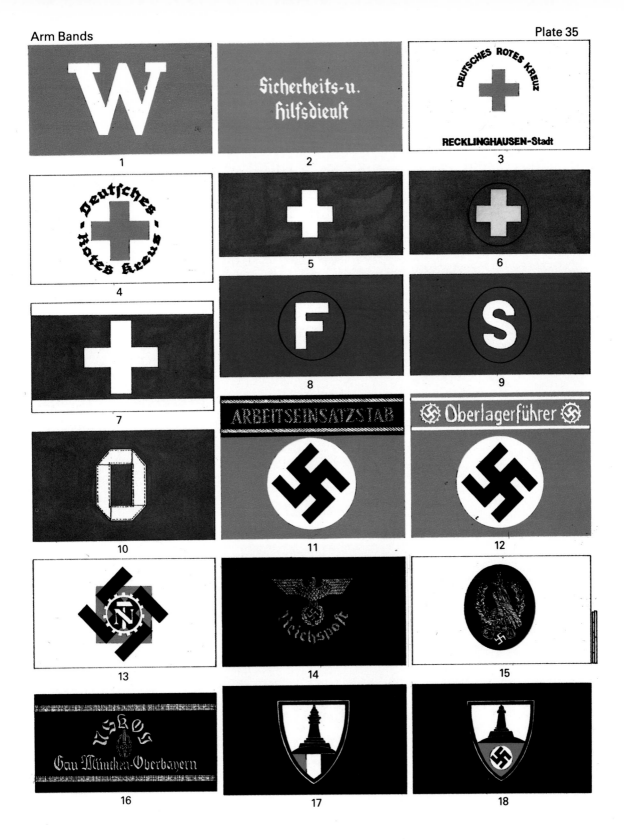

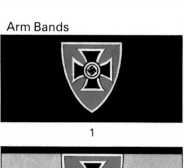

1

2

3

4

ORG.TODT

5

ORG.TODT

6

ORG.TODT

7

O. T.
2059

8

O. T.
5908

9

Org. Todt

10

Org. Todt

11

Org. Todt

12

Org. Todt

13

Reichsbahn

14

D.R.

Arzt

15

16

Zug-
Begleitung

17

W. V. D.
446

18

NSDAP Political Leaders Insignia

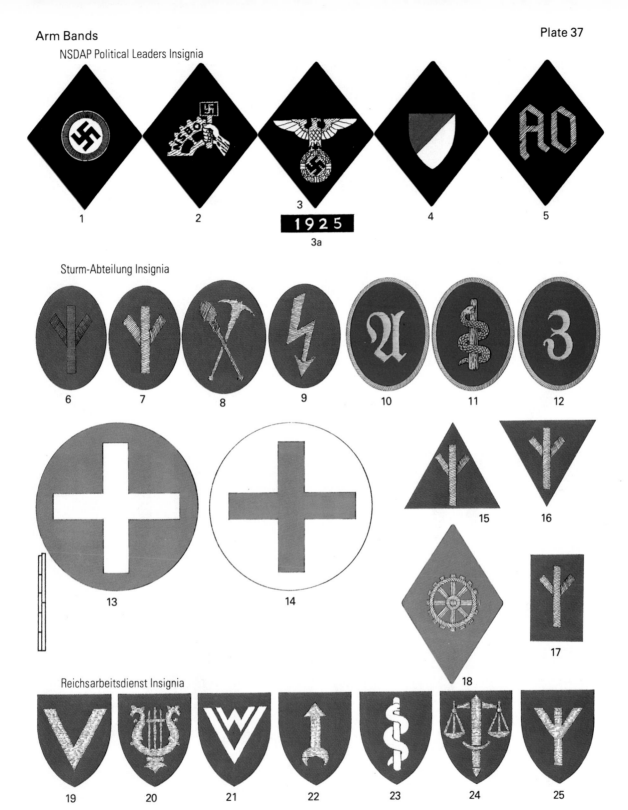

1

2

3

1925

3a

4

5

Sturm-Abteilung Insignia

6

7

8

9

10

11

12

13

14

15

16

17

18

Reichsarbeitsdienst Insignia

19

20

21

22

23

24

25

Reichsarbeitsdienst Service Unit Badges

Nationalsozialistische Kraftfahr Korps Badges

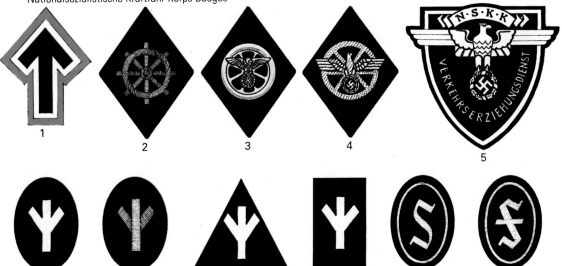

1
2
3
4
5

6
7
8
9
10
11

Brigade Ehrhardt and Stahlhelm District Arm Badges

12
13
14
15

Waffen-SS and Auxiliary Security Police Arm Badges

16
17
18
19

Allgemeine-SS, SS-Verfügungstruppe, Waffen-SS, and SD Sleeve Diamond Insignia

1

2

3

4

5

6

7

8

9

10

11

12

Hitler-Jugend, Deutsche Jungvolk, and Bund Deutsche Mädel Arm Triangle Unit Insignia

13 — Ost Sudetenland

14 — West Köln-Aachen

15 — Nord Nordsee

16 — Süd Baden

17 — China Schanghai

18 — USA

19 — Landjahr

20 — Kap-Stadt

21 — HJ Stab

Deutsche Jungvolk Insignia

Deutsche Jungvolk and Marine-Hitler-Jugend Rank Insignia

Bund Deutsche Mädel Rank Insignia — Breast Badges

Reichsarbeitsdienst Rank Insignia, Fatigue Clothing

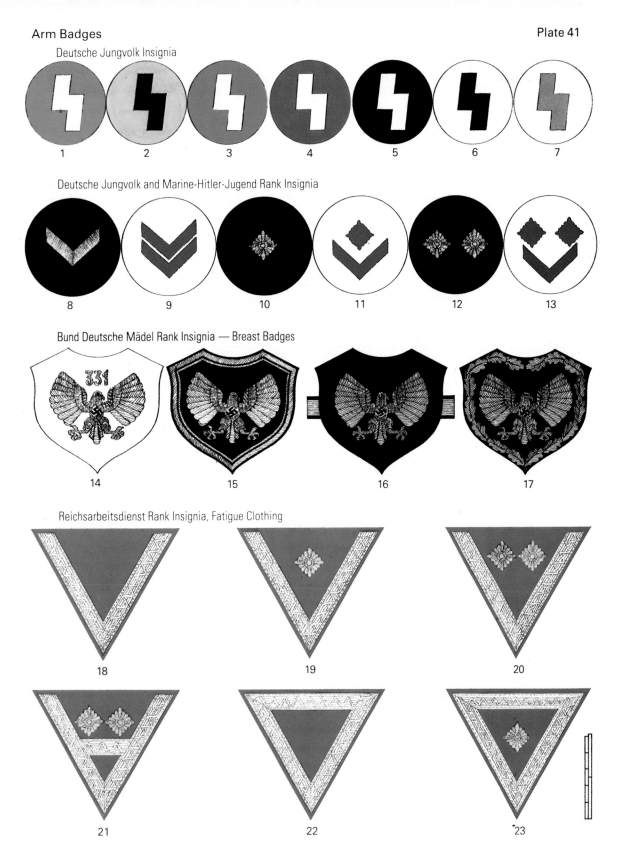

Hitler-Jugend and Marine-Hitler-Jugend Trade and Proficiency Badges

1

2

3

4

5

6

7

8

9

10

11

12

13

Police Formation Proficiency Badges

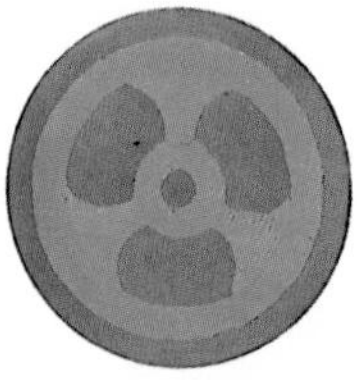

14

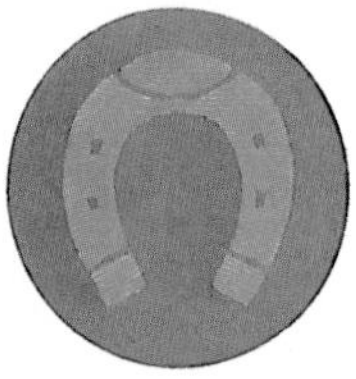

15

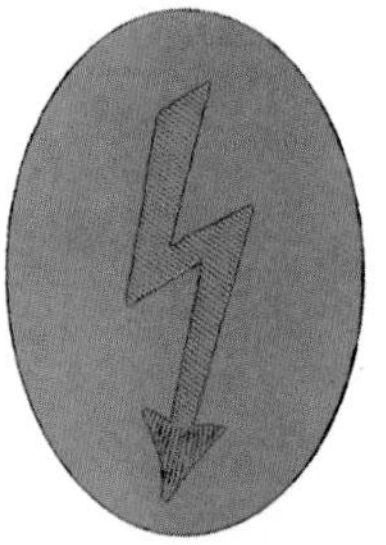

16

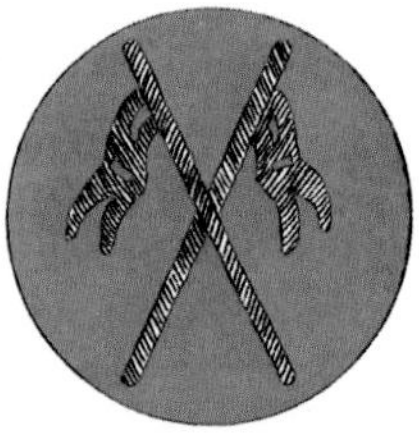

17

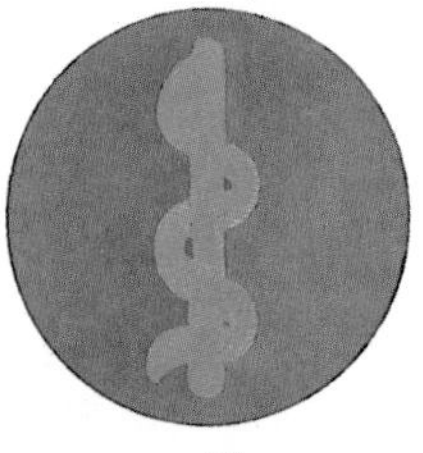

18

Organisation Todt Female Communication Personnel Qualification Badges

19

20

21

Hitler-Jugend, Marine-Hitler-Jugend, and Deutsche Jungvolk Proficiency and Speciality Badges

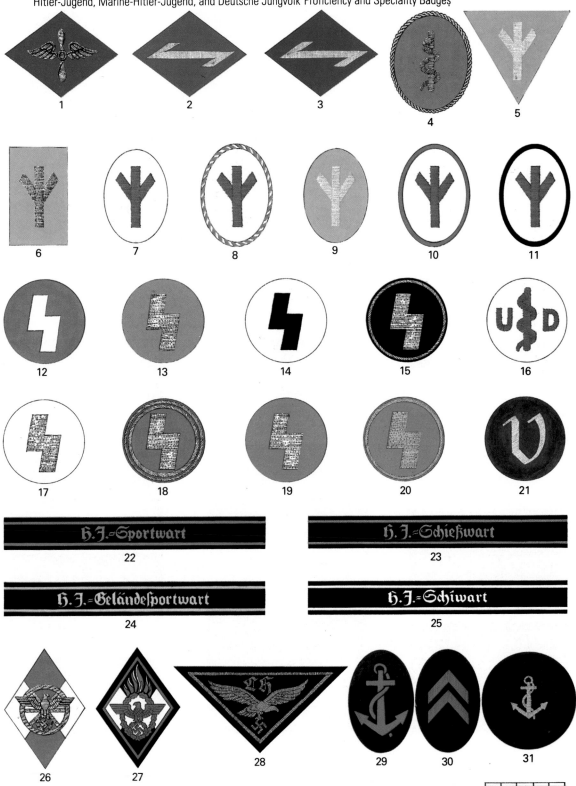

Plate 44

Army Unit Arm Badges

1

2

3

4

5

6

7

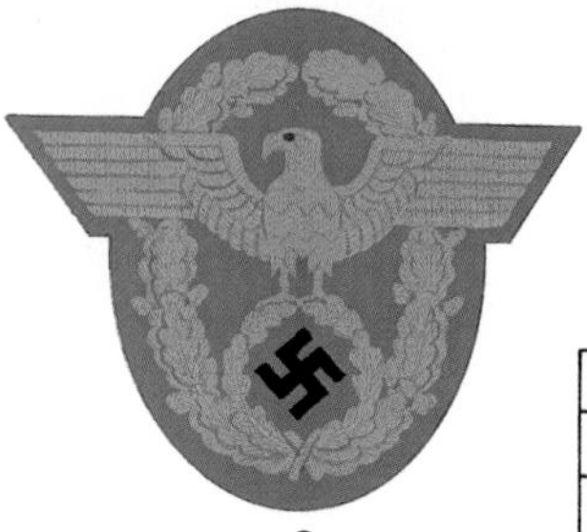

8

Army and Waffen-SS Rank Badges

9

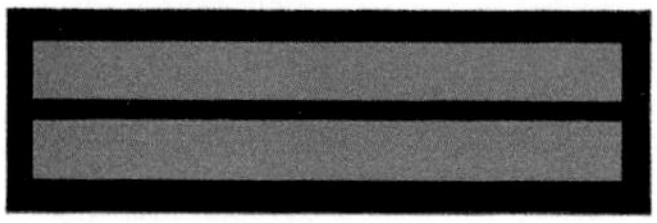

10

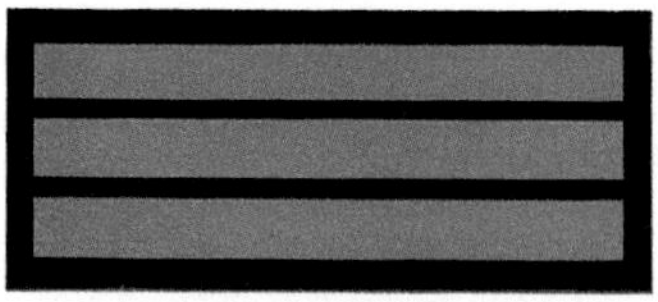

11

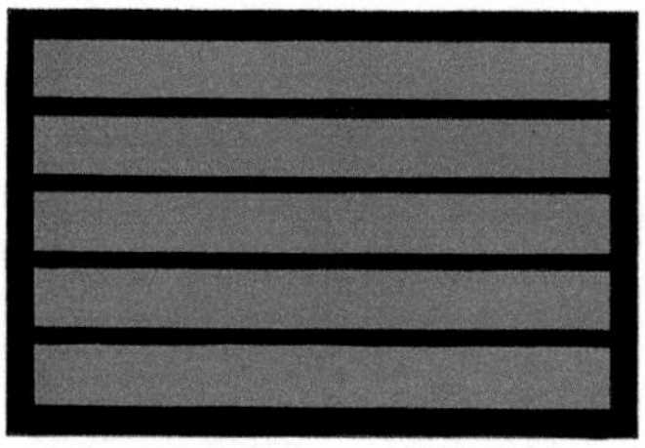

12

13

14

15

16

17

18

19

Army Trade and Proficiency Badges

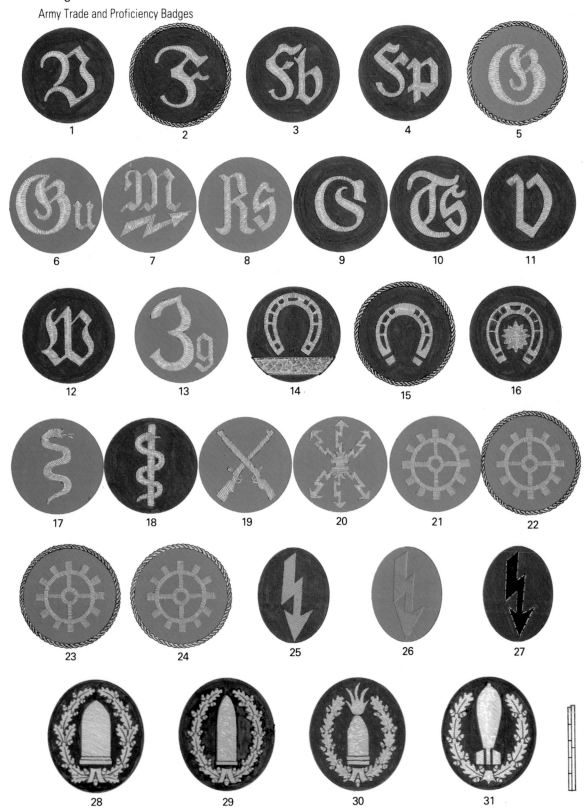

Army Proficiency and Qualification Badges

1 2 3 4 5

Nationalsozialistische Flieger Korps Proficiency, Qualification, and Trade Badges

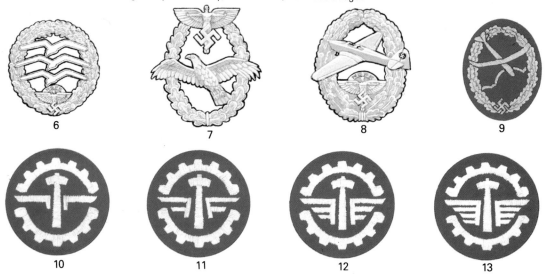

6 7 8 9

10 11 12 13

Deutsche Luftsports Verband Proficiency Badges

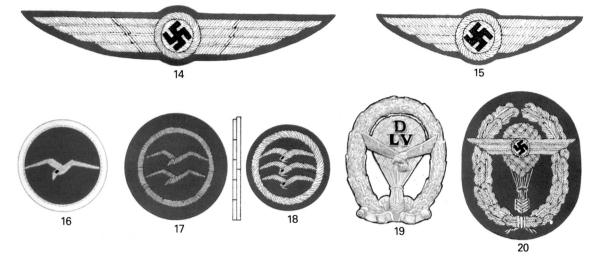

14 15

16 17 18 19 20

Deutsche Luftsports Verband Arm, Trade, and Proficiency Badges

1

2

3

4

5

Abteilung-Segelflug Breast Rank Insignia

6

7

8

Legion Condor Breast Rank Insignia

9

11

13

10

12

Luftwaffe Specialist Qualification Arm Badges

14

15

16

17

18

19

Luftwaffe Trade and Proficiency Badges

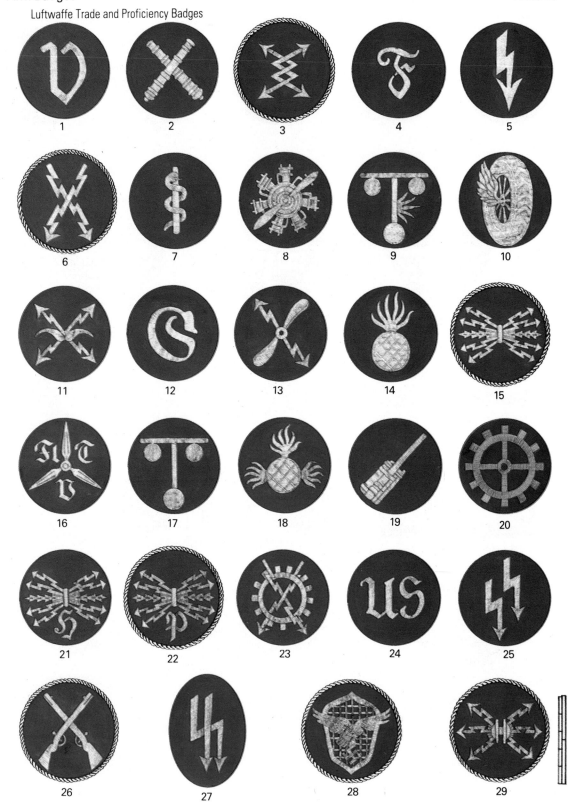

Luftwaffe School and Rank Arm Badges

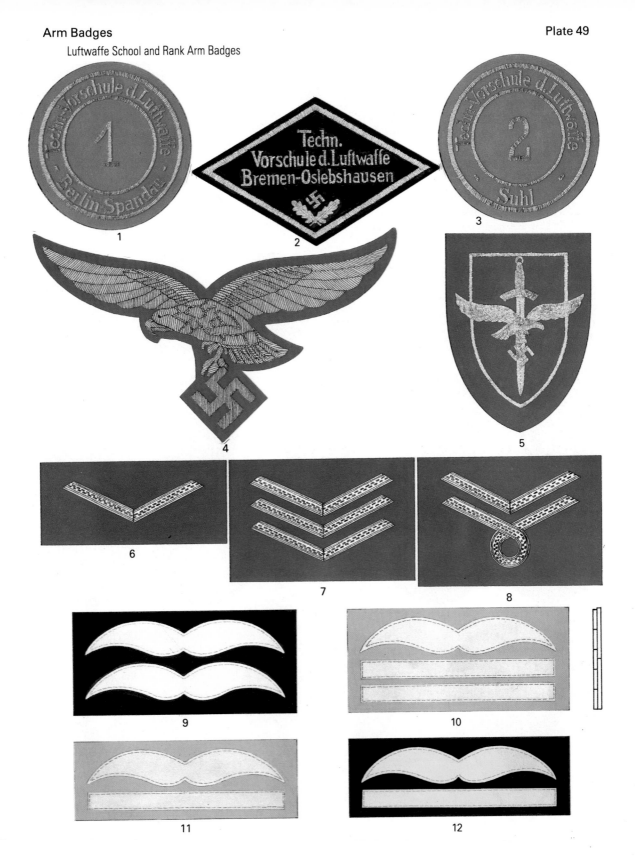

German Navy Trade, Proficiency, and Rank Badges

1

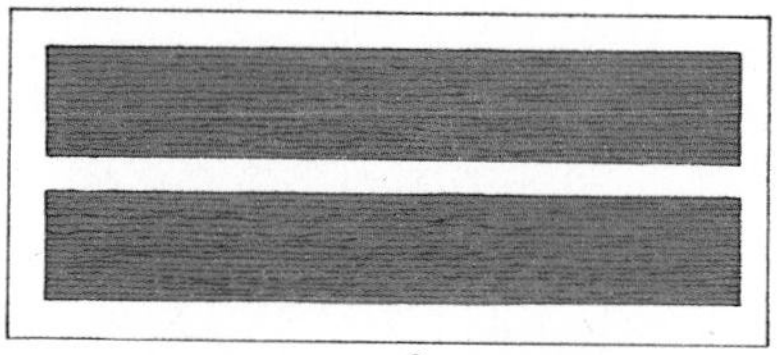

2

3

4

5

6

7

8

9

10

11

12

13

14

15

16

17

18

19

20

21

22

23

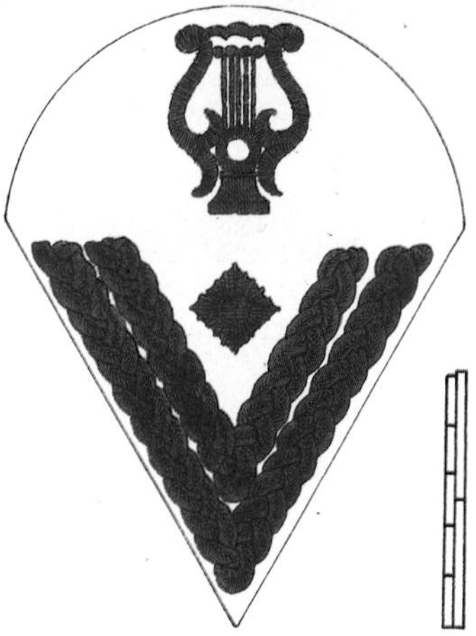

24

German Navy and Marine-Artillery Trade, Proficiency, and Rank Badges

Customs Officials Sleeve Chevrons

Government Administration Officials Sleeve Badges

1

2

3

4

5

6

7

8

9

10

11

12

Reichsluftschutzbund, Werkschutz, Deutsche Rotes Kreuz, Sicherheits
und Hilfdienst and Luftschutz Warndienst, and Technische Nothilfe Arm Badges

1

2

3

4

5 Lemgo 1

6

7

8

9

10

11

12

13

14

15

16

17

18

19

20

Reich Kusten Schutz, Reichs autobahn-Strassenmeister, Reichspost, Deutschen Falkenorden, Deutsche Jägerschaft, and Organisation Todt Arm Badges, Rank Chevrons, and Trade Badges

Organisation Todt, Deutsche Arbeits Front, and Transportflotte Speer Rank Insignia

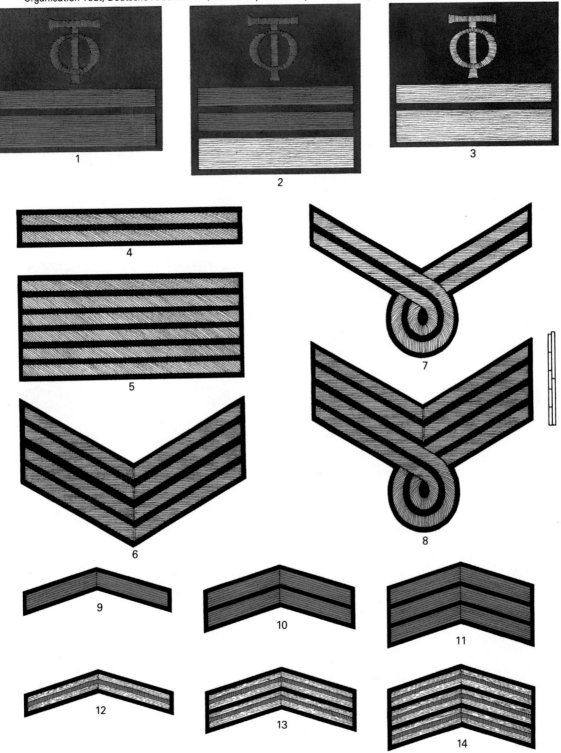

German National Railways and Railway Protection Police Arm Badges, Trade and Speciality Badges

1 RBD Nürnberg

2 RBD Villach

3 Ostbahn

4 RVD Dnjepropetrowsk

5 HVD Brüssel

6 WVD Paris

7

8

9

10

11

12

13

14

15

16

17

18

19

20

21

22

Police Formation Arm and Breast Badges, Fire Police Trade Badges

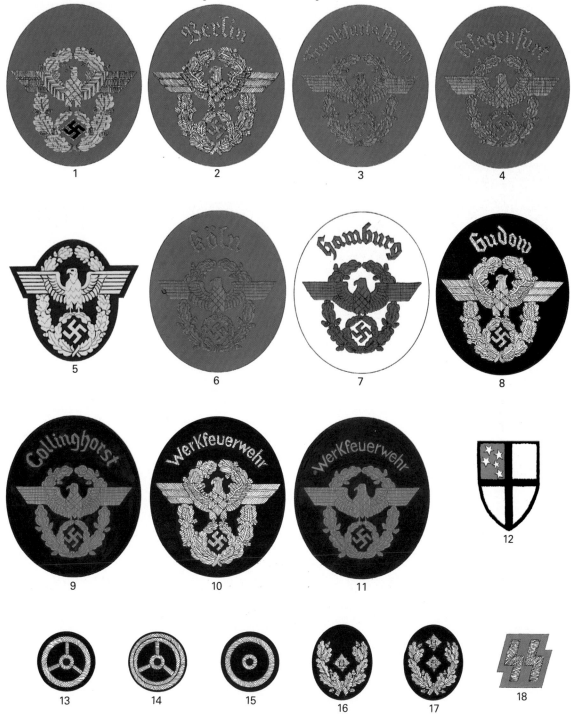

'Old Fighters' Chevrons

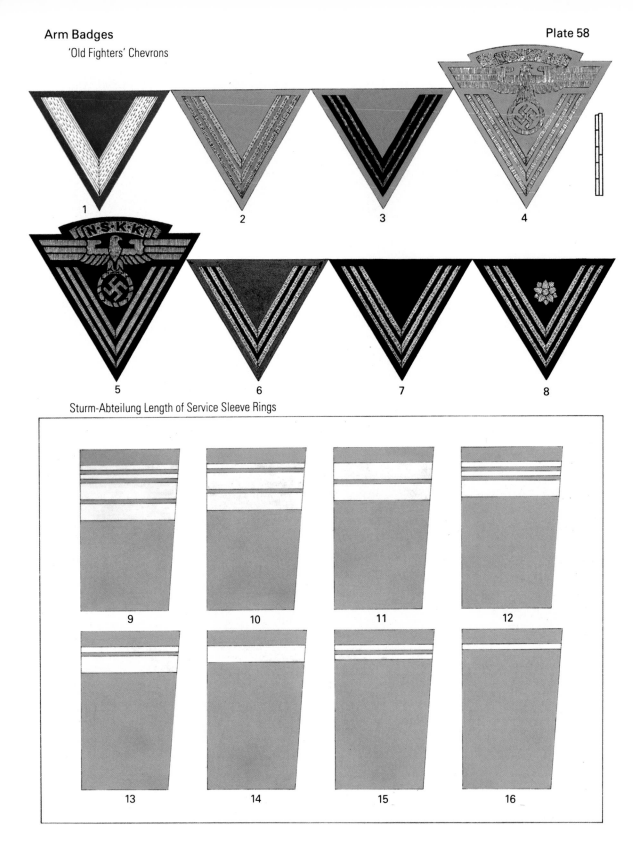

Sturm-Abteilung Length of Service Sleeve Rings

Foreign Volunteer Arm Shields

FRANCE

1

FLANDERN

2

WALLONIE

3

ESPAÑA

4

HRVATSKA

5

Y B B

6

GEORGIEN

7

BERGKAUKASIEN

8

T B

9

P O A

10

LATVIJA

11

ARMENIEN

12

ASERBAIDSCHAN

13

TURKISTAN

14

FREIES INDIEN

15

FREIES ARABIEN

16

Foreign Volunteer Arm Shields

1

2

DON

TƏŊRİ BİZ MENENİ
TURKISTAN

3

4

Eastern Workers Insignia

OST

5

6

7

8

Campaign Arm Shields

NARVIK
1940

9

KRIM
1941 1942

10

DEMJANSK
1942

11

19 43
KUBAN
LAGUNEN
KRYMSKAJA

12

Army Unit Tradition Badges, Foreign Volunteer and Waffen-SS Insignia

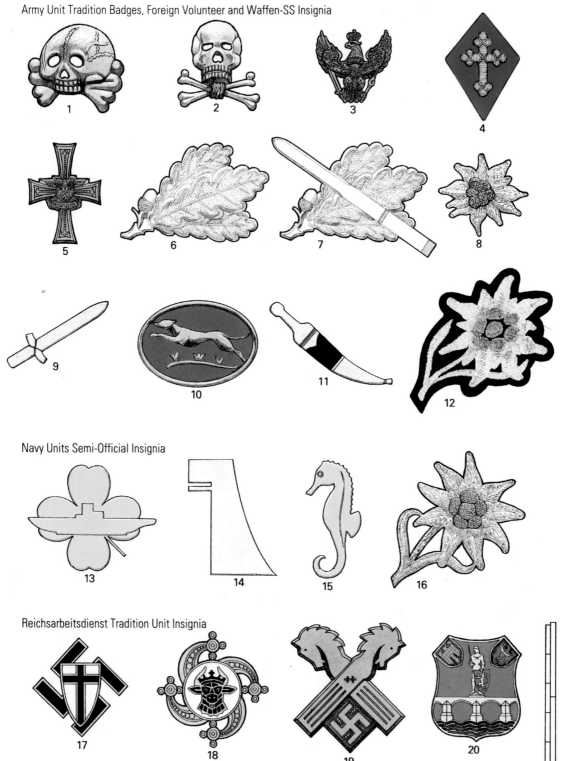

Navy Units Semi-Official Insignia

Reichsarbeitsdienst Tradition Unit Insignia

Plate 63

Plate 64

Trade, Rank, Proficiency and Specialist Arm Badges

Trade badges were usually worn by uniformed personnel who were qualified in a particular trade.

Proficiency badges were those worn by uniformed personnel proficient in a particular skill.

Rank badges worn as arm ornaments were either in the form of chevrons or stripes, or were combined with an emblem.

Plate 37. Arm Badges

NSDAP Political Leaders

1 NSDAP Stabswalter Identification badge, worn on the left forearm.

2 The NSBO (National Socialist Betriebszellen Organisation) arm badge worn on the upper left arm of the NSBO shirt and tunic. The NSBO was a Party organisation of cells in industrial plants composed of Party member workers and foremen in factories.

3 The NSDAP Political Leaders arm insignia as worn by all Political Leaders from Blockwart to Reichsorganisationsleiter on the upper left sleeve. It was for a short period of time worn on its own. Later, in 1933, it was worn together with and above the Swastika arm band but eventually it was done away with and only the arm band continued in use.

3a The small date badge worn below the NSDAP Political Leaders arm insignia showed the wearer's date of entry into the Nazi Party. This date badge was replaced by a cuff-title known as a 'Verdienstabzeichen' (see Plate 29,

no. 7), but this, too, was eventually discontinued.

4 Fraktionsführer arm insignia worn on the left forearm by those NSDAP Political Leaders who were leaders of parliamentary factions in the German State Parliament (Reichstag). The coloured emblem on the black diamond represented the wearer's state colours. Parliamentary Political Leader members who were Fraktionsführer of the Reichstages, the Prussian Landtages, the Bavarian Landtages, and the Austrian Nationalsrats held the rank of NSDAP Landesinspekteur. Fraktionsführer of other Länder were Gauleiter, and Fraktionsführer of town and country areas were Kreisleiter.

5 Auslandsorganisation Raute. It was worn on the left lower sleeve by Party members who were members of the Reich Organisation responsible for the control and welfare of German Nationals living outside the German Reich.

SA

6 Qualified medical SA member below the rank of SA-Sturmführer. This red 'Life-Rune' badge was worn on the left forearm 5 cm above the wearer's cuff. (Sanitäts SA Unterführer und SA Männer), c. 1937.

7 Sleeve badge for SA Doctors (SA-Ärzte), c. 1937. It was worn on left forearm.

8 Pionier-SA badge, worn on the left forearm by holders of Engineering (Pioneering) qualification certificate for the SA. c. 1937.

9 Nachrichten-SA badge, c. 1937. It was worn on the left forearm by qualified SA signals officer personnel. The badge for holders of the signals qualification certificate for the SA for members other than officers had the 'Blitz' emblem in red silk threads.

10 Badge for a qualified chemist, c. 1933, the letter 'A' standing for Apotheker. It was worn on the left forearm by members of the SA and up to July 1934, by members of the SS.

11 Badge for a qualified doctor, c. 1933. It was worn on the left forearm by members of the SA and, up to July 1934, by qualified doctors in the SS.

12 Badge for a qualified dentist, c. 1933, the letter 'Z' standing for Zahnarzt. It was worn on the left forearm by members of the SA and, up to July 1934, by qualified dentists in the SS.

13 Arm badge for an SA medical orderly who had not passed the State medical examination, c. 1933. This comparatively large size badge was worn on the attendant's upper left arm above the Swastika arm band.

14 Arm badge for a qualified SA medical orderly, c. 1933. It was also worn on the upper left arm above the Swastika arm band.

60 The Führer and his SA Chief of Staff, Lutze, on the right, who wears the 'Tyr-rune' arm badge just below the shoulder line on the upper left arm of his tunic (20 April 1938).

15 SA pharmaceutist (SA-Apotheker), c. 1937. This badge was worn on the left forearm.

16 SA veterinary surgeon (SA-Veterinär), c. 1937. This badge was worn on the left forearm.

17 SA dental surgeons and SA dentists (SA-Zahnärzte und Dentisten), c. 1937. This badge was worn on the left forearm.

18 Members of the SA Technical Instruction Unit (SA-Technischen-Lehrsturm), c. 1937. This diamond-shaped badge was worn on the left forearm.

RAD Trade Badges

These Reichsarbeitsdienst trade badges, known as 'Dienstzweig-abzeichen', were worn on the left forearm. They were divided into two groups, those which were worn by RAD ranks from RAD-Arbeitsmann to RAD-Obertruppführer and which were machine-woven in white cotton thread (Group 2), and those which were worn by RAD ranks from RAD-Unterfeldmeister to RAD-Oberstarbeitsführer and whose designs were machine-woven in silver-aluminium thread (Group 1).

19 Sleeve badge for Administration personnel of RAD Staff Detachments (Verwalter bei Abteilungen). It was worn by Group 2 personnel only.

20 Sleeve badge for Bandmaster and Senior Bandmaster (Musikzug und Obermusikzugführer). It was worn by Groups 1 and 2 in the appropriate quality.

21 Administration Staff Personnel of Reich or Gauleitung Group Staff (Group 2) (Verwaltung Reichs-und Gauleitung Gruppenstab). This badge was also worn by both Groups 1 and 2 in the appropriate quality.

22 Sleeve badge for Planning personnel (Group 1) (Planung). It was worn by Groups 1 and 2.

23 Sleeve badge for Medical personnel, 1st design (Group 2) (Heildienst). It was worn by Groups 1 and 2.

24 Sleeve badge for RAD Legal Branch personnel (Group 1) (Rechtshof), also worn by Groups 1 and 2.

25 Sleeve badge for RAD Medical personnel, second design (Group 1). A Group 2 quality badge is known to have existed. This badge was probably introduced during 1940.

Plate 38. Arm Badges

Reichsarbeitsdienst Service Unit Badges

Arm badges displaying an emblem in the shape of a pointed shovel blade known as 'Dienststellenabzeichen' were a universal feature worn on all Reichsarbeitsdienst uniforms and greatcoats. They were worn by all personnel on the left upper arm and, by a system of numbers or letters, identified the wearer, amongst other appointments, as belonging to a particular RAD unit or school.

All the spade emblems in machine-woven silver aluminium thread on a black background were worn by RAD personnel from the rank of Unterfeldmeister up to and including the rank of Oberstarbeitsführer (nos 3, 5, 7, 9, 11, 12, and 13). The spade emblem machine-woven in white cotton thread on to a black or earth brown background was worn by the remaining personnel from Arbeitsmann to Obertruppführer (nos 4, 6, 8, 10, 14 and 15).

1 Worn by Reichsarbeitsführer, Obergeneralarbeitsführer, and Generalarbeitsführer from the Reich Leadership of the RAD.

2 Worn by a Generalarbeitsführer as an Arbeitsgauführer.

3 Worn by Reich Leadership personnel from Unterfeldmeister up to and including the rank of Oberstarbeitsführer.

4 Worn by Reich Leadership personnel from Arbeitsmann up to and including Obertruppführer.

5 Worn by Arbeitsgauleitung personnel, Unterfeldmeister to Oberstarbeitsführer.

6 Worn by the staff personnel of Group 120,

Arbeitsmann to Obertruppführer.

7 Worn by Abteilung personnel of the 6th Detachment, Group 120, Unterfeldmeister to Oberstarbeitsführer.

8 Worn by the staff personnel of the Reichsschule, the training school for highest RAD ranks.

9 Worn by the staff personnel of the training school for senior RAD officers. The small Arabic number below the initial letters 'BS'. (standing for Bezirksschule) indicates the number of the school. There were four such schools in operation in 1937.

10 Worn by the staff personnel of the fourth of four junior training schools, Feldmeisterschule Nr. 4.

11 Worn by the staff personnel of the 5th

61 Party, Para-Military and Police officers at an open air meeting held at Saargemund, October 1943. The RAD officer second from right in the foreground wears the arm spade badge bearing a captial 'M' was a senior officer on the staff of the RAD Head Communication Unit.

Truppenführerschule. There were six such schools for training RAD NCOs.

12 Worn by personnel of RAD Head Communication staff.

13/14/15 No definite reference has been established as to the purpose or meaning of these arm spade badges. It is possible that no. 13 may well have been worn by permanent guard troop personnel ('W' = Wache), and nos 14 and 15 may have had something to do with RAD Lagers, Administration and Lager personnel ('L' = Lager Verwaltung, 'LA' = Lager Abteilung).

Reichsarbeitsdienst der weiblichen Jugend – RADwJ

The Reichsarbeitsdienst der weiblichen Jugend – RADwJ – was the female section of the German Labour Service. They wore on the left upper sleeve of their service uniform a badge, the design of which was peculiar to their organisation.

16 A black Swastika set between the angle made by two black ears of wheat all on a white circular background, an emblem that was used on their unit flags as well as in the design used on their throat brooches. Below the organisational emblem appeared a Roman numeral, the number of the wearer's unit (Bezirksnummer). The background colour to these badges tended to vary from brown to brown-green. This was purely a manufacturing variation. The badge was designed by the Berlin artist Egon Jantke and was introduced for wear in late 1936.

There were three official variations of the badge as follows: white cotton and coloured thread with the Bezirksnummer in white for wear by RADwJ ranks of Arbeitsmaid, Kameradschaftsälteste, and apl.Gehilfe; in silver and coloured threads with the Bezirksnummer in silver for the ranks of Gehilfin and Lagerführerin; and in gold and coloured thread with the Bezirksnummer in gold for the senior RADwJ ranks of Lagergruppenführerin and Bezirksführerin.

Plate 39. Arm Badges

NSKK

1 The 'Tyr-rune' arm badge for those NSKK officer personnel as well as SA and SS officer graduates – who had successfully passed through the SA-Reichsführerschule (SA-State Leadership School) at Munich.

The runic badge was worn on the upper left arm above the Swastika arm band on the brown shirt and the tunic. It was of the same design and colouring for all services. In German mythology Tyr was the son of Odin, the old Germanic god of war.

2 Sleeve insignia of Marine-NSKK Motor Boat unit personnel. The diamond was worn on the left forearm. This is the first model; the second had an eagle superimposed.

3 NSKK Qualified Drivers insignia (NSKK-Kraftfahrraute), first pattern. Worn on the left forearm of the NSKK tunic it had a white metal emblem mounted on to a black cloth diamond-shaped backing.

4 Second pattern NSKK Qualified Drivers insignia. Also worn on the left forearm but this emblem was machine-woven in silver-grey silk threads on to a black silk diamond. The major difference in the two patterns was the shape of the eagles.

5 The NSKK-Verkehrserziehungsdienst badge. A metal arm badge worn by NSKK officers and men with at least six months service in the Driving Instruction Branch of the NSKK. It was worn on the upper right arm, in conjunction with the NSKK traffic duty gorget (not illustrated).

6 NSKK medical personnel below the rank of officer, c. 1942. This cloth badge was worn on the left forearm.

7 NSKK doctors with officer status, c. 1942, worn left forearm.

8 NSKK pharmacists, c. 1942, worn on the left forearm.

9 NSKK dental surgeons and dentists, c. 1942, worn left forearm.

10 NSKK motor transport (Schirrmeister) badge, worn on the right forearm.

11 NSKK driving master (Fahrmeister) badge, worn on the right forearm.

Brigade Ehrhardt and Stahlhelm

12 Second type metal arm badge worn on the upper left arm by all ranks of the 2nd Marine-Brigade Ehrhardt, c. 1920–23.

Of the 25 types of Stahlhelm district arm badges known to have existed, three are illustrated here. All Stahlhelm district badges were worn on the upper right arm of the field-grey Stahlhelm tunic by all ranks.

13 Landesverband Gross Hessen (Land Unit Greater Hessen).

14 Landesverband Ostpreussen (Land Unit East Prussia).

15 Hamburg.

Waffen-SS and Auxiliary Security Police

16 Waffen-SS mountain troops arm badge, worn on the upper right arm by all qualified ranks of SS mountain troop units and formations. Introduced in October 1943, it was machine-embroidered. (See also Plate 61, no. 12).

17 Waffen-SS mountain guide (SS-Bergführer) arm badge. It was worn by qualified Waffen-SS staff personnel of the Senior Mountaineering School of the Mountain Troop Schools of the Waffen-SS.

18 Arm badge for other ranks personnel of the Auxiliary Security Police.

19 Arm badge for officers of the Auxiliary Security Police.

Both badges (nos 18 & 19) were worn on the upper left arm of the Auxiliaries uniforms. The motto 'Treu Tapfer Gehorsam' translates: 'Faithful, Valiant, Obedient'. The similar and

distinctive cap badges as well as the specially designed shoulder straps for members of these units have not been illustrated here. See, however, Plate 34, no. 9.

Plate 40. Arm Badges

Allgemeine-SS, SS-VT, Waffen-SS and SD

Arm Badges (Raute) were worn on the left forearm of the appropriate uniform 3.5 cm above the cuff-title – if worn.

1 Arm Badge for the Staff of the SS Main Security Office and for all SD personnel, the letters SD standing for 'Sicherheits Dienst' (Security Service).

2 Arm badge for the staff of the SS Main Race and Rehabilitation Office (introduced 25 November 1935). The device on the arm badge was known as an 'Odel-rune'.

3 Arm badge for leaders with the rank of SS-Standartenführer and above from the 87th SS Foot Regiment (Innsbruck), and on the staff of SS-Abschnitte (SS Sub-district) XXXVI. The emblem used was a stylized Edelweiss flower.

4 Arm badge as worn by Allgemeine-SS Pioneer personnel.

5 Arm badge worn by German Police NCOs serving in the Waffen-SS.

6 SS Recruitment, Procurement, and Education arm badge displaying a 'T-rune'.

7 Settlement group badge. (In Reichskommissariat für die Festigung deutschen Volkstums-Stabshauptamt.)

8 Economic Enterprise group badge of the SS-Wirtschaft-und Verwaltungshauptamt.

9 Agricultural Economic Administration group badge (Gruppe Landwirtschaftliche Verwaltung).

10 Arm badge for officers of the SS-Totenkopfverbände with the rank SS-Standartenführer and above.

11 Arm badge as worn by former members of the SA who had volunteered for service with the SS Death Head Units. The emblem was

the runic form of the initial letters 'S' and 'A'.
12 Waffen-SS armourer NCO (Waffenunter-führer), introduced sometime after February 1937.

Hitler-Jugend, Deutsche Jungvolk, and Bund Deutsche Mädel Arm Triangles and Unit Insignia

Sleeve or shoulder triangles were a feature of Hitler Youth uniforms. They were also worn by DJ and BDM members. Hitler Youth and DJ personnel had black cloth triangles with lettering and edging machine-woven in bright yellow thread. Girls of the BDM wore black cloth triangles with their lettering and edging machine-woven in white thread. These triangles were worn on the upper right arm of the HJ brown shirt, the BDM white blouse, and the HJ, BDM, and DJ tunics and jackets alike by all but the most senior echelons of the HJ and BDM membership personnel.

The lettering on these triangles was usually in two lines. The upper line, consisting of a single word, showed the wearer's Obergebiet: Nord (no. 15), Süd (no. 16), Ost (no. 13), West (no. 14), or Mitte (not illustrated). The lower line of lettering showed the individual Gebiete, such as Köln-Aachen (no. 14) or Baden (no. 16), there being about 36 such Gebiete in 1939–40, and more with the later annexation of foreign territory.

HJ or BDM units that had been in existence before 1933, known as 'Tradition Units', were distinguished by having a gold yellow braided bar for HJ units (no. 14) or a silver-aluminium braided bar for BDM units (no. 16) sewn along the base line of the arm triangle.

German youths, or children of German parents born or living in countries outside the Greater German Reich were encouraged to belong to the Hitler Youth movement including the BDM.

Where they were permitted to do so they wore their respective uniforms in these foreign countries for official functions. On returning to

62 BDM members from Berlin greeting front-line soldiers returning from the Eastern Front.

Germany or when just visiting the German Reich they also used their uniforms. These youths were distinguished from members of the HJ and BDM resident in the German Reich by the wearing of special 'foreign' arm triangles. Nos 17, 18, and 20 are based on actual items seen in private collections.

17 HJ personnel from HJ unit in Shanghai, China.

20 BDM personnel from Cape Town, South Africa.

18 HJ personnel from the United States of America. This last item may well have been an early pattern of foreign HJ arm triangles. It is almost certain that individual HJ and BDM units existed in the more important cities within the USA and as such would have been distinguished by the use of the name of their town or city, together with the title 'USA'.

From a collecting point of view these 'foreign' arm triangles are amongst the hardest of the HJ/BDM insignia to find, probably because there were so few of them in the first instance and secondly because once war had broken out many of these youth units conveniently disappeared from view, especially in those countries that were not in sympathy with the German cause.

19 Other arm triangles existed, the most notable being this unusual green-coloured Landjahr triangle. This was worn by members of the HJ and BDM who were voluntarily serving for a year working on the land. (See also Plate 28 no. 1, Landdienst der HJ cuff-title.)

21 Reichsjugendführer staff member. Worn by an HJ member on the staff of the Reich Youth Leader.

Plate 41. Arm and Breast Badges

Deutsche Jungvolk and Bund Deutsche Mädel Unit, and Rank Arm and Breast Badges

Personnel of the Deutsche Jungvolk, the junior section of the Hitler Youth, were identified as belonging to a particular 'Oberbann' or DJ district by the wearing of arm badges which displayed a single black or white rune on a circular patch of coloured material. The whole badge, always machine-woven in coloured cotton threads, was worked on to a square background of light tan-coloured material (not illustrated).

These Oberbann badges were worn on the left upper arm directly below the HJ arm triangle badge (see Plate 40). They were in use at least as early as 1934 and were probably phased out, if not discontinued altogether, at the beginning of World War II.

1 Oberbann 1.

2 Oberbann 2.

3 Oberbann 3.

4 Oberbann 4.

5 Oberbann 5.

6 Oberbann 6.

7 Leader of Youth Bann, c. 1937.

DJ Rank Badges and Marine-HJ Rank Badges

Ranks in the Deutsche Jungvolk and the Marine-HJ were primarily displayed by the use of small circular cloth badges worn on the upper right arm and on which were featured a system of chevrons, pips, or combinations of both. These were worked in grey cotton thread on a dark blue background for wear by the DJ, and in mid-blue thread on white material for use by members of the Marine-HJ.

8 Hordenführer (DJ), Rottenführer (M-HJ).

9 Oberhordenführer (DJ), Oberrottenführer (M-HJ).

10 Jungenschaftsführer (DJ), Kameradschaftsführer (M-HJ).

11 Oberjungenschaftsführer (DJ), Oberkameradschaftsführer (M-HJ).

12 Jungzugführer (DJ), Scharführer (M-HJ).

13 Oberjungzugführer (DJ), Oberscharführer (M-HJ).

BDM Rank Badges

The style of clothing worn by members of the BDM did not lend itself to displaying the wearer's rank in the usual way by means of shoulder straps or collar patches. Instead, a system of breast badges was employed and these, worn over the left breast of the jacket or blouse, showed the BDM representation of the German National Emblem combined with a system of embroidery in silver or gold thread indicating an ascending series of ranks.

14 BDM (and JM) breast badge for Gruppenführerin. The white background to these badges was for use on the BDM-JM summer uniform or white blouse. The silver numerals indicate the wearer's unit number.

15 Rank of Gauführerin, as worn on the normal dark blue-black uniform jacket and winter top coat.

16 Breast badge for rank of Untergauführerin z.V. The 'bar' positioned behind the badge indicated the wearer was 'zur Verfügung' or 'z.V.', that is, 'subject to recall in case of an

63 A BDM-Ringführerin in her office, clearly showing the distinctive BDM rank badge, the small figure '6' indicating her unit number.

emergency'. This was a device borrowed from the Armed Forces and the Police.

17 Rank badge for Reichsreferentin, the most senior BDM rank.

Reichsarbeitsdienst Fatigue Dress Arm Rank Badges

Rank was indicated on the fatigue dress of the RAD by the use of arm chevrons worn on the left upper arm. These were in use during World War II and were probably introduced during 1940.

18 RAD Vormann.
19 RAD Obervormann.
20 RAD Hauptvormann.
21 RAD Untertruppführer.
22 RAD Truppführer.
23 RAD Obertruppführer.

Plate 42. Arm Badges

Hitler-Jugend and Marine Hitler-Jugend Trade and Proficiency Badges

The Hitler Youth insignia for graduates of the Reichsführerschule (RFS) was similar in purpose to the SA/SS Tyr-Rune badge (see Plate 39, no. 1). The RFS badge was authorised, probably during 1935, to be worn by those Hitler Youth Leaders who, as graduates, had successfully passed through the Reich Leadership School.

The insignia, which was in cloth form only, was worn over the upper right breast pocket of the khaki-brown and the navy-blue HJ tunics, and the HJ tan-coloured shirt. The device of two sprays of silver-aluminium oakleaves outlined in black threads with a central motif of the letters 'RFS' was hand-embroidered on to a backing of appropriate coloured uniform cloth.

1 The Hitler Youth Leaders Reichsführerschule graduates badge for wear on the khaki uniform and tan-coloured shirt.

2 The same badge for wear on the navy-blue winter uniform.

The Hitler Youth, in keeping with almost all other uniformed organisations, rewarded its members who possessed particular qualifications, skills or trades with insignia to be worn on their uniforms.

3 Arm badge for a qualified driver (HJ-Fahrer).

4 Arm badge for Motor-HJ personnel. The wheel was in grey cotton thread.

5 Arm badge for HJ vehicle instructors. (Motor-HJ Ausbildungsabzeichen); wheel in yellow cotton thread.

6 Arm badge for district inspector of motorised Hitler Youth (Motor-HJ Gebiets-Inspekteure); gilt thread wheel.

7 HJ horse riding proficiency badge (Reiter-scheinprüfung).

8 Hitler Youth communication personnel,

qualification 'A'.

9 Hitler Youth communication personnel, qualification 'B'.

10 Hitler Youth communication personnel, qualification 'C'.

All the above badges, nos 3 to 10 were worn on the left forearm of the HJ shirt and tunic.

11 Marine-HJ signaller (Seefunkabzeichen).

12 Marine-HJ signals qualification class 'A' badge, as worn on the blue-black Marine-HJ uniform.

13 Marine-HJ signals qualification class 'B' badge, as worn on the Marine-HJ white working rig.

German Police Formation Proficiency Badges

Police proficiency badges were worn by personnel of the Reich Protection Police and the Gendarmerie. They were worked in green silk

64 An attractive young woman, a member of the Organisation Todt engaged as signals communication personnel.

or cotton thread for wear by other ranks of the Schutzpolizei (Protection Police) and in orange silk or cotton thread for other ranks of the Rural or Gendarmerie Police. Officers of both Police branches displayed their proficiency badges worked in silver wire.

14 Steering wheel proficiency badge worn by Police officials of the Protection Police qualified as drivers of motorised vehicles.

15 Horse-shoe proficiency badge worn by qualified farriers of the Reich Protection Police.

16 Lightning 'Blitz' badge worn by qualified signallers of Rural or Gendarmerie Police.

17 Arm badge of silver embroidered crossed cavalry lances as worn by a qualified Police officer proficient in horsemanship.

18 Snake and staff badge worn by Protection Police personnel qualified as medical assistants.

All these five badges were introduced in August 1937. They were worn on the left forearm of the Police tunic.

Organisation Todt Female Communication Personnel Qualification Badges

By 1943 women volunteers were being employed within the Organisation Todt as communication personnel. They were used as telephone switchboard operators, trained in wireless and telegraph communication work and worked as clerical staff. They wore a dark blue uniform with a matching-coloured side cap, greatcoat, and suit, in dark blue cloth. The clothing authorities intended to design, manufacture, and issue rank insignia in some form for these women but it is not known if this was ever achieved. They did, however, wear a form of arm eagle badge.

19 Arm badge as worn by enlisted Signals girls of the Organisation Todt. Worn on the upper left arm of their jacket, greatcoat, and service blouse.

20 Arm badge as worn by female leaders of

the Nachrichtenmädel der Organisation Todt, and also worn on the upper left arm of their jacket, greatcoat, and service blouse.

21 Service badge. Identical to the Service brooch except that the badge was in cloth and the brooch in enamelled metal, it was worn by all qualified female communication personnel on the left arm and the left side of the side cap. The OT and blitz were on yellow metal.

Plate 43. Arm Badges

Hitler-Jugend, Marine-HJ and DJ Proficiency and Speciality Badges

65 Hitler Youth wartime volunteers serving as Luftwaffenhelfer being presented with the Luftwaffe Anti-Aircraft badge (25 April 1944). The special blue on black breast badge worn by these HJ personnel can be seen.

1 HJ Flying Branch personnel (Flieger-HJ), badge worn on left forearm, c. 1933 but probably earlier.

2 HJ Adjutant. A silver-grey 'Wolfstongue' rune on a red cloth diamond worn on the left forearm. Examples of this badge in postwar collections are always of the oval variety.

3 HJ Adjutant attached to the Political Leadership Corps (HJ-Adjutant bei den Politischen Leiter), worn on the left forearm.

4 Hitler Youth doctor (HJ-Arzt), c. 1933, worn on the left forearm.

5 HJ pharmacist (HJ-Apotheker), c. 1943.

6 HJ dentist (HJ-Zahnarzt), c. 1943.

7 HJ medical orderly (HJ-Feldscher), 2nd pattern badge worn on left forearm. (First pattern medical badge was as illustrated above under item 4.)

8 Senior HJ medical orderly (Gefolgschaftsfeldscher), also worn left forearm, c. January 1941.

9 HJ doctor (HJ-Arzt), c. 1943.

10 HJ unit medical orderly (Bannfeldscher), worn left forearm, c. January 1941.

11 HJ district medical orderly (Gebietsfeldscher), also worn left forearm c. January 1941.

12 General DJ (Allgemeine-DJ), c. 1943, worn on upper left arm.

13 Staff of DJ (Mitglieder des DJ in Stäben), c. 1943, also worn on upper left arm.

14 DJ in the NPEA (Nationalpolitische Erziehungssanstalten), c. 1943, worn on upper left arm.

15 DJ Leadership Corps (DJ-Führerkorps), c. 1943, also worn on upper left arm.

16 HJ First Aid Service (Unfall Dienst), worn left forearm.

17 DJ Unit Leader (DJ Jungbannführer), c. 1937, worn upper left arm.

18 DJ district leader (Gebietsjungvolkführer als Führer des DJ im Gebiet), c. 1937, worn upper left arm.

19 DJ leader on District Staff (Jungbannführer im Gebietsstab), worn upper left arm, c. 1937.

20 Senior DJ leader on the Staff of the Reich Youth Leader (Oberjungbannführer im RJF-Stab), c. 1937, worn upper left arm.

21 HJ Administration Branch personnel (HJ-Verwalter), worn on left forearm.

At an undetermined date, probably around 1940, a set of four very narrow arm stripes were brought into use for wear by personnel of the Hitler Youth. They cannot be classed as cuff-titles in the strict sense of the word, although they were, in fact, referred to as 'Ausbildungs-

Ärmelstreifen'. Each of these arm stripes were worn on the right forearm and it was possible for more than one to be worn at the same time, one above the other.

22 HJ sports attendant (HJ-Sportwart).

23 HJ shooting attendant (HJ-Schiesswart).

24 HJ field sports attendant (HJ-Geländesportwart).

25 HJ skiing attendant (HJ-Schiwart).

26 Hitler Youth member under training with the NSKK. This cloth badge, a combination of the Hitler-Jugend emblem and the NSKK drivers emblem (see also Plate 39, no. 4), was worn on the left forearm. The date of introduction is uncertain, but it must have been during the early war years.

27 Sleeve badge as worn by Hitler Youth members of the HJ Fire Fighting Squads (HJ-Feuerwehrabzeichen). Introduced in 1941 this silk machine-woven badge combined the Hilter Youth emblem over which was superimposed a Police style eagle and wreath. Worn on the left forearm of the khaki-brown HJ Fire Fighting tunic, this badge indicated that the wearer had successfully passed a Fire Service test. White edging distinguished leaders, while carmine edging indicated enlisted personnel.

28 Breast badge for HJ Volunteer members of the Luftwaffenhelfer and Flakhelfer units. The black triangular badge with its blue, machine-embroidered Luftwaffe eagle and Gothic letters 'L H' was worn over the top edge of the right breast pocket on the special HJ blouse and in the same position on the special HJ top coat. Hitler Youth employed in these two formations served as helpers to the Luftwaffe and anti-aircraft batteries.

29 Marine Hitler Youth sea sports badge (Seesportabzeichen der Marine-HJ).

30 Marine Hitler Youth musician (Marine-HJ Spielmannabzeichen).

31 Marine HJ arm emblem for wear on best dress uniform (Fahrtenanzug). It is of gold embroidery on navy-blue circular cloth patch.

Plate 44. Arm Badges

Army Units

1 Gebirgsjäger Edelweiss arm badge. Standard pattern BeVo quality item worn by qualified members of mountain troop units of all ranks, including generals, of mountain troops on the upper right arm of the field, service and parade uniform, including the greatcoat. It was introduced into service on 2 May 1939. (See also Plate 61, nos 8 and 16.)

2 A variation of the BeVo quality mountain troop arm badge as worn on the tropical uniform and especially the light weight tan-coloured uniform worn by members of the Deutsche Afrika Korps. This item was also worn on the upper right arm but only on the field uniform and the tropical greatcoat. It was not permitted to be worn on temperate climate clothing.

3 A hand-embroidered version of the Gebirgsjäger arm badge.

4 The Ski-Jäger arm badge. This comparatively rate item was worn on the upper right arm of the military uniform of those troops from rifle units qualified in the use of snow skis. (See also Plate 61, no. 7.) It is only known to exist as a BeVo quality item.

5 The Jäger arm badge introduced by an order dated 2 October 1942 for use by personnel of Jäger (Rifle) Divisions and Jäger (Rifle) Battalions was also worn on the upper right arm of the greatcoat, the field, service and uniform tunics. The item illustrated here is of BeVo quality.

6 Arm badge introduced in January 1942 for wear by members of Army technical units who had formerly been members of the TeNo – the Technische Nothilfe or Technical Emergency Corps. It was worn on the upper right arm of the Army field and service uniforms and the greatcoat. The badge is of BeVo quality, the only quality known to exist. (See also Plate 27, no. 12).

7 Army flak artillery unit arm badge. An extremely rare item about which little is known. It was worn on the upper right arm.

8 Feldgendarmerie arm badge, worn by all ranks of the German Army Field Police up to the rank of Leutnant. Officers wore the same design badge but worked in silver thread. The Police Eagle badge was worn on the upper left arm of the Army field and service tunics. (For comparison with Police badges see Plate 57.)

Army and Waffen-SS Rank Badges

Nos 9 to 19 are rank insignia as used on new forms of camouflage and special combat clothing that did not display the wearer's rank by means of shoulder straps. Those items illustrated here were part of a new and complete system of rank insignia, introduced by an order dated 22 August 1942, which covered Army ranks from Unteroffizier to Generalfeldmarschall. They were worn on the upper left arm of the following items of Army clothing:

The new winter uniform;
The snow camouflage uniform;
The snow shirt;
The wind blouse;
Animal skin uniforms;
The denim overalls for armoured troops;
The reed-green overalls for gun crews of batteries and operators of 2 cm anti-aircraft guns;
The denim overalls for the crews of armoured reconnaissance vehicles;
The protective flight overalls for the Balloon Service;
The tropical shirt;
Denim jackets;
Training uniforms;
Jackets of work uniforms.

In February 1943 the same system of rank insignia badges in use by the German Army were introduced into the Waffen-SS. For all intents and purposes they were the same as the Army items, only the Waffen-SS rank terms replacing those used by the Army. In the captions listed below both Army and Waffen-SS ranks are given.

9 Unteroffizier – SS-Unterscharführer.
10 Unterfeldwebel – SS-Scharführer.
11 Feldwebel – SS-Oberscharführer.
12 Stabsfeldwebel – SS-Sturmscharführer.
13 Leutnant – SS-Untersturmführer.
14 Hauptmann – SS-Hauptsturmführer.
15 (No equivalent Army rank) – SS-Oberführer.
16 Generalmajor – SS-Brigadeführer und Generalmajor der Waffen-SS.
17 General der Infanterie, etc. – SS-Obergruppenführer und General der Waffen-SS.
18 Generaloberst – SS-Oberstgruppenführer und Generaloberst der Waffen-SS.
19 Generalfeldmarschall – (no equivalent Waffen-SS rank).

66 Generalfeldmarschall Busch, Commander-in-Chief of an Army Group, seen on the Eastern Front, wearing the special rank insignia for a Field Marshal designed to be worn on those items of clothing that did not display the wearer's rank by the usual method of shoulder straps (16 March 1944).

Those rank badges for Unteroffizier to Oberst (not illustrated) were usually silk-screen-printed on thin cotton cloth. From the rank of Generalmajor to Generalfeldmarschall they were worked in yellow and in yellow and white threads together with yellow braiding on to black woollen material.

Plate 45. Arm Badges

Army Trade and Proficiency Badges

1 Paymaster trainee (Zahlmeisteranwärter).
2 NCO artificer or ordnance technician (Feuerwerker).
3 Fortress construction sergeant-major (Festungsbaufeldwebel).
4 Fortress engineer sergeant-major (Festungspionierfeldwebel).
5 Supply administration NCO (Gerätverwaltungsunteroffizier).
6 Gas defence NCO (Gasschutzunteroffizier).
7 Signals mechanic (Nachrichtenmechaniker).
8 Regimental NCO saddler (Regimentsuntersattlermeister).
9 Motor transport NCO (Schirrmeister).
10 Troop NCO saddler (Truppensattlermeister).
11 Administration NCO (Verwaltungsunteroffizier).
12 Fortifications sergeant-major (Wallfeldwebel).
13 Clothing stores NCO (Zeugmeister).
14 Farrier candidate (Hufbeschlagmeister, Geprüfteanwärter).
15 Qualified farrier (Geprüftes-Hufbeschlagpersonal).
16 Farrier instructor (Hufbeschlag Lehrmeister).
17 Veterinary personnel (Veterinärpersonal).
18 Medical personnel (Sänitätsunterpersonal).
19 Ordnance NCO (Waffenfeldwebel).
20 Radio operators (Funkmeister).
21 Motor or armoured mechanic, 2nd class (Kraftzeug oder Panzer Wärte II).
22 Technical artisan (Handwerker).
23 Motor or armoured mechanic, 1st class (Kraftzeug oder Panzer Wärte I).
24 Master technical artisan (Vorhandwerker).

All the above 24 Army trade badges were worn on the right forearm of the field tunic, service tunic, uniform jacket, and the greatcoat.

25 Signals operator with anti-tank units (Nachrichtenpersonal).
26 Signals operator with artillery units (Nachrichtenpersonal).
27 Signals operator with engineer units (Nachrichtenpersonal).

The above three examples, together with other badges of this type, were worn on the upper right arm. These lightning 'Blitz' badges existed in other colours for use by signals operators from other branches of the German Army. They were: white for infantry units; gold-yellow for cavalry units; light blue for supply units; Bordeaux-red for smoke troop units; light green for mountain troop units; grass-green for armoured infantry units; and copper brown for certain reconnaissance units. None of these have been illustrated here.

28 3.7 cm anti-tank gunner, 4th grade (Panzer-Abwehr Geschutze), c. 1936.
29 2 cm tank gunner, 1st grade (Kampfwagenkanone .30), c. 1936.
30 Gun layer, artillery (Richtabzeichen für Artillerie-Richtkanonier).
31 Smoke-projector operator (Richtabzeichen für Nebeltruppen).

The above four badges were worn on the recipient's left forearm.

Plate 46. Arm and Breast Badges

Army Proficiency and Qualification Badges

1 Qualified helmsman for engineer assault boats (Steuermann). A number of manufacturing variations exist of this badge. The finest quality had the anchor and ship's wheel pressed out of white metal with a frosted silver finish and silver highlights. This metal emblem was mounted on to either an oval of dark blue-green badge cloth or field-grey cloth reinforced from behind by an oval backing plate through which passed the prongs – five in number – affixed on the underside of the metal emblem. Examples of this badge are known to have been manufactured by C. E. Junker of Berlin, one of the finest badge manufacturers operating during the Third Reich. There were silver wire hand-embroidered versions and silver-grey cotton thread machine-embroidered versions, both of which types were worked on to dark blue-green and field-grey cloth. All versions of the badge were worn on the upper left sleeve.

2 Army anti-aircraft range-taker arm badge (Heeresflak E-Messer), introduced on 18 May 1944 and worn on the left forearm. (See also Plate 44, no. 7, and Plate 9, no. 18.)

3 The motor vehicle driver's badge of Merit (Kraftfahr-Bewährungsabzeichen). Instituted on 23 October 1942 but made retroactive to 1 December 1940, the motor vehicles driver's badge of Merit, often referred to as the driver's service badge, was awarded to military and civilian drivers who had distinguished themselves during periods of combat as drivers. It was also awarded to those persons who had taken exceptional care of their vehicles under adverse conditions. The award to military personnel was authorised by military unit commanders. Civilians were recognised by the Minister of the Interior.

The metal badge was instituted in three classes, bronze, silver, and, the highest award, gilt. The design of a motor vehicle steering wheel surrounded by a wreath of laurel leaves was mounted, with the aid of two metal prongs and a small metal backing plate, on to a circular or diamond-shaped piece of cloth, the colour of which matched the colour of the

67 An SS-Rottenführer of the Waffen-SS photographed on the Eastern Front on the occasion when he was awarded the Motor Vehicles Driver's Badge of Merit (7 June 1943).

wearer's uniform. The award was sewn to the left forearm of the field, service, and, where it was possessed, the parade uniform.

The requirements for the award of the bronze class badge (as illustrated here) were: 90 days unbroken service as a motor-cycle dispatch rider; 120 days of unbroken service as a front line supply driver; 135 days of unbroken service as a driver of any other military transport vehicle.

The silver and the gilt versions were awarded for longer periods of service. Service under extreme climatic conditions or across very difficult terrain, or where the service carried out was of an exceptional nature could result in the required periods of service being shortened. The award of the badge required that the driver maintained his level of performance. Any driving convictions or neglect of his vehicle could result in the award being withdrawn.

4 Arm badge worn by German Army women of the rank of Stabsführerin and Oberstabsführerin serving in the 'Nachrichtenhelferinnen des Heeres'. It was worn on the left upper arm of their uniform tunic and service dress. (See also Plate 2, no. 4.)

68 The 'Lightning Blitz' arm badge worn by members of the Nachrichtenhelferinnen des Heeres.

5 The snipers' badge (Scharfschützenabzeichen), 1st Class. The snipers' badge was instituted by an order dated 20 August 1944. It was awarded in one of three classes depending on the recipient's qualifications and only those marksmen employed in the capacity of a sniper were eligible. The badge was worn on the right forearm above all other insignia on the field and the service tunic and the uniform coat but not on the greatcoat. Eligibility for the third

class award required the recipient to have made 20 kills. The second class award required 40 kills and the first class snipers' badge, as illustrated here, meant that the holder had killed 60 or more of the enemy. The 2nd Class Badge had a silver border to the oval badge and the 3rd Class award was without a border. The design was the same for all three items. This badge in any of the three classes was also permitted to be worn by qualifying personnel of the German Air Force (ground troops), the Navy, and the Waffen-SS.

NSFK Proficiency, Qualification and Trade Badges

The NSFK was founded on 17 April 1937. It was first commanded by Korpsführer General der Flieger Friedrich Christiansen (he later commanded the German Occupation Forces in the Netherlands), who in turn was succeeded by Korpsführer Generaloberst Alfred Keller. Membership to the NSFK was voluntary. Its paramount purpose was to stimulate, encourage, and foster interest in flying and aeronautics amongst the youth of Germany, especially the DJ and the Hitler Youth members of the flying section who were the potential future air and ground crews of the Luftwaffe. The most important aspect of the work undertaken by the NSFK was that of instruction and indoctrination.

A very large proportion of the NSFK personnel were instructors. The NSFK maintained pilot training and aircraft maintenance schools. It encouraged model aircraft and model glider construction and flying. It had aircraft workshops and built full size gliders, and gave instruction in glider flying and flying power driven aircraft. Insignia and prizes of varying kinds were devised as awards to encourage the youths under instruction to strive for perfection in whatever field of aviation they had chosen.

6 The NSFK Grosses Segelfliegerabzeichen (Greater Glider Pilots Badge). Instituted on

26 January 1942 by Korpsführer Christiansen, the purpose of the badge was to further distinguish advanced gliding achievement beyond the already existing NSFK award. Persons in the Luftwaffe, the Hitler Youth, and the NSFK were eligible for this award which was bestowed in one of two groups:

Group 1.   As recognition of the achievement of the advancement of military flight proficiency through gliding.
Glider pilot achievement.
Achievement in hand work.

Group 2.   The recipient must already have been awarded the 2nd Class Glider Pilot's Certificate and have successfully achieved a glider endurance flight of five hours, returning to the starting point.
The contestant must have reached an altitude of 3300 feet three times during the course of a single glider flight.

The metal and enamelled badge was presented with an award document (certificate) and the badge was worn on the lower part of the left breast of all uniforms.

On 12 July 1938 Korpsführer Christiansen instituted a new badge to be awarded to NSFK pilots and NSFK trained pilots. Known as the Abzeichen für Motorflugzeugführer (badge for pilots of powered aircraft), it was originally produced as a silver thread embroidered cloth badge (not illustrated). On 1 May 1939 the blue-grey cloth badge underwent a change both in its design and its manufacture. It was re-issued as a metal badge (as shown in no. 8) and the original embroidered Swastika emblem at the base of the wreath of laurel leaves and oak leaves was changed to that of the NSFK Flying Man symbol on the new badge at the base of an all-oak leaf wreath.

In 1942 the badge underwent a third and final change in design (as shown in no. 7), and in place of the two-seater, low-winged monoplane as featured on the second pattern badge an eagle in an attitude of soaring flight was substituted with the NSFK Flying Man emblem, slightly larger and without the arched ribbon, being moved from the base of the badge to the top section of the oak leaf wreath. All three versions of the badge were worn on the left breast pocket of the NSFK uniform, the first pattern being sewn into position with the other two being pinned on.

7 3rd design of the NSFK 'badge for pilots of powered aircraft'.

8 2nd design of the NSFK 'badge for pilots of powered aircraft'.

9 The NSFK aero-modelling proficiency badge, Grade 'B' (NSFK Modellflugleistungsabzeichen, 'B' Prüfung). This was one of three grades of aero-modelling proficiency badges. Members of the Hitler Youth and the DJ organised special modelling groups for model glider flying. These groups were controlled by members of the NSFK and at times of competitive flying were often supervised by representatives of the Luftwaffe, in whose ultimate interest it was to encourage this type of activity. To encourage the youths and to reward them for their skill and ability in building and flying prize winning model gliders the three grades of aero-modelling proficiency badges were established.

To have been awarded this 'B' Grade badge meant that the competitor had to perform aerial manoeuvres with his model glider which required his sailplane to make a 90 degree and a 360 degree turn at least five times out of twenty flights.

10 Trade badge for NSFK workshop leader in glider construction workshop. This cloth badge with its grey cotton embroidery on a base of blue-grey badge cloth was worn on the left forearm of the NSFK tunic. These badges were known to have been in use from at least 1940 to 1942 and were probably introduced before the earlier date and probably continued in use after the later date.

11 Trade badge for NSFK work shop leader in a sailplane workshop.
12 Trade badge for sailplane examiner, 2nd Grade.
13 Trade badge for sailplane examiner, 1st Grade.

DLV Proficiency Badges

In 1933, long before the relevant clauses of the Versailles Treaty had been denounced by Adolf Hitler, Hermann Göring had set about organising his new Air Force. It was his proud boast that his 'boys in blue-grey' were to be the lynch-pin of the war of the future, a war of aggression which would be won by Germany within the first few days by her possession of vast numbers of bombers.

Nominally his 'boys' belonged to the Deutsche Luftsports Verband. This was the German Air Sports Organisation which had been formed in March 1933 by the amalgamation of German civilian flying clubs. The organisation was commanded by Bruno Loerzer, a World War I fighter ace, former Commander of Jagdgeschwader 3 and holder of the Pour le Mérite – the Blue Max. It was obvious, however, that this organisation was just a cover for the training of the future German Luftwaffe. Indeed, when conscription was introduced in 1935, the same year the DLV was dissolved, entry into the Luftwaffe was restricted to members of the DLV.

The task of the DLV was similar to that of the NSFK, the organisation that was to replace the DLV. Members of the DLV promoted civilian interest in model building and flying, gliding, ballooning, and motor-powered aircraft flight. They instructed German youth – especially the Flieger-HJ and the DJ – in all aspects of aviation, flying, and ground maintenance.

Personnel of the DLV of whatever rank wore uniforms of blue-grey. Much of their insignia was very similar to that which the Luftwaffe

adopted a few years later (see Plate 11, nos 17 to 27). Pilot-observers and wireless operators in the DLV were distinguished by wearing silver bullion wings.

14 DLV pilot-observer breast 'wings' (Flugzeugführer und Orterabzeichen).
15 DLV wireless operator 'wings' (Bordfunker).

Both types of 'wings' were worn above the right breast pocket of the DLV tunic. However, photographic evidence indicates that at some time during the formative months of the DLV these wings were worn on the left breast. The reason for the change over has not yet been established.

With the possession of anything remotely approaching a military air force strictly prohibited to Germany under the stringent terms of the Versailles Treaty, Germans who were air-minded had only commercial or private flying open to them, alternatives which for many were well outside their means or ability to pursue. Glider flying, however, offered these Germans the opportunity of comparatively inexpensive flying experience. The sport of gliding also proved very useful training for future Luftwaffe pilots. Civil pilots under instruction were tested, judged and, where successful, were awarded one of three Civil Gliding Proficiency Badges (Segelflieger-Abzeichen).

16 Glider pilot 'A' level proficiency badge (Segelflieger-A-Abzeichen Gleitfliegerprüfung 'A'). To be awarded this level required that the recipient had made a 30-second free flight without manoeuvre. The badge illustrated here was machine-stitched in white cotton thread on to blue material. In this quality it was intended to be worn on the lower part of the left breast of the DLV brown shirt—the HJ and NSFK brown shirts.
17 Glider pilot 'B' level proficiency badge (Segelflieger-B-Abzeichen Gleitfliegerprüfung 'B'). To be awarded this badge meant that the

recipient had made a 6o-second free flight and executed an 'S' turn manoeuvre. The badge shown here was machine-embroidered on to blue-grey uniform cloth and was normally worn on the DLV, the NSFK, and the Luftwaffe blue-grey tunic. It too was worn on the lower left breast.

18 Glider Pilot 'C' Level Proficiency Badge (Segelflieger-C-Abzeichen Gleitfliegerprüfung 'C'). To qualify for this award the recipient had to pass a test first in order to enter for the award and this in turn was followed by stringent flight testing and oral examination. This badge was intended to be worn on the blue-grey DLV, NSFK, and Luftwaffe uniform in the same position as the previous two badges. This badge, the senior of the three, is illustrated here as having hand-embroidered aluminium thread worked on to a circular base of blue-grey badge cloth.

The DLV instituted two badges at different times for those members who had passed proficiency tests as balloon pilots. The first pattern DLV Balloonist Badge (not illustrated) was a cloth badge with its motif of a balloon flanked by oak leaves worked in aluminium threads on to an oval of blue-grey badge cloth. The second pattern DLV Balloonist Badge was in metal.

19 2nd pattern DLV balloonist badge. A bronzed metal badge depicting a hot air balloon surrounded by a wreath of oak leaves, and upon which, on the upper surface of the balloon appeared the black enamelled letters 'DLV'. This badge was worn on the left breast pocket of the tunic.

20 On 10 March 1938 the NSFK instituted the first of a series of badges of distinction for members of the NSFK. This first badge, the badge for free ballooning pilots (Abzeichen für Freiballonführer) was in cloth and took the form of a hot air balloon surrounded by a wreath of oak leaves across which appeared stylized wings of the same pattern as used for the DLV pilot-observer's breast wings (see no.

14 above). The embroidery work was in silver-aluminium thread worked on to an oval of blue-grey badge cloth. The badge was worn sewn on to the left breast tunic pocket.

Plate 47. Arm and Breast Badges

DLV Arm Badges, Trade and Proficiency Badges

1 The DLV National Emblem as worn on the upper left sleeve of the DLV service and uniform tunic and the working-dress blouse, the shirt, and the uniform tunic of the 'Abteilung-Segelflug' – the gliding section of the DLV. The early pattern eagle and Swastika emblem was in grey-white cotton thread for use by lower ranks, in silver-aluminium thread for DLV officer classes, and in gilt wire embroidery for general officers.

2 Proficiency badge worn by DLV flying personnel (Fliegendes Personal), worn on left forearm of DLV tunic and greatcoat.

3 DLV drivers badge (Kraftfahrer). Note similarity to the item used by the Luftwaffe as illustrated on Plate 48, no. 28.

4 DLV balloonist (Ballonfahrer).

5 DLV technical personnel (Flugzeug Personal).

Nos 2 to 5 above were worn by men and non-commissioned DLV personnel only.

Abteilung-Segelflug Breast Rank Badges

6 Segelflugscharführer breast badge.

7 Segelflugsturmführer breast badge.

8 Leiter der Abteilung Segelflug bei Präsidium breast badge.

The three items above were diamond-shaped badges worn above the right breast pocket of the working shirt and acted as a form of rank insignia, the shirt not having shoulder straps or collar patches. In all there were five of these badges, the remaining two Abteilung-Segelflug ranks of 'Segelflug-Truppführer' and 'Referent bei Landesverband' not being illustrated.

Legion Condor Rank Insignia

German Air Force volunteers who were sent to Spain in 1936 to assist Generals Mola and Franco in their rebellion against the Republican government of the day were known collectively as the 'Legion Condor'. In an effort to conceal their true identity these Luftwaffe volunteers wore olive-brown uniforms very similar to those worn by the Spanish Nationalist forces. The Legion also adopted rank insignia for their troops that was the same as that in use with the Spanish Army. German volunteers were all stepped up by one rank when serving in the Legion, so that a Luftwaffe Oberleutnant in Germany wore the three six-pointed stars of a Spanish Capitán when in Spain. Branch-of-service colours were used with these Spanish-style rank badges, appearing as a border of colour around the actual rank badge. All Legion Condor badges of rank were worn above the left breast pocket of the Legion shirt and tunic as well as on the front of the 'Fliegermütze' (side cap).

The Legion Condor branch colours were: leadership personnel — black; flying branch personnel — gold-yellow; flak Artillery troops — bright red; and signals personnel — light brown;

9 Anti-aircraft Legionär (Legionario-Voluntario).

10 Signals Unteroffizier (Cabo).

11 Hauptmann, flying branch (Capitán).

12 Oberstleutnant (Teniente Coronel) and Oberst (Coronel) from the Legion's leadership/staff branch.

13 Spanish-speaking German interpreters (Dolmetscher) were attached to the Legion and they were distinguished by wearing a small diamond-shaped cloth badge worn in the centre of the right breast pocket and on the front of their side cap. The badge, which displayed a vertical bar of silver lace surmounted by a silver dot, was sewn to an upright lozenge of cloth in the branch colour of the unit to which the interpreter was attached. Shown here is the badge as worn by an interpreter from a flak-artillery unit.

Luftwaffe Specialist Qualifications

These arm badges were worn on the left forearm of the Luftwaffe flying blouse, service tunic, parade uniform, and greatcoat.

14 Sound location operator (Horcher). The twisted gold-corded border indicated that the wearer had one year's service in this particular speciality. This practice was used for other badges in this category where this ruling applied. This badge was introduced in April 1942.

15 Military boat personnel (Seemännisches Bootspersonal) introduced March 1935 for Luftwaffe personnel of tenders, crash-boats, and the like.

16 Rangefinder (Entfernungsmesser), introduced in April 1942.

17 Flying technical personnel (Fliegertechnisches Personal) introduction date March 1935.

18 Flying Personnel (Fliegendes Personal), except those entitled to wear the Luftwaffe pilot's, observer's, or the radio operator's metal breast badge (not illustrated). The introduction date was between March 1936 and April 1937.

19 Flak (anti-aircraft) personnel (Flakartilleriepersonal), worn only after nine months service. The introduction date was August 1937. It exists in yellow on dark blue backing, probably for female auxiliaries.

Plate 48. Arm Badges

Luftwaffe Trade and Proficiency Badges

1 Administration NCO (Verwaltungsunteroffizier).

2 Ordnance – heavy weapons – NCO in anti-aircraft units and Regiment 'General Göring' (Waffenunteroffizier für Flakartillerie und Regiment 'General Göring').

3 Qualified telephone operator NCO (Geprüfter Fernsprechunteroffizier).

4 NCO artificer or ordnance technician (Feuerwerker).

5 Signals personnel of flying and anti-aircraft branches (Truppennachrichtenpersonal der Flieger und Flaktruppe).

6 Qualified telegraphist NCO (Geprüfter Fernschreibunteroffizier).

7 Medical personnel (Sanitätspersonal).

8 Aircraft equipment administration branch personnel (Geräteverwalter für Flugzeuggerät).

9 Searchlight equipment administration branch personnel (Geräteverwalter für Scheinwerfergerät).

10 Mechanized transport equipment (Kraftfahrzeuggerät).

11 Air raid warning personnel (Flugmeldepersonal).

12 Transport sergeant (Schirrmeister).

13 Aircraft radioman (Funkmeister).

14 Aerial light bomb armourer NCO (Waffenunteroffizier für leichte Bomben).

15 Qualified radio NCO operator (Geprüfter Funkunteroffizier).

16 Graduate from a Technical Flight Preparatory School (ehemaliger Militärschüler der Fl. Techn. Vorschulen).

17 Unestablished badge.

18 Aerial heavy bomb armourer NCO (Waffenunteroffizier für schwere Bomben).

19 Flak crews, such as gun loaders, fuze setters, etc. (Geschützbedienung, Ladenkanonier, Zündereinsteller).

20 Technical sergeant (Technischer Unteroffizier).

21 Qualified sound location operator (Geprüfter Horchfunker).

22 Qualified directional radio operator NCO (Geprüfter Horchfunkerunteroffizier).

23 Signals equipment branch personnel (Luftnachrichtengerät).

24 Luftwaffe NCO schools student (Unter-offizierschüler der Luftwaffe).

25 Unestablished badge.

26 Small arms ordnance NCO – flying branch personnel and air signals troops (Waffenunteroffizier für Flieger Truppe und Ln. Truppe).

27 Unestablished badge.

28 Transport driver (Kraftfahrer).

29 Master radioman (Funkmeister).

All the badges as listed above were, with the exception of nos 16 and 24, worn on the left forearm of the Luftwaffe service tunic and flight blouse. No. 16 was worn on the upper left sleeve and no. 24 was worn on the right forearm. Only 29 of the known 36 items have been illustrated here.

Plate 49. Arm Badges

Luftwaffe School and Rank Arm Badges

1 Technical Preparatory School for the Luftwaffe at Berlin-Spandau.

69 A switchboard operator of the Luftwaffe Nachrichtenhelferinnenschaft. The arm insignia, both qualification badge and rank chevrons, are not dealt with in the text.

2 Technical Preparatory Air Force School at Bremen-Oslebshausen, sleeve diamond worn on left forearm of wearer's blue-grey service tunic.

3 Technical Preparatory School for the Luftwaffe at Suhl.

4 Air Force general officers cloak eagle. It was worn on the right side of the (sleeveless) cloak approximately half way between the wearer's shoulder and elbow. Officers of the Luftwaffe below the rank of general wore the same pattern of eagle, but worked in silver-aluminium threads. This item was very much a pre-war item as the Luftwaffe officers cloak was seldom used during the war years.

5 Arm badge for female personnel serving as members of anti-aircraft gun crews (Flakwaffenhelferinnen). The badge was worn on the upper right sleeve of the blouse type jacket and greatcoat.

Rank insignia for female personnel of the 'Luftnachrichten-Helferinnenschaft'. This service consisted of the 'Flugmeldedienst' (Air Raid Warning Service) and the 'Fernsprech-und Fernschreibbetriebsdienst der Luftwaffe' (Telephone and Teletype Departments of the Luftwaffe.) The third and final pattern of rank insignia was introduced on 28 July 1941, and the items were worn on the upper left arm of the blouse type jacket, tunic and greatcoat.

6 Rank badge for Luftnachrichten-Flugmeldehelferin and/or Luftnachrichten-Betriebshelferin.

7 Rank badge for Luftnachrichten-Flugmeld haupthelferin and/or Luftnachrichten-Betriebshaupthelferin.

8 Rank badge for Luftnachrichten-Flugmeldoberführerin and/or Luftnachrichten-Betriebsoberführerin.

Rank insignia was displayed on Luftwaffe flying suits by means of a series of arm badges. Ranks from Unteroffizier to Generalfeldmarschall were represented by a series of stylized 'wings' and bars in various combinations and

70 Luftwaffe officers from an He 111 bomber unit wearing different patterns of flying suits, but both with their Luftwaffe rank insignia on the upper arms. The three wings over a bar all in white represented the Air Force rank of captain (Hauptmann).

in two basic colours, white cloth for all ranks up to Oberst, and in gold-yellow cloth from Generalmajor to General der Flieger. The two most senior ranks of Generaloberst and Generalfeldmarschall wore oval cloth badges with an emblem consisting of a gold-yellow wreath of oak leaves with a gold-yellow Luftwaffe eagle and Swastika (not illustrated). The rank badge for the field marshal had the addition of crossed batons at the base of the wreath.

These rank badges were sewn on to an oblong of cloth that usually matched the colour of the flying suit. The badges were worn in pairs, one on each upper arm of the flying suit.

9 Rank badge for Unterfeldwebel and Luftwaffe Fähnrich used on the winter flying suit.

10 Rank badge for Leutnant as used on the summer flying suit.

11 Rank badge for Major as used on the summer flying suit.

12 Rank badge for Generalmajor as used on the winter flying suit.

Flying suit rank badges existed for other branches of the German Air Force. Administration officials, Corps of Air Force Engineers, and the Navigational Corps of the Luftwaffe all wore rank badges of a special design representing their own particular ranks. These have not been illustrated here.

Plate 50. Arm and Breast Badges

Navy Trade, Proficiency and Rank Badges

Division and watch strips were worn by German seamen, petty officers and senior petty officers serving aboard larger ships in the German Navy. They were worn on either arm of the naval uniform as a single strip or in pairs or in groups of three strips depending on their Division.

The badges consisted of strips of red ribbon worn, on both the dark navy-blue and the white summer uniform, high up on either arm depending on whether starboard or port watch. When worn on the right upper arm, just below the wearers shoulder seam, they indicated that the person was on Starboard Watch, one strip for the 1st, two strips for the 3rd, and three strips for the 5th Division. When worn on the left upper arm, just below the wearer's shoulder seam, they indicated that the person was on Port Watch, one strip for the 2nd Division, two strips for the 4th Division, and three strips for the 6th Division.

1 Starboard 1st Division or port 2nd Division watch strip for use on the dark navy-blue rig.

2 Port 4th Division or starboard 3rd Division watch strips for use on the white working rig and white uniform.

3 The immediate junior staff personnel of the German Naval Commander-in-Chief wore a special distinguishing badge. The dark navy-blue circular cloth badge displayed, embroidered in coloured threads, a German Naval admiral's flag flying from a yellow staff. The badge was worn by the staff personnel on the left upper arm above all other badges on all forms of naval uniform dress except the greatcoat.

4 The officer of the watch identification badge. This oval-shaped, gilded metal badge was worn by watch-keeping officers in the button-hole of the left lapel of the frock-coat, in the second buttonhole from the top on the greatcoat, just above the top button on the left side of the blue reefer jacket and in the buttonhole of the left breast pocket on the white summer tunic. It was not the personal property of the officer but was passed from one watch officer to the next whenever one relieved the other. An arm band of white material with a machine-woven coloured representation of this badge was also worn, intended to take the place of the metal badge.

5 Naval NCOs preparatory school badge. Not a great deal is known about this badge. It is possible that it was worn by Naval pupils attending engine-room artificer courses for promotion from ordinary seaman to petty officer and chief petty officer. The purpose of the gilt chevron is uncertain. The exact manner of wear is unknown. The date of its introduction is also not known. However, if the supposition that this type of badge could have existed for seamen at engineer-room artificer instruction schools can be proved to be correct, why is it that other badges of a similar pattern for other possible courses have not so far been recorded?

Naval Officers Branch of Service Sleeve Badges (Laufbahn Abzeichen)

These small oval badges with their hand embroidered gilt thread motifs were worn on both forearms on the Naval officers frock-coat, the blue reefer jacket and the officer's blue mess kit jacket.

6 Line officers represented by a five-pointed gold star.

7 Engineer officer.

8 Defensive ordnance officer has the motif of a mine.

9 Administrative officer.

10 Gunnery officer represented by an emblem of a flaming winged shell.

These branch-of-service badges, including others not illustrated, were worn above the sleeve rings of rank displayed on Naval officers uniform clothing.

Naval cadet branch-of-service badges (of intended branch) were similar to regular officers' branch-of-service badges. Of the same size and quality of manufacture, they were distinguished by having an edging to the oval badge of gold-coloured strands of fine twisted cording representing coiled ropes. Naval officer cadets – or aspirants wore these badges in place of the standard naval trade badge as worn by naval ratings. They were worn on all forms of uniform clothing except fatigue dress and the greatcoat. They were produced in gold on dark navy-blue for normal use and in cornflower blue on white for wear on the white uniform. The Naval cadets intended branch-of-service badge was worn on both forearms in the same position as that used for regular officers branch-of-service badges, with the obvious exception that there were no sleeve rank rings used.

11 The badge illustrated is for a Naval cadet undergoing training in naval construction.

Sleeve Insignia for the Corps of Civilian Naval Officials attached to the Navy for the duration of the war, and civilian naval officials.

12 Civilian Naval administrative official of the highest group attached to the Navy for the duration of the war.

13 Civilian Naval technical official, advanced group.

14 Civilian Naval legal official of the highest group.

15 Civilian Naval official, highest group of instructors.

16 Civilian Naval pharmacist of the highest group attached to the Navy for the duration of the war.

All civilian Naval officials were distinguished from Regular Naval officers by the silver-coloured buttons and insignia they wore. The distinction made between those civilian naval officials attached to the Navy for the duration of the war and civilian Naval officials was that the former had the addition of silver twisted cording around the edge to their oval-shaped sleeve badges. Both types of officials badges were worn on the forearms of the Naval officials uniform tunics.

German Naval service department badges for ratings were worn by all seamen who had completed their preliminary training. They were worn on the upper left arm above rating insignia, if worn. Their purpose was to indicate the wearer's department of service.

17 Signals rating badge (flags show the letter 'c'), (Signal-Laufbahn).

18 Carpenter's badge (Zimmermanns-Laufbahn).

19 Hydrographer's badge (Vermessungs-steuermanns-Laufbahn).

20 Defence ordnance Artificer (Sperrme-chaniker-Laufbahn).

21 Gunlayer rating badge – marine-artillery (Marineartillerie-Laufbahn).

When the department of service badge was worn directly above rank chevrons, or when the department of service emblem was incorporated into the chevron badge, as illustrated below, these indicated that the wearer was an able seaman or a leading seaman.

22 Able seaman. A rank badge of issue quality of yellow-coloured felt chevron.

23 Qualified radio telegraphist leading seaman with four and a half years seniority. The badge was of dress uniform quality chevrons of gilt braiding, often privately purchased by the wearer.

24 First class leading seaman bandsman with eight years seniority. Chevrons as worn on the white summer uniform.

Plate 51. Arm Badges

German Navy and Marine Artillery Trade, Proficiency and Rank Badges

Petty officers (Maat) and senior petty officers (Obermaat) in the German Navy were distinguished by wearing arm badges bearing a sea anchor with, in the case of the senior petty officers version, the addition of a chevron. These badges, which not only showed the wearer's rank but also his particular trade, were produced in two qualities and came in two colour combinations. For use on the dark navy-blue rig the oval arm badges had their design either machine-embroidered in yellow silk threads on to a flat oval badge of navy-blue badge cloth or they were produced in gilded metal mounted on to an oval of dark navy-blue cloth backed with a metal backing plate. This later type was used on their uniform jacket and the pea jacket. The badges used by petty officers and senior petty officers on their white summer rig had the same design of badge as for their navy-blue rig – whatever that was – but in place of the yellow-coloured emblem the design was now worked in royal blue cotton threads on to an oval of white cloth. All badges were worn on the upper left arm.

1 Boatswain petty officer (Steuermanns-maat), shown here as a gilt metal badge.

2 Petty officer (Bootsmanns-maat), shown here as an example of the yellow silk embroidered badge for everyday wear.

3 Writer petty officer (Schreibersmaat).

4 Sick berth petty officer (Sanitätsmaat).

5 Radio telegraphist petty officer (Funk-maat), summer uniform.

6 Defence ordnance artificer petty officer (Speerwaffen-Mech. Maat).

7 Aircraft spotter petty officer (Flugmelde-maat).

8 Chief petty officer armourer (Oberfeuer-werksmaat).

Lower deck ratings with specialist skills wore specialist badges on the left sleeve of their naval uniforms below their rank badges and Laufbahn badges. These specialist badges were very distinctive, having their various emblems worked in red silks on to either dark blue

71 Ships Writer Leading Seaman Walther Gerhold who received his Knights Cross for his one-man submarine torpedo attack against an Allied cruiser, part of the Normandy invasion fleet (22 July 1944). The Writers trade badge (Schreiber Laufbahn) shown here forms an integral part of the two chevron Obergefreiter sleeve badge.

badge cloth or white cloth for summer rig.

9 Underwater detector specialist (Unterwasserhorcher).

10 Small calibre anti-aircraft director (Waffenleitvormann für Fla.).

11 2nd class motor engineer (Motorlehrgang II).

12 Anti-aircraft gun commander (Geschutzführer II).

13 Assistant torpedo instructor (Torpedohilfslehrer).

14 1st class electrical artificer (Elektro-Maschinen-Lehrgang I).

15 Gunlayer 'E' with six years seniority (Geschutzführer – sechs-jährige Bewährung).

16 Submarine and salvage diver (U-Boots und Bergungstaucher).

Personnel of the German marine-artillery and lower-deck ratings undergoing training at Naval shore-based establishments were provided with field-grey clothing. To a limited extent these marine-artillery troops were entitled to wear trade and speciality badges. These badges were confined to the expertise and skills required of these troops. Where they applied, these badges had the same design of emblem as those used by the sea-going members of the German Navy, the only difference being that the background colour to the badges was field-grey and not dark navy-blue.

17 Driver petty officer (Kraftfahrmaat).

18 Marine-artillery rating trade badge (Marineartillerie-Laufbahn).

19 Writer (Schreiber-Laufbahn).

20 Range taker (Entfernungsmesser mit Fla. E Messausbildung).

Plate 52. Arm Badges

Customs Officials Sleeve Chevrons

1 Sleeve chevron worn by leading supervisory Customs officials.

2 Sleeve chevron for Customs officials with special employment.

3 Sleeve chevron for Customs detachment leaders.

All three types of chevrons were worn on the left cuff of the Customs officials tunic and greatcoat. They were introduced in January 1939.

Government Administration Officials Sleeve Badges

A very distinctive feature of both the dark blue-black Government officials uniform as well as the grey service uniform was the large sleeve eagle badge. Worn on the left forearm the four basic designs were based on the four

72 The Imperial Japanese Foreign Minister, His Excellency Matsuoka taking his leave of Foreign Minister von Ribbentrop (right foreground) on 30 March 1941 at the end of his official visit to Berlin. Von Ribbentrop wears the very special arm badge peculiar to him as head of the Foreign Office.

pay groups. The four designs were further sub-divided by the addition of 'stars'.

4 Sleeve badge for ap.Regierungsinspektor, Group IV officials of the lowest pay grade.

5 Sleeve badge for Regierungsoberinspektor, Group IV officials of pay grade A4b1.

6 Sleeve badge for Regierungsamtmann, Group III officials of pay grade A3b.

7 Sleeve badge for Regierungsdirektor, Group III officials, pay grade not known.

8 Sleeve badge for Ministerialrat, Group II officials, pay grade A1a.

9 Sleeve badge for Ministerialdirigent, Group I officials, pay grade B6.

10 Sleeve badge for Ministerialdirektor, Group I officials, pay grade B5.

11 Sleeve badge for Staatssekretär, Group I officials, pay grade B3a.

12 Sleeve badge for Reichsminister, Group I officials, pay grade not known.

Plate 53. Arm Badges

RLB, Werkschutz, DRK, SHD-LSW and TeNo

1 Reichsluftschutzbund (RLB) arm eagle emblem, machine-woven quality.

2 Reichsluftschutzbund arm eagle emblem, hand-embroidered quality. Both these items, which were the same badge, despite their differences in quality, were worn on the left cuff of the RLB (National Air Protection League) uniform tunic just above the cuff facing. The exact purpose of the single (no. 1) and double (no. 2) silver braid chevrons worn below the RLB eagle is unknown. They may well have indicated that the wearer held a particular position of responsibility. It is unlikely that they represented rank insignia as RLB ranks were indicated by the use of collar patches and shoulder straps (see Plate 17). The most obvious explanation is that the chevrons indicated length of service.

3 Arm badge worn by members of the Factory

Protection Service (Werkschutz) on the upper left sleeve of their tunics and greatcoats. The emblem represented a Nazi shield protecting a stylized factory.

4 Sleeve badge worn by male or female doctors. Thought to have been worn on the lower left sleeve.

5 Deutsche Rote Kreuz (DRK) district unit sleeve triangle. Worn by female personnel on the upper right arm of nurses' clothing, working dress, and tunic. Usually these badges were machine-woven in white grey cotton threads. However, silver-aluminium hand-embroidered badges existed. It is doubtful if these represented a more senior rank, but rather were privately purchased in preference to the machine-woven issue items.

6 Sleeve badge thought to have been for use by qualified medical specialists, probably volunteers in the DRK. Worn on the left forearm.

73 Nurse and matron from the DRK (the German Red Cross) treating lightly injured civilians after a daylight raid on the German town of Dusseldorf (21 July 1943).

170

7 DRK emblem worn on upper right arm by, at least, male Red Cross uniformed personnel.

Personnel of the five branches of the Sicherheits und Hilfsdienst – the Security and Help Service (SHD) – wore specialist badges on their left upper arm and occasionally on the left forearm of their uniforms. These specialist badges indicated the type of qualification the wearer held. All badges were machine-woven in coloured silks. The badges were introduced during 1941.

8 White Gothic letter 'F' on a red oval with green edging. Sleeve badge worn by SHD Fire Fighting personnel (Feuerlöschdienst).

9 White Gothic letter 'J' on brown oval with green edging. Badge worn by SHD Repair and Maintenance personnel (Instandsetzungsdienst).

10 White Gothic letter 'V' on lilac oval with green edging. Sleeve badge worn by SHD Veterinary Service personnel (Veterinärdienst).

11 Black Gothic letter 'G' on yellow oval with green edging. Badge worn by members of SHD decontamination squads (Entgiftungsdienst für im Gasspüren und Entgiften Ausgebildete.)

12 White serpent and staff emblem on pale blue oval with green edging. Badge worn by SHD medical personnel (Sänitätsdienst).

TeNo trade badges 'Dienstabzeichen' were smallish machine-woven silk badges, with their design of a white emblem or Gothic type letters set inside a white cogwheel all on a black circular silk backing.

13 Allgemeiner Dienst (AD) badge for general branch service personnel. The branch colour is green.

14 Luftschutz-Dienst (LD) badge for civil air-defence branch personnel. The branch colour is red.

15 Verwaltungsdienst (V) badge for administrative branch personnel.

16 Arzt-und Sanitätspersonal badge for medical branch personnel (doctors and medical orderlies).

17 Musikzugführer badge for TeNo musicians.

18 Technicher Dienst (TD) badge for technical branch personnel. The branch colour is blue.

19 Bereitschafts-Dienst (BD) badge for Emergency Service personnel. The branch colour is orange-yellow.

20 Arm badge for TeNo staff at, and graduates from the TeNo Reich Training School. Worn on the upper left arm of the dark blue-black tunic and greatcoat above the TeNo arm eagle badge (see Plate 2, no. 10).

Plate 54. Arm Badges

RKS, RAB, Reichspost, DFO, Deutsche Jägerschaft, OT Arm Badges, Rank Chevrons and Trade Badges

1 An 'RKS' arm badge. Little is known about this badge or the organisation it represented. The initial letters are thought to stand for Reich Kusten Schiffe – National Coastal Shipping – related to the Railways. The badge was worn on the upper left arm of a double-breasted jacket of dark navy-blue material with gilt buttons.

The maintenance, repair, and administration of the German Autobahn system was, in 1937, undertaken by persons attached to the German National Railways. In 1940 a special uniform was introduced for the Directors of Autobahn Work Camps. Construction squad overseers wore a military style uniform in blue-grey cloth worn with a light blue shirt and black tie. They wore an arm band with the legend '1.Lagerführer' or '2.Lagerführer'. This item, where appropriate, had the addition of strands of silver braiding of varying width depending on the wearer's years of service with the construction unit. A band of silver braid 1 cm wide indicated three years service, a 2 cm wide braid stood for five years' service, and eight years was rewarded by the use of a 3 cm wide braid.

In 1942 a completely new system of uniforms and insignia was introduced for use by three types of Autobahn officials, control officers known as Strassenmeister (Street Masters), all drivers (Kraftfahrer), and auxiliaries (Amtsgehilfe und Pförtner).

2 Arm badge worn by senior drivers (Fahrmeister) and head auxiliaries (Botenmeister) only. (For RAB officers rank insignia, see Plate 21, nos 17 to 22).

3 Arm badge worn by RAB-Strassenmeister. Assistants to the Reichs Autobahn street masters wore the same type of badge but with a half wreath of four oak leaves. Both badges were worn on the RAB service tunic on the upper left arm.

4 Arm badge for Post Office personnel who were not qualified as full Post Office functionaries.

74 German Falconry officials collecting money on the streets of Berlin in aid of the Wartime Winter Relief Work (W.H.W.) on 4 November 1939. Both the Falconry arm badge and the arm band are shown.

5 Arm badge for use by female Post Office personnel, worn on upper left arm as part of the introduction of the new uniform items in 1940. (See also Plate 35, no. 14.)

6 Arm badge for uniformed officials of the Deutsche Falkenorden (Order of German Falconers), a sub-division of the Deutsche Jägerschaft. (See also Plate 35, no. 15.) It was worn on upper left arm.

7 Arm badge for uniformed members of the Deutsche Jägerschaft (German Hunter's Association) from the rank of Hegeringsführer (Local Surveyor) to Landesjägermeister (Provincial Leader). It too was worn on the upper left arm.

8 Arm badge for senior uniformed rank of the Deutsche Jägerschaft for the rank of Reichsjägermeister (National Hunting Master). It was also worn on the upper left arm.

9 Org. Todt rank chevron for rank of OT-Vorarbeiter and OT-Stammsanitäter, worn in conjunction with plain OT collar patches.

10 Org. Todt rank chevrons for rank of OT-Meister and OT-Obersanitäter, worn in conjunction with plain OT collar patches.

11 Org. Todt rank chevrons for rank of OT-Obermeister and OT-Hauptsanitäter, worn in conjunction with plain OT collar patches.

These chevrons were part of the new Organisation Todt insignia introduced in 1943 (for other details see Plate 19).

Organisation Todt speciality and service insignia introduced in April 1942 were intended to recognize the various skills and qualifications of their work personnel and OT Leaders.

12 Speciality badge for Organisation Todt bricklayer-mason (Maurer).

13 Speciality badge for Organisation Todt carpenter (Zimmermann).

14 Speciality badge for Organisation Todt scaffolder or possibly specialist worker in iron work used in re-inforced concrete casting (Eisenflechter).

15 Specialist badge for Organisation Todt machinist (Maschinist).

16 Specialist badge for Organisation Todt driver (Kraftfahrer).

All Organisation Todt speciality badges were worn on the right forearm.

17 Unestablished badge, probably a specialist badge which may have been for a surveyor, the design probably being of a plumb-line bob, or for a joiner, the design probably representing a wood chisel cutting into a block of wood.

18 Unestablished badge, also probably a specialist badge for a mechanic.

19 Service badge for Organisation Todt musicians.

20 Service badge for Organisation Todt medical attendant.

21 Service badge for Organisation Todt signaller.

All Organisation Todt service badges were worn on the left forearm.

Plate 55. Arm Badges

Organisation Todt, Deutsche Arbeitsfront, and Transportflotte Speer Rank Insignia

1 Organisation Todt rank insignia for ranks of OT-Vorarbeiter and OT-Stammsanitäter. It was worn on the work uniform on upper right arm.

2 Organisation Todt rank insignia, worn on the work uniform on the upper right arm.

3 Organisation Todt rank insignia, worn on the upper right arm of the work uniform.

4 DAF rank insignia for DAF-Rottenführer.

5 DAF rank insignia for DAF-Werkscharmeister.

6 DAF rank insignia for DAF-Ortsobmann.

7 DAF rank insignia for DAF-Kreiswerkscharführer.

8 DAF rank insignia for DAF-Gauobmann.

All five of the above DAF rank bars and chevrons, together with the other seven ranks not illustrated, were worn on the upper right arm.

Rank chevrons worn by 'seamen' and 'petty officers' of the Transportflotte Speer. These chevrons were worn in conjunction with certain collar patches for individual ranks of the Transport Flotilla 'Speer'. (See Plate 21, nos 1, 2 and 3.)

9 Matrosen.

10 Vollmatrose.

75 A delegation of members of the DAF (German Labour Front) marching through the streets of Rome. Various DAF rank chevrons can be seen.

11 Hauptmatrose.

12 Unterbootsmann. Chevron worn in conjunction with collar patches (Plate 21, no. 1).

13 Bootsmann. Chevrons worn in conjunction with collar patches (Plate 21, no. 2).

14 Oberbootsmann. Chevrons worn in conjunction with collar patches (Plate 21, no. 3).

Plate 56. Arm Badges

Uniform clothing for personnel of the German National Railway system underwent a number of changes during the period 1933 to 1945, but even more changes were made upon the various items of insignia worn on these uniforms.

The German Railway cuff-titles already dealt with (see Plate 29, nos 3 to 6), and which were worn in conjunction with an arm eagle (see Plate 1, no. 9), were very short lived. Introduced in February 1941, these items were replaced in September of the same year by a new system of arm badges. These arm badges combined the German National Emblem set above the name of the railway division and the initial letters of the particular railway directorate to which the wearer belonged. The German National Railway system, which together with the railway systems of the annexed territories and occupied countries were divided up into Railway Divisions usually based on large and important marshalling yards or railway areas. The Railway Division badges were worn on the left upper arm of the uniform tunic and working jackets. The four sets of initial letters stood for:

RBD – Reichsbahndirektion (State Railway Directorate);

RVD – Reichsverkersdirektion (State Traffic Directorate);

HVD – Hauptverkehrsdirektion (Central Traffic Directorate);

WVD – Wehrmacht Verkehrsdirektion (Armed Forces Traffic Directorate).

76 Three members of the German State Railways based in Paris. The official with the duelling scars wears the Reichsbahn arm badge emblem for the Armed Forces Traffic Directorate Paris. This photograph precisely illustrates the complete mix of uniform items, caps and cap insignia, collar patches and shoulder straps that continued to be worn seemingly at all times throughout the period covered by this book.

Reichsbahn

1 Reichsbahndirektion Nürnberg (Southern Germany).

2 Reichsbahndirektion Villach (Austria).

3 Ostbahn, worn by railway personnel operating in the Eastern occupied territories, the 'Generalgovernment', and based on Cracow (Krakow).

4 Reichsverkehrsdirektion Dnjepropetrowsk (an important railway administrative centre in the Ukraine).

5 Hauptverkehrsdirektion Brüssel (capital of Belgium).

6 Wehrmacht Verkehrsdirektion Paris (capital of France).

Many more of these badges existed, all of exactly the same design, size, and colouring, only their railway divisional names and directorate letters being different.

Reichsbahn Trade Badges

There were ten German Railway trade badges, correctly referred to as 'branch and specialist badges' (Sparten und Fachabzeichen); eight are illustrated here. All were machine-embroidered in yellow threads on to a circular cloth badge of black material. These badges were worn on the left forearm of the dark blue tunic.

7 Badge for wagon supervisor (Wagenaufseher), Wagon Master (Wagenmeister), senior wagon master (Oberwagenmeister), and wagen works master (Wagenwerkmeister).

8 Badge for railcar driver (Triebwagenführer), and senior railcar driver (Obertriebwagenführer).

9 Badge for shunting supervisor (Rangieraufseher), shunting foreman (Rangiermeister), and senior shunting foreman (Oberrangiermeister).

10 Badge for plate gang leader (Rottenführer), plate gang supervisor (Rottenaufseher), plate gang foreman (Rottenmeister), and senior plate gang foreman (Oberrotten-

meister).

11 Badge for a driver of rapid travel vehicle, and driver and mate of lorries for public use (Fahrer der Schnellreisenwagen und Fahrer und Begleiter der Lastkraftwagen für den öffentlichen Güterverkehr).

12 Badge for train conductor (Zugschaffner), senior train conductor (Oberzugschaffner), train guard (Zugführer), senior train guard (Oberzugführer), loading conductor (Fahrladeschaffner), senior loading conductor (Fahrladeoberschaffner), railcar conductor (Triebwagenschaffner), and senior railcar conductor (Triebwagenoberschaffner).

13 Badge for National Railways technical inspector (Technischer Reichsbahninspektor), National Railways senior technical inspector (Technischer Reichsbahnoberinspektor), and National Railways supervisor – in outdoors technical construction services (Reichsbahnamtmann – in bautechnischer Aussendienst).

14 Badge for senior machinist (Obermaschinist), works leader, and operating works leader (Werkführer – Betriebswerkführer), works master and operating works master (Werkmeister – Betriebswerkmeister), senior operating works master (Betriebsoberwerkmeister), technical railway inspector (technischer Reichsbahninspektor), senior technical railways inspector (technischer Reichsbahnoberinspektor), and National Railways supervisor (Reichsbahnamtmann).

Railway Protection Police Speciality Badges

Early in 1941 new uniforms and uniform regulations were introduced for all ranks of the Bahnschutze. The colour of these new uniforms was officially described as 'blau meliert' but it became commonly referred to as 'horizon blue'. The introduction of new insignia was very complete, with new cuff-titles (see Plate 27, nos 2–5) and rank insignia in the form of new shoulder straps and collar patches (see Plate 14) and a range of fifteen speciality

77 Two members of the Railway Protection Police – the Bahnschutzpolizei. Both wear an un-identified arm badge as illustrated on Plate 56.

arm badges. Illustrated here are seven of these items. All were worn on the right forearm of the tunic just above the turn back cuff.

15 Music Leader (Musikführer), a lyre hand-embroidered in silver-aluminium threads.

16 Staff district leader (Stabsbezirksführer), a 'star' within a wreath also embroidered in silver-aluminium threads. The badge for senior district leader (Oberbezirksführer) – not illustrated – had just the 'star' without the wreath. These two positions were administrative appointments, not ranks.

17 Weapons specialist for other ranks (Waffenmeistergehilfe) For these personnel the badge was machine-embroidered in white cotton thread. For weapons specialist officers (not illustrated) the crossed rifles were in aluminium thread and for weapons specialist officer instructors at Bahnschutze Schools (not illustrated) the crossed rifles were surrounded with a wreath, all worked in silver-aluminium threads.

18 Administration personnel (Verwaltungsführer) up to the rank of Bzp.Oberzugführer, as illustrated, machine-embroidered in white cotton thread. For Administrative personnel from the rank of Bzp-Abteilungsführer and above (not illustrated) the same device of a letter 'V' was hand-embroidered in silver-aluminium thread.

19 Dog handler specialist trainer (Hunde-abrichtwart der Reichsbahndirektionen) from each of the railway directorates. This badge, as illustrated, shows the head of an Alsatian, in red threads with a silver piping to the edge of the badge. Dog handlers (Hundeführer) had badges machine-woven in white cotton with blue piping, and national dog trainers had badges hand-embroidered in silver-aluminium with silver-corded edging (last two not illustrated).

20 Driver (Kraftfahrer) up to the rank of Bzp-Oberzugführer machine-embroidered in white cotton thread. Drivers from the rank of Bzp-Abteilungsführer and above wore badges with the vehicle steering wheel hand-embroidered in silver-aluminium thread (not illustrated).

21 Bahnschutzepolizei Arzt – Railway Protection Police doctor. Life-rune hand-embroidered on to dark blue backing cloth. Medical personnel up to the rank of Bzp-Oberzugführer had the same emblem machine-woven in white cotton thread on to an oval of 'horizon blue' cloth and for medical personnel from the rank of Bzp-Abteilungsführer had the same emblem hand-embroidered in silver-aluminium thread also on 'horizon blue' cloth, these last two badges not being illustrated.

22 Unidentified arm badge. From contemporary photographic evidence this badge can be seen being worn by armed Bahnschutz personnel, on the upper left arm of the tunics that were in use prior to those introduced in 1941.

Plate 57. Arm Badges

Police Formation Arm and Breast Badges, Fire Police Trade Badges

July 1936 saw the introduction of new uniforms for all ranks of the Schutzpolizei (Protection Police), Gendarmerie (Rural Police), Gemeindepolizei (Local Municipal Police), Gendarmerie-Bereitschaften (Rural Stand-By Police) and the Wasserschutzpolizei (Water Protection Police). The new Police Eagle arm badge was a feature of these, and later, uniforms. They were produced in three qualities according to the wearer's rank and the design in the range of colours corresponding to the Police branch colour (for lower ranks) and with the badge cloth colour to match the colour of the wearer's uniform.

1 Arm badge worn, as were all Police Eagle arm badges, on the upper left arm by Police General Officers. Before the latter part of 1942 Police generals were ranked as Generalmajor, Generalleutnant, and General der Polizei. After 1942 their rank terms were changed to SS/Police style and an extra rank was introduced. They were: SS-Brigadeführer und Generalmajor der Polizei, SS-Gruppenführer und Generalleutnant der Polizei, SS-Obergruppenführer und General der Polizei, and SS-Oberstgruppenführer und Generaloberst der Polizei. All pre- and post-1942 generals wore the same pattern of gold bullion hand-embroidered badge.

2 Arm badge as worn by an officer of the Berlin Schutzpolizei. The emblem was hand-worked in silver-aluminium threads for all officer ranks from Leutnant up to Oberst for all Police service with the exception of the Wasserschutzpolizei. However, Werkfeuerwehr officers never wore the name of a city or locality, just the eagle.

3 Arm badge as worn by police personnel up to the rank of Leutnant from the Frankfurt-am-Main Schutzpolizei.

4 Arm badge for lower rank Gendarmerie policemen based on Klagenfurt.

5 Machine-woven arm badge for lower rank personnel of the Waterways Protection Police. The use of yellow had nothing to do with rank. Yellow was the branch colour allotted to Waterways Protection Police. Wasserschutzpolizei officers wore the same badge but hand-embroidered in yellow silks and Generals in gold bullion threads.

6 Arm badge for lower rank personnel of the Cologne city Municipal police.

7 Arm badge for lower ranks of the Hamburg Traffic Police. This badge was worn on the distinctive white jacket used for traffic duty.

8 Arm badge for an officer of the Fire Police. (*The illustration should not show 'Gudow': Fire Police officers' arm badges bore no name.*)

9 Arm badge as worn by lower rank members of the Collinghorst Fire Police.

10 Arm badge as worn by an officer in charge of a fire fighting detachment attached to a large industrial factory.

11 Arm badge as worn by lower rank fire police personnel acting as part of a fire fighting unit attached to a large factory complex.

12 The 'Kreuz des Südens' – the Southern Cross or Cross of the South – sleeve badge was a 'Tradition Badge' worn by personnel of selected German Police units chosen to perpetuate the 'traditions' of German Police formations that had served in some of Germany's former overseas colonies. The badge was worn on the left forearm 1 cm above the cuff.

A series of five new badges were introduced in November 1942 for use by personnel of German Volunteer Fire Police units. All had silver-aluminium embroidery on dark blue-

78 An Oberwachtmeister of the Berlin Schutzpolizei distributing Axis national flags to onlookers waiting to see the arrival of the Italian Foreign Minister Count Ciano on 27 September 1940.

black uniform cloth.

13 Kraftfahr (driver).

14 Maschinisten mit Führerschein (machinist with driving licence).

15 Kraftspreitzenmaschinist (fire engine driver operator).

16 Unterkreisführer (under-district leader).

17 Stellv.Kreisführer (deputy district leader).

18 The Sig-runen der SS breast badge.

Authorised by order of the Führer and Reichs-chancellor on 16 January 1937 to be worn on the Order Police uniform, this runic badge in hand-embroidered silver-aluminium thread on a backing of green uniform material was worn in the middle of the left half of the left breast tunic pocket, 1 cm below the base of the breast pocket, by all Police who had once been members of the Allgemeine-SS.

178

Length of Service Chevrons and Sleeve Rings

Plate 58. Arm Badges

'Old Fighters' Chevrons

The date 30 January 1933 was an important one in the historical calendar of the Nazi Party. It was on this day that Adolf Hitler, until then the leader of the Nazi Party, became the Chancellor of Germany. It was an important watershed in the history of the German National Socialist movement. The party membership referred to it as the 'Seizure of Power'.

The date was also chosen to mark the divi-

sion between what the Nazis looked upon as their years of struggle and the period when their movement had achieved political respectability.

Membership of the Nazi Party and any of its affiliated uniformed formations was on a voluntary basis. However, to have become a Nazi Party member prior to 30 January 1933 was a decision taken out of conviction and at real personal risk. Membership after that date was without risk, deemed by many Germans to be expedient, and in many cases it was a positive

79 The NSKK Old Fighters chevron seen here being worn by the NSKK officer fourth from left in the front row.

179

advantage, as the sharp increase in membership enrolment testified.

Membership before 1933 could, and often did cost individuals their jobs. Active members risked injury from political opponents and, very often, the Police. While the Nazis themselves excelled at intimidation, torture, beatings and killings, there were many hundreds of instances of Nazis being maimed, killed, or murdered by other political extremists either in street brawls, at political meetings, or by being 'ambushed' or hunted down.

Thus, in order to distinguish those persons who were classed as 'Old Fighters' – 'Alte Kämpfer' – a simple 'winkle' or chevron introduced during 1933 was worn on the upper right arm of the brown shirt, tunic, jacket, and greatcoat. It varied in colour between different formations but was usually a 1 cm-wide braid either stitched directly on to the sleeve of a garment or on to a backing of cloth that matched the tunic or coat upon which it was worn.

1 NSFK, as worn on the NSFK blue-grey uniform. For wear on the NSFK brown shirt the chevron would be mounted on brown cloth.

2 SA chevron.

3 Chevron for former members of the Stahlhelm serving in the SA. Worn on the left forearm above the cuff.

4 NSKK, worn on the NSKK brown shirt, and khaki tan tunic.

5 Marine-NSKK worn on the navy-blue tunic and greatcoat.

6 German Police, wearer having been a member of the NSDAP before 30 January 1933.

7 Worn by members of the Allgemeine-SS and later the Waffen-SS who had joined the SS, the NSDAP, or any one of the Party affiliated formations before 30 January 1933. It was also worn by Austrian nationals who had volunteered and had held SS membership in the Austrian SS before 12 February 1938 – the date when Austria was 'incorporated' into the Greater German Reich. It was also worn by former members of the German Armed Forces and the German Police up to 25 July 1935 when, for them, it was replaced by the following pattern, no. 8.

8 Chevron with star (pip) introduced on 25 July 1935 and worn by members of the Allgemeine-SS and later the Waffen-SS, who had been former members of the German Police or the Armed Forces before 30 January 1933.

SA Length of Service Sleeve Rings

The SA went one step further than any other Party formation in that, in addition to wearing 'Old Fighters' chevrons, they introduced a series of sleeve rings worn to indicate the members exact length of unbroken service in the SA

80 Hans Hieronymus, General Secretary of the German branch of the FIBA (International Federation of Amateur Boxing), wearing General-SS uniform complete with the SS Alte Kampfer Winkle.

81 SA-Obergruppenführer Wilhelm Scheppmann saluting a departing German Army General. The rings worn around the sleeves indicate that Scheppmann had been a member of the SA anytime from 1 January 1925 to 31 December 1925.

or the Marine-SA prior to 30 January 1933.

These sleeve rings were worn in various combinations of narrow and/or wide bands of grey-aluminium braiding sewn on to the cuffs of their uniform jackets, brown shirts, and greatcoats. The principle was that the more sleeve rings worn, the earlier the wearer had joined up and the longer his service. They were worn by all ranks eligible to wear them.

	Time period	Sleeve ring details
9	1.1.25 to 31.12.25	two 12 mm, two 4 mm
10	1.1.26 to 31.12.26	two 12 mm, one 4 mm
11	1.1.27 to 31.12.27	two 12 mm
12	1.1.28 to 31.12.28	one 12 mm, two 4 mm
13	1.1.29 to 31.12.29	one 12 mm, one 4 mm
14	1.1.30 to 31.12.30	one 12 mm
15	1.1.31 to 31.12.31	two 4 mm
16	1.1.32 to 30.1.33	one 4 mm

Foreign Volunteers Arm Shields

Within the ranks of the German Armed Forces, including the Waffen-SS and certain front-line Police Regiments, there served as 'Volunteers' many hundreds of thousands of non-German personnel. There were two distinct groups of 'Volunteers', those from the Western European countries and those from the Eastern territories. Generally speaking there were two distinct types of 'Volunteers'. There were those that volunteered out of a sense of conviction to fight alongside the German Armed Forces against what they saw as the 'Bolshevik threat', and there were those that joined 'Volunteer' units in order to escape inevitable death in the dreadful conditions of their prisoner of war camps.

Contingents of these 'Volunteers' were formed into military units of varying size, depending on the strength of their troops, but conveniently called 'Legions'. Other 'Volunteers' served with German Naval units and Air Force squadrons, either as integral parts of the German units or as separate volunteer units serving alongside the German units. The German authorities issued these volunteer units with clothing and equipment of the same pattern as worn by their own troops. They were distinguished, however, by wearing certain items of insignia, the most common being the Foreign Volunteer Arm Shields. Certain of these Volunteer Troops when not actually fighting for the Germans wore the uniform of their parent force, especially when they returned to their country of origin. The rest, having no indigenous uniform of their own to don, would either continue wearing their German garb or put on civilian clothing.

Plate 59. Arm Shields

Foreign Volunteers Arm Shields

1 A blue-white-red tricolour arm shield surmounted by the legend 'FRANCE', worn on the upper right arm of the German Army uniform tunics and greatcoat by the members of the Légion Volontaire Français contra la Bolshévisme. The French volunteers served in Infanterie-Regiment 638 France.

82 Generalleutnant Freiherr von Gablenz (right) talking to officers and men of the French Volunteer Legion.

2 A black rampant lion, the historical emblem of the Flemings set on a gold yellow shield surmounted with the name 'FLANDERN' (Flanders). This pattern of BeVo quality shield was issued to Flemish-speaking volunteers serving in a battalion strength 'Legion' alongside the German Army. After only nine months the

Flemings were transferred into the Waffen-SS and the emblem was probably never worn. The shield was to be worn on the upper left arm.

3 A black-yellow-red tricolour arm shield representing the ancient and national colours of Belgium and surmounted by the name 'WALLONIE' (Walloon) was worn by French-speaking Belgium volunteers under the leadership of Leon Degrell in a 'Legion' formed from Walloons. Shield worn on the upper left arm of their German Army and later Waffen-SS uniforms.

4 A red-yellow-red horizontal tricolour, the nationalist colours of Franco's Spain surmounted with the Spanish for Spain, 'ESPAÑA', was the arm shield worn by the personnel of the Spanish Blue Division (Division Azul). The Blue Division, so named after the colour of the blue shirts worn by the Falangist volunteers, was given the German military designation of Infanterie-Division 250. The arm shield was worn on the upper right arm of both the German Army and Spanish Army uniforms. Spanish volunteers in the German Luftwaffe wore the same arm shield on their Air Force uniforms.

5 Croatian volunteers serving with the German Army (Infanterie-Division 369), Navy, and Air Force wore German military uniforms but they were distinguished from their German comrades by wearing an arm shield on the left upper arm of their uniforms. The red and white chequer board design of the shield was taken from the arms of Croatia and was surmounted by the word 'HRVATSKA', Serbo-Croatian for Croatia. Another arm shield existed for wear by these same personnel which was of the same red and white design but had the word 'KROATIEN', the German spelling of Croatia, along the top.

6 Arm shield for Ukrainian volunteers. The colours of yellow and light blue are the national colours of the Ukraine and the Trident of Vladimir is the Ukrainian national emblem.

The letters 'У П А' are the Cyrillic letters standing for the Ukrainian name 'Ukrains'ka Povstans'ka Armyia' – the Ukrainian Insurgent Army. The arm shield was worn on the upper arm of the German Army uniforms worn by these Ukrainian volunteers.

7 Volunteers from the province of Georgia in southern Russia, an area that had once been an independent nation until annexed by the Soviets, wore an arm shield bearing the colours of red, white and black on the upper right arm of their German Army uniforms. It is of interest to note that Joseph Stalin came from Georgia.

8 The second pattern arm shield, introduced sometime during 1943, as worn by volunteers from North Caucasia, on the upper right arm.

9 Four separate arm shields with a two colour diagonally separated design existed for four Cossack Volunteer Units. These were: Siberian Cossacks ('СВ'), Kuban Cossacks ('КВ'), Don Cossacks ('ВД') as illustrated on Plate 60, no. 1, and Terek Cossacks ('ТВ') as shown here. All arm shields were worn on the upper left arm. The letters placed above the colours of the shield were cyrillic letters.

10 This arm shield is probably the most common of all volunteer shields encountered in collections, and various qualities exist. There is a printed version with the design and colours, as featured here, silk screen-printed on to white linen, a common practice found amongst quite a number of other volunteer unit arm shields. The type of shield illustrated here represents the BeVo silk-woven variety. A third variety had the design embroidered in coloured threads on to a backing cloth of blue-grey material. This last type is said to have been used by POA volunteers serving with the German Luftwaffe.

The Cyrillic letters 'Р О А' stand for the Russian title of this organisation, the 'Russkaia Osvoboditel'naia Armiia', or Russian Army of Liberation. The Imperial, pre-Soviet colours of red, white, and blue were chosen together

83 A Major in the Russian Army of Liberation interrogating a Soviet prisoner of war (6 August 1943).

with the Imperial Russian emblem of the Cross of St Andrew (Russian version) as a fitting emblem to represent all the various Osttruppen factions that went to make up the 'Vlasov Army' of the POA. The arm shield was worn on the upper left arm of the German military tunics and greatcoats worn by these volunteers of all ranks.

11 Arm shield worn by Latvian volunteers on the right upper arm of their German military uniforms. The diagonal tricolour of dark red, white and dark red was taken from the colours of the ancient thirteenth century flag of the Letts. The word 'LATVIJA' stood for Latvia.

12 Volunteers originating from Armenia wore a BeVo quality arm shield. They were formed into a battalion-strong unit given the designation 812th Armenian Battalion. They saw service in Holland as well as on the Eastern Front.

13 Aserbaijani volunteers were formed into two battalions, the 804th and 807th Aserbaijanian Battalions. Personnel of these two units wore volunteer arm shields on the right upper arm of their German military uniforms. There were, in fact, three separate versions of these shields, one of which is illustrated here. All had the same horizontal tricolour of blue-red-green, but on the two patterns not illustrated here there were two different emblems, one featuring a large yellow crescent moon and an eight-pointed star, the other a smaller white crescent moon and an eight-pointed star set on the red portion of the tricolour.

14 Volunteers from the province of Turkestan had three patterns of arm badge, one in the shape of a shield, as shown here, while the other two were arm ovals (see Plate 60, no. 3). The pink and blue shield with the design of a bow and arrow was the second pattern arm

184

shield issued in 1943. It was worn on the upper right arm by these volunteers on their German Army uniforms.

15 Personnel, both Indian and their German Officers and Instructors, of the Azad Hind, or Free Indian Legion, wore an arm shield that bore the colours of the Indian National Congress, a horizontal tricolour of saffron, white, and green superimposed with a 'Springing Tiger', the emblem of the Azad Hind Fauj. The shield was worn on the upper right arm of the German uniforms. The Indians were formed into a 'Legion' which had the German designation Infanterie-Regiment 950.

85 A Muslim volunteer in the Free Arab Legion.

16 The arm shield as worn by personnel of the Free Arab 'Legion' displayed the sacred Islamic colours of red-white-green-black. The device was almost identical to the flag used by the Hashemite Kingdom of Jordan, except that in the red trapezium there appeared two seven-pointed white stars in place of a single Jordanian star. The arm shield was worn on the upper right arm of the German uniforms.

Plate 60. Arm Shields

Foreign Volunteer Arm Shields

1 Arm shield for Don Cossacks. These volunteers formed part of the Nr. 2 Kosaken-Division which existed from 1944 to 1945.

84 A young Sihk volunteer in the Free India Legion, the Azad Hind Fauj, photographed in the area of Monte Cassino, Italy.

2 Arm shield for Don Cossacks worn by personnel of the Divisional Supply Troops of the 1st Kosaken-Division.

3 Arm shield, third and final issue, for members of the Turkestan Legion (162nd Division) introduced in 1944. The inscription around the upper part of the oval badge is in the Turkestan language and is the equivalent of the German Army motto, 'Gott mit uns' – 'God is with us'. The badge was worn on the upper right arm of the service tunic and greatcoat.

4 Arm shield worn by Hungarian personnel attached to German forces. There was no 'Hungarian Legion', and it is thought that this BeVo-produced silk badge was worn as an identifying badge by Hungarian troops.

86 Two young Eastern Workers wearing their German inspired National Emblems. The girl on the left is from the Ukraine whilst the girl on the right hails from Russia.

Eastern Workers Insignia

5 The much despised Ostabzeichen was introduced on 20 February 1942. The idea of a special identifying badge to be worn by Eastern workers originated mainly from the Germans' fear of their civilian population becoming contaminated by the Soviet civilians, considered by the Nazi authorities as sub-humans (Untermensch). These workers had been transported into the Reich from the occupied Eastern territories to work in German factories and homes, and on farms.

The Ost patch had to be worn on every outer garment these workers brought with them to the Reich. As all Jews and inmates of concentration camps were already compelled to wear identifying insignia of one sort or another the Ost patch was considered by both Germans and Eastern workers alike as an odious symbol reflecting its wearer's inferior status.

By 1944 circumstances within Germany had changed. The German attitude towards these Eastern workers who, by now, they considered essential to their war effort was one of encouragement. The Ost patch was abolished and in its place three separate emblems intended to be worn as a mark of pride and tradition were introduced for use by the three main Eastern worker national groups.

6 The Volksturmsabzeichen for · Ukrainian workers. The symbolic Ukrainian trident surrounded by sunflowers.

7 The emblem for Russian workers of the Cross of St Andrew, also surrounded by sunflowers.

8 The Belorussian emblem consisting of an ear of corn and a cog wheel surrounded by sunflowers.

Military Campaign Arm Shields

Plate 60. (Continued)

Campaign Shields

As has already been mentioned, the three main methods the German authorities employed in order to recognize and reward their fighting troops who had taken part in particular battles or campaigns was by awarding medals, cuff-titles (see Plate 24), and campaign shields. Each type of award was for a different campaign or battle and as the war progressed it was not uncommon to encounter battle hardened individuals who had received more than one of these awards, in some cases two items of the same kind. If a person had been awarded two campaign shields he wore both on the upper left arm, one above the other, the earliest award uppermost, separated by a gap of approximately 5 mm

9 The Narvik Shield (Narvikschild) was in-

87 A German Naval Maat wearing the gilt naval version of the Narvik Campaign shield.

stituted on 19 August 1940 and was awarded to all personnel of the Army, Navy, and Air Force who had taken part in the Battle for Narvik in Norway between 9 April and 9 June 1940.

Two versions of this badge were produced, one in a gilt-coloured finish for wear by Naval personnel, and the more common version in a matt grey metal finish for use by Army and Air Force personnel. The three branches of the German Wehrmacht were represented on the design of this shield; the Edelweiss for the Army units – many of whom were predominately Mountain Troops, the propeller for Air Force units, and the fouled anchor for Naval units. The awards were made by and on the approval of General-of-Mountain Troops Eduard Dietl, Commander of Army Group 'Narvik'.

The shield was worn mounted on to a backing of appropriately coloured uniform cloth, re-inforced by a metal plate. The cloth was dark navy-blue for Navy, blue-grey for the Air

88 Two musicians taken prisoner in North Africa; both wear the Krim or Crimea campaign arm shield.

Force, and field-grey for the Army. It was worn on the upper left arm.

The Narvik shield, as well as all other campaign or battle shields, could also be worn on any of the Nazi Party uniforms, including Police uniforms. Those who had received a shield and had later transferred out of the Armed Forces and were serving in any of the Nazi Party formations or the Police forces, were also permitted to wear their award on their Party or Police uniform. In the case of the Party formations, the shield was usually worn 2 cm above the Swastika arm band on the left upper arm.

10 The Crimea Shield (Krimschild). This 'Battle Badge' was instituted on 25 July 1942 and awarded to all members of the Wehrmacht, including the Waffen-SS and members of Police Regiments, who had been engaged against the enemy on the land, in the air, or at sea between 21 September 1941 and 4 July 1942. To have been eligible the recipient had to have taken part in one major engagement or to have served at least three months in the area. These requirements were shortened if the recipient had been wounded. The design used on the shield showed a map of the Crimea bearing the German word 'Krim'. This 'Battle Badge' was also worn with a backing cloth in the appropriate uniform colour and was worn sewn on to the wearer's left upper arm of all tunics and the greatcoat. The badge had a bronzed, metallic finish and was awarded by Feldmarschall von Manstein.

11 The Demjansk Shield (Demjanskschild) was instituted on 25 April 1943 and was awarded to the men of the 100,000-strong 2nd Army Corps who, for fourteen months, had successfully defended the town and encircled district of Demjansk. Demjansk lay directly north of the Kholm area where the German garrison there held out against overwhelming odds for 105 days. Like the defenders of Demjansk, they too received a 'Battle Badge' (not illustrated). Both defensive pockets were supplied by air throughout the German winter retreat of 1941–42. The award which was approved and made by General Graf von Brockdorff-Ahlefeldt was in dull grey-white metal with a backing cloth and was worn on the upper left arm. The design of two crossed swords surmounted by an aeroplane represented the ground defence forces and the Air Force.

12 The Kuban Shield (Kubanschild) was instituted on 20 September 1943. It was awarded to all members of the armed forces who had taken part in at least one major engagement in the defensive fighting within the Kuban bridgehead area since 1 February 1943 or who served at least 60 days in that theatre of operations. The time period was shortened if the recipient had been wounded. The bronze-coloured metal shield was worn mounted on to a cloth backing sewn to the wearer's upper left arm. The design on the shield showed a stylized representation of the Kuban bridgehead front-line running from the lakes in the north (Lagunen), through Krymsk (Krymskaja) and across the Kuban river, that runs east to west through this area, to Novorossiysk (Noworo-Ssijsk) in the south. The award was authorised and presented by Feldmarschall von Kleist, Commander of the Kuban area.

Other campaign and battle shields existed but which are not illustrated here. These were Cholm and Lappland which were definitely instituted and awarded, Lorient which was known to have been awarded, and Warschau, about which there are doubts.

Tradition and Unit Cap Badges

Plate 61. Head-Dress Insignia, Tradition Badges, Official and Semi-Official Unit Insignia

Three types of insignia were worn on German military soft head-dress, apart from the standard eagle and Swastika, Reich cockade and wreath. These were tradition badges worn only by Army personnel, official unit badges worn by Army, Waffen-SS, and RAD personnel, and semi-official unit badges worn by Army, Navy, Air Force, Paratroop, and Cossack units.

Army Tradition Badges and Units Semi-Official Insignia

Army tradition badges were worn during the 1933–45 period in order to perpetuate the traditions of former Imperial and pre-Imperial German army units. These tradition badges as worn on the soft head-dress of the new German Army were a miniaturized form of the old emblems originally worn by past élite regiments.

1 The Totenkopf (Death's Head) with the crossed bones positioned directly behind the skull was originally worn by the Prussian 1st and 2nd Bodyguard Hussars. The insignia worn by 1.Leib-Husaren-Regiment was continued by 1st Squadron of 5.Reiter-Regiment in 1921. In 1933 it was worn by the Regimental Staff and 1st, 5th and 11th Squadrons of 5.Kavallerie-Regiment. (See also Plate 9, no. 17.) The insignia worn by 2.Leib-Husaren-Regiment was, in 1921, worn by 2nd Squadron of 5.Reiter-Regiment. In 1933 this insignia was

89 Major Nobis, RKT wearing the standard pattern metal Edelweiss cap insignia worn by all German Mountain troops.

worn by the Regimental Staff, 1st Abteilung, and 2nd and 4th Squadrons of 5.Kavallerie-Regiment.

2 The Totenkopf with bones crossed directly below the lower jaw of the skull was originally worn by the Brunswick Infantry Regiment Nr.92 and, sometime after 1921 during the Reichswehr period, this traditional emblem was passed on to the 1st and 4th Companies of the 17.Infanterie-Regiment. On 10 February 1939 this honour was extended to include the

90 Oberfeldwebel Wriedt, RKT talking to Hitler-Jugend members.

Regimental Staff, the 1st and 2nd Battalions, and 13th and 14th Companies of 17.Infanterie-Regiment.

The insignia worn by the 17th Brunswick Hussar Regiment was continued in use in 1921 by 4th Squadron of 13.Reiter-Regiment, and in 1939 by 2nd Abteilung of 13.Kavallerie-Regiment.

3 The 'Dragoon Eagle', correctly known as the Schwedter Adler, was originally worn by 1st Brandenburg Dragoon Regiment Nr.2, sometimes referred to as the 'Schwedter Dragoons'. In 1921 this tradition badge was worn by the Regimental Staff and 2nd Squadron of 6.Reiter-Regiment; in 1926 the honour was extended to include the 4th Squadron of

the same regiment. There was a change of units holding the traditional emblem sometime during 1933, but on 12 October 1937 3rd Kradschützen (motorcycle) Battalion was also given this distinction.

4 The German Army Chaplains 'Gothic Cross' (Gotisches Kreuz) was worn on the front of the soft head-dress of Army chaplain and Field bishops in either white metal or white cotton embroidery.

All four items of insignia described above were worn on the front of the peaked cap and the field cap positioned between the eagle and Swastika emblem above, and the Reichskokade, with or without the oak leaf wreath, below.

5 The Hoch und Deutschmeister Kreuz, normally found mounted on to the shoulder straps of personnel from the Grenadier-Regiment 'Hoch und Deutschmeister' was also used as a semi-official cap insignia, by both regular and replacement battalion troops.

6 Introduced on 2 August 1942 the Jäger cap badge was issued to all troops of German Army Jäger divisions and Jäger battalions. In white metal, the official cap emblem was worn on the left side of the field cap and the mountain cap.

7 The Ski-Jäger cap badge was introduced on 21 August 1944 for wear by German Army troops of 1.Ski-Jäger Brigade. The white metal official cap badge was worn on the left side of the Feldmütze and the Bergmütze, like the Jäger badge.

8 The Edelweiss metal cap badges introduced for wear by all personnel of mountain troop formations on 2 May 1939 were in two types. The type which is illustrated here was worn on the front of the peaked caps worn by the mountain troop personnel, positioned between the eagle and Swastika cap emblem, and the oak leaf wreath with its cockade. The other type illustrated under no. 16 below was worn on the left side of the Bergmütze. Both these emblems were introduced at the same time

91 General der Panzertruppe Hasso von Manteuffel (left) listening to the reports of officers from the 116th Panzer-Division. Two of the officers wear the semi-official divisional emblem badge on the left side of their peaked caps.

as the Gebirgsjäger Edelweiss arm badge (see Plate 44, no. 1).

9 Semi-official unit emblem worn by Army personnel from an un-identified Infantry Division, probably the 290th Infantry Division. Worn on the left side of the peaked cap and field service cap.

10 Semi-official unit emblem worn by personnel of the 116th Panzer-Division, the 'Windhund' Division.

11 Semi-official unit emblem worn by certain Eastern Volunteer units, a representation of the Arabic Jambiya, a short, curved-bladed, knife in its sheath. From photographic evi-

dence, this emblem was worn by members of the Georgian and Aserbaijanian Legions on the left side of their field caps.

12 The Waffen-SS cloth version of the Edelweiss cap insignia, worn on the left side of the Waffen-SS Bergmütze.

Navy Units Semi-Official Insignia

13 Semi-official cap emblem thought to have been worn by the crew of the German submarine *U-802*.

14 Semi-official cap emblem worn by the crew of a German submarine, thought to be *U-270*. Made from flat, white sheet metal it was worn

92 Knights Cross Holder with Oakleaves Generaloberst Rendulic, Commander-in-Chief of a German Army on the Finnish Front, talking to an officer of the Waffen-SS Mountain Troops who wears the SS cloth version of the Edelweiss cap insignia.

on the left side of both the peaked cap and the 'little boat' (Schiffchen) side cap.

15 Semi-official cap emblem believed to have been worn by the crew of *U-97*.

16 Army pattern Edelweiss cap emblem worn as a popular emblem by crews of U-Boats and other sea-going vessels, usually by those who had taken part in the Norwegian campaign, especially Narvik.

Reichsarbeitsdienst Tradition Unit Insignia

In 1943 a series of thirteen tradition badges for wear by certain Arbeitsgau of the Reichsarbeitsdienst were introduced. These metal badges, some in plain metal, others elaborately finished in coloured enamels, were worn on the left side of the RAD head-dress.

17 RAD Tradition badge for personnel of Arbeitsgau I, Ostpreussen.

18 RAD Tradition badge for personnel of Arbeitsgau VI, Mecklenburg.

19 RAD Tradition badge for personnel of Arbeitsgau XVIII, Niedersachsen-Ost.

20 RAD Tradition badge for personnel of Arbeitsgau XXXVIII, Sudetengau-Ost.

93 On their return to their naval base, the crew of a German U-Boat avidly read the first newspaper that they have seen in weeks. All wear the Army pattern Edelweiss cap emblem chosen as the crew's semi-official emblem.

Flag Bearer's Insignia

94 The Army Flag Bearers arm insignia.

Plate 62. Flag Bearers Arm Shields

Only six uniformed organisations made use of special arm badges to be worn by Flag and Standard bearers: the German Army, Navy, and Air Force, and the Regiment 'General Göring', the Hitler Youth, and the National Socialist War Veterans Association (NS-RKB). All badges were worn on the upper right arm.

1 BeVo quality arm badge for Army standard bearers from Panzer (armoured) and Panzer-Abwehr (anti-tank) units.

2 BeVo quality arm badge for Army Flag bearers from Jäger (Rifle) and Gebirgsjäger (Mountain Troop) units.

3 Hand-embroidered quality arm badge for Naval Flag bearers for wear on the navy-blue rig, introduced on 28 August 1936.

4 Hand-embroidered quality arm badge for Naval Flag bearers for wear on the summer, white uniform, introduced 28 August 1936.

5 Hand-embroidered arm badge for Air Force Flag bearers from flying branch units, introduced on 11 May 1936.

6 Hand-embroidered arm badge for Air Force Flag bearers from anti-aircraft units, introduced on 11 May 1936.

7 Hand-embroidered arm badge for Flag bearers from the Regiment 'General Göring'.

8 Machine-woven arm badge for Flag bearer from a Hitler Youth Gefolgschaft.

9 Machine-woven arm badge for Flag bearers from a Hitler Youth Bann and a Deutsche Jungvolk Jungbann.

194

95 German Hitler Youth and Finnish Sports youth in Breslau. The HJ member on the left is wearing the arm badge for a flag bearer from an HJ-Gefolgschaft.

96 HJ flag bearers in Nürnburg, the one on the right wearing the arm badge of a flag bearer from a Hitler Youth Bann.

Musicians 'Wings'

Plate 63. Musicians Wings

Almost all German uniformed organisations possessed military or military-style bands. Many of these organisations had separate bands for their individual units or formations. With only a few exceptions, the German Navy proper being the most notable, musicians in these bands were distinguished from other uniformed personnel by wearing on the shoulders of their uniform dress musicians wings or 'Schwalbennester' – swallow's nests, an allusion to the shape of these items being somewhat akin to the mud nests made by swallows built under the eaves of buildings.

Distinctions were usually made between three grades of musicians. Generally speaking, bandsmen of drum and fife bands wore wings without a fringe and with the braiding on the swallow's nests in a dull grey finish. Trumpeters and musicians had wings with bright braiding and again were usually without a fringe, although there were exceptions. Finally, buglers and drum-majors wore wings that were more elaborate in that they had a deep fringe and bright braiding.

All German musicians wings conformed in overall shape and usually consisted of upright 'bars' of braiding, normally seven in number, set against an arch of coloured cloth, the lower edge of which was invariably finished with a length of the same braiding.

The wings were worn in matching pairs, one to each shoulder. They were affixed to the uniform either by being sewn permanently into the upper shoulder seam of the tunic or, as was the more common practice, by being attached to the wearer's uniform by a series of hooks fastened to the backs of the 'nests' which hooked into a matching series of loops sewn around the shoulder seam of the wearer's uniform tunic.

The coloured background cloth used on these swallow's nests usually indicated either the wearer's service or organisational colour, or their unit or formation branch-of-service colour.

1 Early NSDAP Political Leadership swallow's nest for a bandsman from an Ortsgruppe, c. 1933–38. The dull grey braiding with a patterning of small Swastikas was on a backing of light brown cloth, the colour chosen to represent Ortsgruppen units.

2 Late pattern NSDAP Political Leadership swallow's nest for trumpeters and musicians from a Kreisleitung, c. 1938–45. The introduction of the fourth and final range of collar patches and arm bands for use by NSDAP Political Leaders also saw the introduction of new patterns of swallow's nests. The earlier dull grey or silver braiding was replaced by gold braiding also with a patterning of small Swastikas for all three groups of musicians and all three areas of Political Leadership. No. 2 has a short fringe 3 cm deep and the dark brown was the colour chosen for a Kreis.

3 Late pattern NSDAP Political Leadership swallow's nest for a drum-major from a Gau, c. 1938–45. The bright red background was the colour used by Gau members. The gilt fringe was 5 cm deep.

97 Side drummers of the NPEA.

4 Early example of a Hitler Youth swallow's nest, c. 1933.

5 Late pattern of Hitler Youth swallow's nest, c. 1938–45.

6 Swallow's nest for a drum-major of the German Protection Police, c. 1936–45, the green background being the branch colour of the Schutzpolizei.

SA swallow's nests of the period 1933–38/39 were in a range of colours, all of which corresponded to the various SA district colours. Each of these district colours were, with just one exception, shared by two individual SA districts. The various SA districts sharing a district colour were further distinguished by the use of gilt- or silver-coloured collar patch insignia (metal) and buttons, and in the case of SA musicians the colour of the braiding used on their swallow's nests.

7 Swallow's nest for SA musician from the SA District of Südwest. The orange background was the district colour used and was shared by the SA districts of Südwest and Mitte. The silver braid (or dull grey 'Litzen') distinguished the SA district of Südwest from the SA district of Mitte who used gilt braid (or dull yellow 'Litzen').

8 Swallow's nest for SA musician from the SA district of Ostmark, c. 1934. The black braiding was peculiar to this district and was only used on early pattern swallow's nests. This braiding was eventually changed to silver and dull grey, according to the wearer's musical status.

9 Allgemeine-SS swallow's nest, c. 1933–36 for an SS drum-major. SS drum-majors were distinguished by having a 7 cm deep white stranded fringe, changed in 1936 to an aluminium-silver fringe. The black cloth backing was universal for all Allgemeine-SS and Waffen-SS swallow's nests.

Reichsarbeitsdienst swallow's nests had no special backing colour, only black being used. The distinctive braiding with its red central strip distinguished these swallow's nests as being for the RAD from other formations that used black backing to their musician's wings.

10 Red striped white braiding was used on the swallow's nests worn by bandsmen of RAD Corps of Drums.

11 Red striped silver braided nests were used by RAD Musicians and Trumpeters.

12 The same quality nests as for no. 11 but with the addition of a 7 cm deep silver-stranded fringe were worn by RAD Drum-Majors.

Plate 64. Musician's Wings

1 Army swallow's nest for infantry drum and fife musicians. Dull grey braiding without fringe on white 'Waffenfarbe', arm-of-service colour for infantry personnel.

2 Swallow's nest for Army artillery regimental bandsmen and trumpeters. Silver braiding on red backing, red being the arm-of-service colour appointed to the artillery arm.

3 Swallow's nest for battalion buglers and drum-majors of Army Veterinary Service. Silver braid with a 7 cm deep silver-stranded fringe on a backing of carmine cloth.

German Air Force swallow's nests followed closely the system used by musicians of the German Army.

4 Swallow's nest for Luftwaffe Spielleute (drum and fife musician) of the Air Force flying branch, gold-yellow being their particular arm-of-service colour. Braiding was in dull grey.

5 Swallow's nest for Luftwaffe Musiker (bandsman) from a medical section band, dark cornflower blue being their Waffenfarbe. Braiding was in bright aluminium.

6 Swallow's nests for Luftwaffe Stabshornisten (staff buglers) of the air signals branch, light brown being their arm-of-service colour. Braiding and 7 cm deep stranded fringe were in bright aluminium.

In addition to the formations of the German

98 A group of Hitler Youth musicians at summer camp before the war.

99 Flemish volunteers in the Waffen-SS photographed at Klagenfurt in May 1942, from left to right: Victor Cochet from Mol, Joris de Smet from Ghent and Jos. Lauf of Brussels. As musicians they are all wearing the Musicians Wings or 'Swallows Nests'.

100 RAD Musicians in Tripoli (25 March 1938).

Air Force that possessed unit bands there existed a separate entity known as Regiment 'General Göring' (later to become a division and then a corps). White was the Waffenfarbe employed by this regiment and their swallow's nests were slightly more elaborate.

7 The drum and fife bandsmen had dull grey braiding but with the addition of a 4.5 cm deep grey wool-stranded fringe.

8 The nests for Bandsmen had bright aluminium braiding with a 4.5 cm deep aluminium stranded-fringe.

9 Battalionhornisten of the Regiment 'General Göring' wore nests which were also braided with bright aluminium but they had the addition of a 7 cm deep aluminium stranded-fringe.

Landespolizeigruppen were para-military Police units which existed in Germany under the Nazis before Hitler openly repudiated the Versailles Treaty and expanded his Armed Forces. A number of 'Green Police' units were raised between 1933–35. Trained and equipped as Police these thinly disguised Police formations were in reality acting in all but name as Infantry battalions.

The Land Police Groups possessed military style Police bands and members of these bands wore swallow's nests. These did, however, differ slightly from the usual pattern in that they were edged along the base of the nest with russa braiding, and not in the same wide, flat braiding used as the 'bars' to the nests. These 'bars' were themselves finished in a point. The backing colour was dark green, the same colouring as used on their cuff-titles (see Plate 26, no. 11) and other items of insignia (not illustrated).

10 Swallow's nest for LPG Drum and Fife Musicians; braiding was in dull grey-white.

11 Swallow's nest for LPG unit bandsmen; braiding was in silver-aluminium.

12 Swallow's nest for drum-major and battalion buglers of the LPG braiding and 7 cm deep stranded fringe were in bright silver-aluminium.

List of Plates

The colour plate section appears between pages 80 and 145.

Index

Organisation	Subject	Plate	Number
	Arm badges	39	16, 17
		40	1–12
		44	9–18
	Length of service chevrons	58	7, 8
	Head-dress insignia	61	12
	Musicians wings	63	9
Hitler-Jugend, Bund Deutsche Mädel, and Deutsches Jungvolk	Organisational emblem	2	9, 18
	Shoulder straps	7	1–22
	Collar patch	7	23
	Cuff-titles	28	1–5
	Arm bands	32	10, 11
	Arm badges	40	13–21
		41	1–17
		42	1–13
		43	1–31
	Flag bearers arm shields	62	8, 9
	Musicians wings	63	4, 5
Reichsarbeitsdienst	Organisational emblem	1	11
	Shoulder straps and collar patches	8	1–25
	Cuff-titles	28	6–15
	Arm Bands	32	13, 14
	Arm badges	37	19–25
		38	1–16
		41	18–23
	Head-dress insignia	61	17–20
	Musicians wings	63	10–12
German Army	National emblem	1	2
	Shoulder straps	9	1–18
	Collar patches	9	20–23
	Cuff-titles	24	5–13
		25	1–5
	Arm bands	33	1–15
		34	6
	Arm badges	44	1–19
		45	1–31
		46	1–3, 5
	Head-dress insignia	61	1–10, 16
	Flag bearers arm shields	62	1, 2
	Musicians wings	64	1–3
German Navy (Kriegsmarine)	National emblem	1	1
	Shoulder straps	10	1–9
	Collar patches	10	10–15
	Cuff-titles	27	8–10
	Arm band	34	10
	Arm badges	50	1–24
		51	1–16
	Head-dress insignia	61	13–16
	Flag bearers arm shields	62	3, 4
Marine-Artillery	National emblem	1	6
	Shoulder straps	10	16–21

Organisation	Subject	Plate	Number
	Collar patches	10	23—25
	Arm badges	51	17—20
NSFK	Organisational emblem	1	5
	Shoulder straps	11	1—4
	Collar patches	11	5—16
	Breast badges	46	6—9, 20
	Arm badges	46	10—13
	Length of service chevron	58	1
Deutscher Luftsport-Verband	Collar patches	11	17—20, 22, 24, 26
	Shoulder straps	11	21, 23, 25, 27
	Arm band	33	16
	Breast badges	46	14, 15, 16—19
	Arm badges	47	1—5
	Organisational emblem	2	8
Luftwaffe	National emblem	1	3
	Shoulder straps	12	1—12
	Collar patches	12	13—24
	Cuff-titles	25	8—14
		26	1—5
	Arm bands	33	17, 18
		34	1—5
	Arm badges	48	1—29
		49	1—4, 9—12
		47	14—19
	Flag bearers arm shields	62	5—7
	Musicians wings	64	4—9
German Police	National emblem	1	13
	Shoulder straps	13	1—15
	Collar patches	13	16—28
	Cuff-titles	26	11—13
		27	1, 6, 7
	Arm bands	33	9, 12
	Arm badges	42	14—18
		57	1—17
	Breast badge	57	18
	Musicians wings	63	6
Landwacht	National emblem	1	14
	Arm bands	34	8
Bahnschutzpolizei	National emblem	2	7
	Shoulder straps and collar patches	14	1—21
	Cuff-titles	27	2—5
	Arm badges	56	15—22
Zollbeamte	Organisational emblem	2	11
	Shoulder strap	15	1—7
	Collar patches	15	8—13
	Cuff-titles	2	11
		27	11

Organisation	Subject	Plate	Number
	Arm chevrons	52	1–3
Deutsche Arbeitsfront	Organisational emblem	2	1
	Shoulder straps	15	14–17
	Arm chevrons	55	4–8
	Arm band	35	12
Government Officials	National emblem	2	17
	Shoulder straps	15	18–21
	Arm badges	52	4–12
Technical Stud Service	Shoulder straps	16	1, 2, 5, 6
	Collar patches	16	3, 4
Labour Operations Executive	Collar patches	16	7–16
	Arm band	35	11
Ostbeamte	Collar patches	16	17–23
Reichsluftschutzbund	Organisational emblem	2	14
		1	12
	Shoulder straps and collar patches	17	1–19
	Arm bands	34	15, 16
	Arm badges	53	1, 2
Sicherheits-und Hilfdienst and Luftschutz Warndienst	Shoulder straps	17	20–24
	Collar patches	17	25–27
	Cuff-title	30	5
	Arm bands	34	17, 18
		35	1, 2, 8, 9, 10
	Arm badges	53	8–12
Deutsches Rotes Kreuz	National emblem	2	15
	Shoulder straps	18	1–6
	Collar patch	18	7
	Arm bands	33	7
		35	3, 4
	Arm badges	53	4–7
Wasserstrassenluftschutz	Shoulder straps	18	8–15
	Collar patches	18	16–19
Organisation Todt	Organisational emblem	2	6
	Shoulder straps	19	1–7
	Collar patches	19	8–21
	Arm bands	36	5–13
	Arm badges	54	9–21
		55	1–3
Womens Signals Organisation Todt	Arm badges	42	19–21
Technische Nothilfe	National emblem	2	10
	Shoulder straps and collar patches	20	1–29
	Cuff-titles	27	12, 13

Organisation	Subject	Plate	Number
	Arm bands	35	13
	Arm badges	53	13–20
Transportflotte Speer	Collar patches	21	1–8
	Arm badges	55	9–14
Transport Korps Speer	Collar patches	21	9–12
	Shoulder straps	21	13–16
Reichsautobahn Strassen-Meister	National emblem	2	21
	Passants	21	17–22
	Arm badges	54	2, 3
Deutsche Falkenorder	Collar insignia	22	1–4
	Shoulder straps	22	13, 14
	Arm band	35	15
	Arm badge	54	6
Deutsche Jägerschaft	Collar insignia	22	5–12
	Shoulder straps	22	13–14
	Arm badges	54	7, 8
		1	15
Forestry Services	Collar patches	22	15–18
	Shoulder strap	22	19
Deutsche Reichsbahn	National emblem	1	9
	Shoulder straps	23	1–11
	Collar patches	23	12–19
	Passants	23	20–29
	Cuff-titles	29	3–6
	Arm bands	36	14–18
	Arm badges	56	1–14
NS-Reichskriegerbund	National emblem	1	10
	Cuff-titles	29	11–13
	Arm bands	35	17, 18
		36	1–4
NS-Studentenbund	National emblem	2	2
	Arm band	32	12
Werkschutz	Organisational emblem	2	16
	Arm bands	35	5, 6, 7
	Arm badge	53	3
Reichspost	Arm band	35	14
	Arm badges	54	4, 5
Postschutz	Organisational emblem	2	12
	Cuff-title	29	1
Brigade Ehrhardt	Cuff-title	29	2
	Arm badge	39	12

Organisation	Subject	Plate	Number
NSBO	Arm badge	37	2
		2	13
Air-Sea Rescue Service	Organisational emblem	2	3
Female Army Auxiliaries	National emblem	2	20
	Cuff-titles	25	6, 7
	Arm badge	46	4
Landespolizeigruppe 'General Göring'	Cuff-title	26	11
	Musicians wings	64	10–12
Frauenschaftsleiterinnen	Arm band	32	18
Deutscher Volkssturm	Arm bands	34	11, 12
State Service	Arm band	34	14
Generalluftzeugmeister	Arm band	34	13
Luftwaffe Flak Helferin	Arm badge	49	5
	Arm chevrons	49	6–8
RADwJ	Arm badge	38	16
RKS	Arm badge	54	1
NSKOV	Arm band	35	16
Auxiliary Security Police	Arm badges	39	18, 19
	Arm band	34	9
Foreign Volunteer Units	Arm shields	59	1–16
		60	1–4
	Head-dress insignia	61	11
Eastern Workers	National badges	60	5–8
Campaign Awards	Cuff-titles	24	1–4
	Arm shields	60	1–4
Segelflug Abteilung	Breast badges	47	6–8
Legion Condor	Breast badges	47	9–13